Palgrave Hate Studies

This series builds on recent developments in the broad and interdisciplinary field of hate studies. Palgrave Hate Studies aims to bring together in one series the very best scholars who are conducting hate studies research around the world. Reflecting the range and depth of research and scholarship in this burgeoning area, the series welcomes contributions from established hate studies researchers who have helped to shape the field, as well as new scholars who are building on this tradition and breaking new ground within and outside the existing canon of hate studies research.

More information about this series at
https://link.springer.com/bookseries/14695

Kim Barker • Olga Jurasz

Violence Against Women, Hate and Law

Perspectives from Contemporary Scotland

palgrave
macmillan

Kim Barker
Law School
The Open University
MILTON KEYNES, UK

Olga Jurasz
Law School
The Open University
MILTON KEYNES, UK

ISSN 2947-6364 ISSN 2947-6372 (electronic)
Palgrave Hate Studies
ISBN 978-3-030-99374-0 ISBN 978-3-030-99375-7 (eBook)
https://doi.org/10.1007/978-3-030-99375-7

This Palgrave Macmillan imprint is published by the registered company Springer Nature Switzerland AG.
The registered company address is: Gewerbestrasse 11, 6330 Cham, Switzerland

To the late Emma Ritch—
with thanks and feminist solidarity.

Acknowledgements

The initial research which contributed to the development of this book was financially supported in 2019 by the Open University's Citizenship and Governance Strategic Research Area funding.

We thank Craig Dalziel for his outstanding (and pernickety) research assistance in the earliest and late stages of this book project.

February 2022 KB & OJ

Contents

List of Figures

Introduction: Becoming Angry (Or Why This Book and Why Now)

Every book has a story. For many, it is arguably the story of the book's becoming which sparks more curiosity than the book itself, but it is also crucial in understanding the shape, content and story filling the pages that follow. It is no different with this book.

The Becoming of This Book

This book is about violence against women (VAW), hate crime and law in post-Devolution Scotland. But that story is the tale that follows. The immediate story (before we get to that) is a story of becoming: becoming angry with relentless, pervasive, everyday acts of violence; becoming increasingly frustrated with the law's stagnation in addressing it and becoming terrified by the speed with which, especially during the final months of writing this book, the footnotes of the manuscript overflowed with reports of misogynistic police behaviours as well as deaths of women such as Sabina Nessa or Ashling Murphy who "just" were going about their everyday life. In some respects, this is a story of the problem with "just": "just" women but now just(ice) for women. None of this is new for anyone involved in researching and writing about VAW, but the constant and invasive barrage of these reports, killings, and 'announcements' made us wonder—frequently—'why do we bother'/'what is *really* going to change'. It also made us angrier whilst providing the motivation to keep going.

As such, this book is more than merely a collaborative research output (to use the despised academic 'descriptor'...). It is written by women, about women. It presents women's challenge to the law over its inaction in light of the VAW women face in everyday life and across the spaces they occupy. The categorisations and diversifications aside, the core problem of legal inaction and pervasive VAW remain. It is not enough to have glossy campaigns and promised law reform. Read it as our version of 'personal is political', if you will—it's something of a 'call to arms', but more of a provocation to 'do better'.

It is also written in spite of the challenges that have been thrown in our direction: the questioning of this research's value, the repeated querying of the 'impact' on our academic career progression ('Are you sure you want to be known for *that*?') or equally on the collaboration underpinning this research ('It may be worth writing something by yourself'; 'Is it still written with X?'). It is unlikely that similar remarks would have been encountered by other colleagues working on other topics. It's important to us, to women, and to the subject, to highlight the context in which (or, rather, in spite of which) research on VAW, especially that with a feminist angle, is situated, including this book. But there is a cost—the cost of *not* 'doing' the research, and as a result, *not* challenging the existing dialogue around VAW—and the attitudes towards not just it, but discussions of it, is greater than the cost of doing it. Women (particularly us) will not stop.

Challenges (and anger) aside, this book is built on five years of engagement with VAW in various forms and fora in Scotland. We have witnessed, as researchers, the unfolding debates and discussions, particularly in Scotland. We have submitted evidence to, and engaged with, the Scottish Cabinet. We have made our expert opinions known to the Bracadale Review, in response to the One Scotland Consultation, but also to the Justice Committee on the Hate Crime and Public Order Bill (Scotland) 2020. We met with the (then) Cabinet Secretary for Justice and the Minister for Equalities in 2019. We gave evidence to the Misogyny and Criminal Justice Working Group in 2021. While we may disagree with the direction law reform has ultimately taken, we have not come at this from a standing start. This book tells part of that story, but also the story of VAW in Scotland.

This book also documents a story of Scotland's efforts to combat VAW and women's activism to make VAW and gender inequality a 'historical curiosity' which continuously makes all the difference. In *Living a Feminist Life*, Sara Ahmed wrote that "we have to make sense of what does not make sense. [...] In making sense of things that happen, we also draw on histories of thought and activism that precede us."[1] Others who came before us were instrumental in documenting Scottish women's voices on this subject—Evelyn Hunter, Dr Esther Breitenbach, Professor Fiona MacKay, to name but a few. We were fortunate to be able to draw on their expertise and work in this book whilst bringing in perspectives from our own research.

But it is also 'our voice'. It will not take long for you as the reader to (perhaps) wonder why two non-Scots wrote a book about VAW in Scotland. This book would probably not have come to fruition if not for challenges thrown in our direction. First, from Professor James Chalmers who politely made us aware of the Bracadale Review (and indirectly sent us down this path), but more recently from the late Emma Ritch (the former Executive Director of Engender) during the launch of our previous book, *Online Misogyny as Hate Crime: A Challenge for Legal Regulation* in Edinburgh in 2019. Emma, who generously took the time to read the book and speak at the launch, remarked that the "[e]ntire time I was reading this timely and important book, I wished that there was an equally robust analysis of the law done for Scotland." We accepted—eventually—that challenge, especially given Emma's unparalleled support. The challenge took on a new meaning given the growing attention to matters surrounding gender and hate crime reform (both in Scotland and in south of the border) as well as attempted developments in law and policy on VAW. In finishing this book, and the 'call to arms' we hope it sounds for Scotland, we note with great sadness that Emma will not see the outcome of the challenge she threw us, nor the analysis of the law for Scotland that it ultimately presents. We hope she would be satisfied with it.

---

[1] Ahmed (2017, pp. 20–21).

This book is ours, and the mistakes in it are ours too. While writing it we've tried to keep our voices in it, as well as presenting a reasoned legal discussion. Before it gets to a detailed discussion of hate crime and harassment, the first two chapters set the scene in Scotland. They tell the story of post-Devolution Scotland and the unfolding approach to tackling VAW. They also engage with what have historically been difficult issues. In this book, we take VAW and Scotland from pre-Devolution politics to discussions of misogynistic harassment, and beyond, with proposals for an alternative approach to harassment generally. In offering this alternative vision, we outline legislative proposals that we *hope* can offer a different society for women, and a different approach to VAW.

Our book examines the phenomenon of VAW—online and offline—and law and policy responses to it in post-Devolution Scotland. In doing so, it incorporates discussions of Scotland's contemporary efforts to address VAW in the context of hate crime, which, over the course of the past five years of so, have not only dominated public debate but also severely polarised it. We engage with the question of Scotland's legislative progressivism in the last two decades and bring the discussion to considerations of the proposed standalone offence of misogynistic harassment and the work of the Working Group on Misogyny and Criminal Justice in Scotland.

The Structure of This Book

A cautious reader may observe that the length of chapters decreases as we progress through the book. This is reflective of the narrowing down of issues examined in the discussions that follow, whilst highlighting the breadth of topic that VAW in Scotland is (Fig. 1).

We do not approach VAW from a siloed nor isolated perspective. We address—as you will see—VAW, hate crime, online VAW (OVAW), misogyny, and harassment. In bringing together these perspectives, we embrace a more holistic discussion—it is also a discussion we had hoped to find in the existing work on VAW in Scotland. In not finding it, we've written it instead.

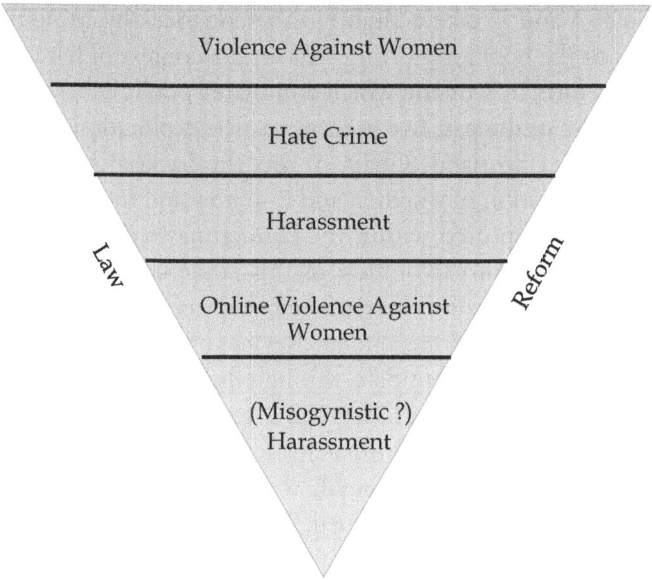

Fig. 1 Pyramid of VAW in Scots Law illustrating the approach taken in this book

Our discussion starts with the exploration of the phenomenon of VAW in Chap. 1 where we analyse the relationships between VAW and concepts of misogyny and hate speech/hate crime, which emerged in the context of recent law reform of the hate crime frameworks in Scotland and in other jurisdictions of the UK. The discussion draws on a variety of influences—local, national and global—which have shaped the law, policy and actions against VAW in Scotland, including the constitutional settlement (Devolution), developments in international law and human rights, and, more recently, the rise of #MeToo. Given the focus on Scotland, it would be difficult (especially for two women lawyers!) to ignore the impact of Devolution on law and policy making in Scotland, especially post-1999. In Chap. 2, we discuss whether the post-Devolution settlement has heralded a new way of doing things and a more progressive approach for women, and their rights, in Scottish society, in Scots Law and in Scotland. In particular, we question whether the frequently claimed 'different' ways of doing things in Scotland reflect political rhetoric rather than legal reality.

Chapters 3 and 4 take a slightly different focus by bringing a hate crime lens to the book, exploring VAW in the context of hate crime and hate crime reform in Scotland which dominated public debate in Scotland over the course of the past five years or so. The exploration of the history of hate crime in Scotland (Chap. 3) sets the background to the (still) controversial question of whether, and if so how and to what extent, gender ought to be captured within the hate crime framework. Chapter 4 focuses exclusively on exploration of this issue, carefully and critically examining consecutive, but incremental, steps of hate crime law reform in Scotland—from the Independent Review of Hate Crime Legislation in Scotland led by Lord Bracadale, through the passage of the Hate Crime and Public Order (Scotland) Act 2021, to the ambit of the Working Group on Misogyny and Criminal Justice in Scotland led by Baroness Helena Kennedy QC and proposals to create a stand-alone offence of 'misogynistic harassment'. Intrigued by this concept, we explore it in greater depth in Chap. 5, setting it against the history of the evolution of harassment in law, from the 1970s to the present. We question whether misogynistic harassment is a desirable avenue of addressing the harassment of women which is motivated by gender-based hate, and whether it merits anything other than praise for legislative creativity. In exploring discussions of harassment, we turn our attention to the often overlooked, but equally important, online context. Chapter 6 offers an analysis of the current provisions capable of applying to forms of OVAW in Scots Law, by examining the communications misuse offences, threatening and abusive behaviours, and other, more nuanced forms of OVAW, including image-based sexual abuse and text-based (sexual) abuse. It suggests that there is a need for an alternative approach, as well as legislation to capture OVAW in particular.

In probing these discussions, but joining together VAW, hate, and harassment, (including their online forms), difficult issues are combined. The polarisation of the debate surrounding sex/gender, especially in relation to hate crime reform, has not made this research particularly easy but challenged us to take a position—unlike the Scottish Government—on the issue. Throughout the book, we advocate for the inclusion of gender as a protected characteristic in the hate crime framework in Scotland and we view VAW, following CEDAW and the Istanbul Convention, as a form of gender-based violence and discrimination. We provide our rationale for this approach, which also forms the basis for our recommendations for alternative law reform in Chap. 7.

As such our book contributes to several debates in history, literature, law and society. Uniquely, it combines several legal perspectives on VAW (Scottish, UK, international, post-Devolution) with discussions surrounding hate crime reform and new dimensions of VAW (online and technologically related) to propose a tangible set of recommendations for alternative law reform in these areas. It does so by engaging with substantive legal issues, some of which have dogged Scotland for decades. This book is not, cannot and should not be the last word on VAW, and Scottish legal responses to it. We may not have *the* answer, but we *do* have the discussion (and some practical recommendations for the way forward).

We have, as we said above, benefitted from the women that have come before us. We have also benefitted from the campaigns, the women's movement and women who were prepared to fight for their voice and their rights. This book is testament to those women—without them, our voices would not appear here. In the 1970s, women Reclaim(ed) the Night; in recent years, women have Reclaim(ed) These Streets and attempted to Reclaim the Internet. We pay their efforts forward and Reclaim the Debate on ending VAW in Scotland.

February 2022 KB & OJ

Reference

Ahmed, Sara. 2017. *Living a Feminist Life*. Durham: Duke University Press.

1

The 'Historical Curiosity' of Violence Against Women in Scotland

1.1 Introduction

> The marginalization of women is a process generated not only by forces inside Scotland—it is also generated by forces outside its borders. Thus, while we do need to explore how Scottish culture and society is gendered, we also need to understand how that culture has been formed in relation to other cultures, in other parts of Britain, in Europe, and throughout the world, particularly through its participation in imperialist domination. We need to understand what it shares with other cultures and how it has been shaped by these, especially by the relationship with England and the consequences of English political and cultural hegemony.[1] (Esther Breitenbach, Alice Brown, Fiona Myers)

Violence against women (VAW) is neither a new phenomenon nor one specific to Scotland. The discussions of law reform in Scotland (or anywhere else for that matter) require consciousness of the broader sociocultural and geopolitical contexts. The beginning of the twenty-first century was a milestone for Scotland becoming a devolved jurisdiction and

[1] Breitenbach et al. (1998, pp. 47–48).

K. Barker, O. Jurasz, *Violence Against Women, Hate and Law*, Palgrave Hate Studies,
https://doi.org/10.1007/978-3-030-99375-7_1

substantively progressing in building its vision for a fair and equal society. However, whilst these developments have a specific focus on Scotland, they have been affected by broader societal problems, phenomena and political changes. The collective ripple effects of these are not to be underestimated and go to show the interconnectedness between global and local spaces of activism, protests and action, specifically against VAW.

Despite decades of women's activism in Scotland (and worldwide) to raise awareness of, and to combat, VAW, it continues to thrive, emerging in new forms, new fora and in response to global phenomena. The sheer volume of VAW, its contexts, types and the spaces in which it is occurring, is not only overwhelming but also supports the well-documented point about its widespread, disproportionate and everyday nature. It is therefore not an exaggeration to say that women experience violence *everywhere*: in the home, at work, in the family, in healthcare, in the intimate partner context, on the streets and online. The types of violence also differ from verbal to written, physical to psychological, sexual to economic, 'private' to 'public' and/or structural.

The numbers alone are concerning, even more so given the generally common underreporting of VAW across the world. For example, it is estimated that globally 736 million (and up to 852 million) women have been subjected to either or both physical and/or sexual violence at least once since the age of 15,[2] and 83 million to 102 million women across the EU have experienced sexual harassment since the age of 15.[3] In 2020–21 in Scotland, the police recorded 65,251 incidents of domestic abuse where "80% of the incidents had a female victim and a male accused,"[4] and in 2019–20, 2343 cases of rape and attempted rape were reported.[5] The violence is also experienced by girls, both online and offline: 58% of 14,000 girls surveyed worldwide have been harassed online on social media platforms,[6] and 50% said that they experience more online harassment than street harassment.[7]

---

[2] WHO (2021, p. xvi).

[3] European Union Agency for Fundamental Rights (2014, p. 95).

[4] Scottish Government (2021a).

[5] Rape Crisis Scotland (2021).

[6] Plan International (2020, p. 16).

[7] Ibid., p. 38.

In 2021, at the height of the COVID-19 pandemic, the UN Secretary General António Guterres reflected on the widespread and significant detrimental impact of the pandemic on women by calling it "a crisis with a woman's face."[8] This alarming rise in the frequency of VAW has long-term term individual and societal impacts: it not only contributes to a significant backlash against women's rights[9] but also slows down (admittedly already stagnated) progress and any hard-won gains in the global fight against VAW. But does it truly take a global pandemic to conclude this? Or is it rather the lived, everyday experience of a range of violent acts—physical, sexual, psychological, verbal, textual, on- and offline, in conflict or in 'peacetime'—being disproportionately directed at and endured by women that is (or at least, should be) sufficiently serious to warrant global concern and prioritise action?

The experience of the COVID-19 pandemic has further highlighted the commonplace occurrence of VAW. The rapidly rising rates of, particularly, domestic violence and online and technologically facilitated VAW,[10] both globally and domestically, have led the UN to call VAW a "shadow pandemic."[11] In the UK alone, the 24-hour National Domestic Abuse Helpline, run by Refuge, reported a 65% increase in logged reports of domestic violence between April and June 2020, with a further 700% increase in visits to their Helpline website.[12] A similar pattern has been recorded in Scotland,[13] across Europe[14] and worldwide too.[15] Furthermore, the pandemic has demonstrated how laws can be used to legitimise VAW and to oppress women, especially in times of crisis.[16] Uniquely, the COVID-19 pandemic also highlighted a shared concern about VAW across all four nations of the UK, albeit showing somewhat divergent

[8] Guterres (2021a).

[9] Barker and Jurasz (2023, forthcoming).

[10] Barker and Jurasz (2020d); Price (2020); World Wide Web Foundation (2020).

[11] UN Women (2020).

[12] Office for National Statistics (2020).

[13] BBC News (2020); Scottish Government (2020c); Crown Office & Prosecutor Fiscal Service (2021).

[14] Gunka and Snitsar (2020).

[15] UN Women (n.d.: https://www.unwomen.org/en/news/in-focus/in-focus-gender-equality-in-covid-19-response/violence-against-women-during-covid-19).

[16] Barker and Jurasz (2023, forthcoming).

approaches to addressing VAW, and women's rights generally, in unprecedented times. This contrast was particularly evident between England and Scotland,[17] with the latter generally being more responsive to the challenges facing women—be it in the context of reproductive health[18] or providing financial support for services for women subjected to VAW.[19]

According to the United Nations Population Fund,[20] this is not a short-term challenge given that the pandemic is likely to result in a one-third reduction in the progress towards ending gender-based violence[21] (GBV) by 2030—a target set by the UN Sustainable Development Goals agenda—with a predicted additional 15 million cases involving GBV globally every three months of lockdown. The pandemic-related rises in GBV and VAW also come at a significant cost. For example, in July 2021, the Scottish Government allocated an additional £5 million to frontline services for women in Scotland affected by GBV,[22] on top of the announcement of the Delivering Equally Safe Fund to tackle VAW in 2020.[23] The personal costs of harms suffered by women subjected to violence, together with the broader societal harms[24] and costs, significantly exceed the available resources, but especially budgets.[25]

This pessimistic status quo is by no means a reflection on women's activism to break the continuum of VAW—rather, it is a painful reminder of how deeply entrenched VAW is in the fabric of society and how the

---

[17] Ibid.

[18] Scottish Government (2020a).

[19] Scottish Government (2020d).

[20] United Nations Population Fund (2020).

[21] Throughout this chapter, terms gender-based violence and violence against women are used. Violence against women is understood here as a form of gender-based violence, as categorised by the CEDAW Committee and the Council of Europe convention on preventing and combating violence against women and domestic violence 2011: see Council of Europe Convention on preventing and combating violence against women and domestic violence (opened for signature 11 May 2011, entered into force 1 August 2014) CETS 210 (Istanbul Convention) Preamble and art 3(a). For clarification of terms used in this book, please see *The Introduction*.

[22] Scottish Government (2021e).

[23] Scottish Government (2020b).

[24] Barker and Jurasz (2021d, pp. 256–259).

[25] Women's Aid estimated that a minimum of £393 million annually is required to fund domestic abuse services in England alone. This figure does not capture the cost of services needed to assist women who have been subjected to other forms of VAW. See Women's Aid (2019).

forces of sexism, gender stereotypes, patriarchy and misogyny continuously fuel its existence on a daily basis. It is also a reflection on how crucial integrated law, social and economic policy and gender-responsive budgeting are to tackling VAW at local, national, regional and international levels. Importantly, given the pervasiveness of VAW, Scotland cannot tackle it alone.

The integration of VAW into law and policy responses is now common, although questions remain about their design, cohesion and effectiveness. Whilst VAW has always been a significant social problem, its visibility and recognition within law and policy is relatively recent.[26]

1.2 Violence Against Women: Law and Policy

The recognition of VAW as a legal and human rights issue in the 1990s, giving rise to State obligations to prevent, combat and remedy such acts, started a seismic shift in relation to how society approached VAW. The emergence of a human rights-based approach to tackling VAW was the result of decades of international campaigning for women's rights and calls to end VAW which continue to this day. The defining moment for the anti-VAW and women's rights movements was the 1995 Fourth World Conference on Women in Beijing where 189 countries unanimously adopted *The Beijing Declaration and the Platform for Action*, which set strategic objectives and actions for the achievement of gender equality and the advancement of women in 12 key areas, including the commitment to tackle VAW.[27] It provided a universal global framework against which the progress in the 12 areas can be monitored and reported upon.[28] The significance of *Beijing Declaration* and its influence on shaping Scotland's policy responses towards VAW has grown in post-Devolution

---

[26] See, for example, Crown Prosecution Service (2012).

[27] Whilst *Beijing Declaration and Programme for Action* was crucial in making a global commitment to tackle VAW, it focused on a number of areas which were – and continue to be – of significant importance and concern to women, including women and the environment, women and the economy, women and the media, the girl child.

[28] See, for example, Engender (2015).

Scotland and is further evidenced by the subsequent reliance on and commitment to its standards.[29]

Since Devolution, not only have Scotland's commitments to international standards concerning VAW become more prominent, but tackling VAW in Scotland has become an important feature of social policy, backed by governmental funding and supported by successive Scottish Governments.[30] Published in 2014, the original *Equally Safe* strategy is a blueprint for Scotland's plan to combat VAW "once and for all."[31] It views VAW as having "no place in our vision for a safe, strong, successful Scotland."[32] Scotland has also been leading the way in implementing initiatives to help tackle VAW—especially where law is concerned. This has included putting forward progressive legislative proposals (e.g., to create an offence of misogynistic harassment, discussed in Chap. 5) and implementing modern laws—such as the Domestic Abuse (Scotland) Act 2018 (asp 5)—somewhat countering the well-established patterns of law generally lagging behind the recognition of women's experiences of violence.[33] The success of the Scottish *Equally Safe* strategy has also had clear impact beyond Scotland, with Northern Ireland proposing to develop and introduce an Equally Safe strategy to tackle violence against women and girls "as an Executive priority."[34]

Despite these clear areas of legislative progressivism, the law and policy responses to VAW in Scotland have been inherently affected by the broader sectoral, societal and attitudinal problems. The UK-wide crisis of the loss of public/women's confidence in the police protecting women from violence and responding to reports of VAW has deepened. The kidnapping, rape and murder of Sarah Everard by the police officer Wayne Couzens[35] is just one—high-profile—example. Other debacles damaging

---

[29] UK Government Equalities Office and UN Women (2020).

[30] Ibid., p. 13.

[31] Scottish Government and COSLA (2014, p. 48).

[32] Ibid., p. 5.

[33] This point has been made in late 1980s by Liz Kelly and still applies today, especially in relation to legislating on contemporary forms of violence, such as online and technologically facilitated VAW. See Kelly (1988, p. 74).

[34] Department of Health, Department of Justice, and The Executive Office (2022).

[35] Dodd and Siddique (2021).

women's trust in the police include investigations into the inappropriate use of social media by some police officers, including contacting victims of crime for sexual activity[36] and sharing grossly offensive and misogynistic messages on WhatsApp groups,[37] resulting in a wave of dismissals;[38] the use of force by Metropolitan Police against women protesting against VAW while paying tribute at Sarah Everard's vigil;[39] and the sexist, derogatory and violent treatment of Dr Konstancja Duff;[40] these are only a few contemporary examples demonstrating police attitudes and institutionalised VAW. Police Scotland has also been criticised for problematic attitudes towards sexual violence,[41] despite being praised for the 'Don't Be That Guy' campaign tackling sexual violence.[42] Concerns have also been raised in relation to the sexist culture in Scotland's armed police, following express recognition of it by the Employment Tribunal in *Malone v. The Chief Constable of the Police Service of Scotland*.[43] Issues of discriminatory attitudes amongst Police Scotland and concerns over the level of their awareness of the experiences of women and together with the needs of specific groups have been highlighted as a barrier to reporting hate crime.[44] Specifically, the reported existence of homophobia, racism and misogyny within Police Scotland has undermined public confidence in, and the credibility of, processes for reporting hate crime.[45] Collectively, this undermines Scotland's other work in tackling VAW, especially amidst claims for progressivism beyond modernising legislation. The mixed messaging resulting from the clash between public commitments to tackling VAW by Police Scotland (for example, the 'Don't Be That Guy' campaign) and the pervasive discriminatory attitudes and practices (such as

36 Independent Office for Police Conduct (2021).

37 Hamilton (2021).

38 Dodd (2021); Priestley (2021).

39 Graham-Harrison (2021).

40 Gayle (2022).

41 Bussey (2021).

42 Mackie (2021).

43 Judgment of the Employment Tribunal (Edinburgh) (Case No: 4112618/18, 4 October 2021).

44 HM Inspectorate of Constabulary in Scotland (2021, p. 49).

45 Ibid., p. 59.

the evident lack of concern for women's public safety during COP26 in Glasgow in November 2021)[46] further reinforce this point. Importantly, the juxtaposition of these attitudes puts in question whether Police Scotland can legitimately claim to have any commitment to, or a progressive approach towards, tackling VAW in Scotland.

Whilst these issues in policing VAW are not new,[47] their implications are significant. These institutionalised discriminatory attitudes towards women, the disbelief in women's experiences of violence and, importantly, the law, its enforcement and the criminal justice system not taking action against VAW effectively, put women's lives in jeopardy. This is especially so given the long history of associating VAW with a socially constructed private/feminine sphere (and therefore outside the scope of legal regulation), rather than public/masculine sphere,[48] which has stood as a barrier to women reporting violence or, even when reported, legal action being taken against the perpetrators. Moreover, it supports the existence and operation of a system whereby the law and institutions of the justice system neither universally nor effectively protect women from violence, but in and of itself reinforce it. This relationship between law, power and violence is neither particular to Scotland nor to VAW. Rather, it is a relationship of a structural nature that crosses geo-political and cultural boundaries, as illustrated by the images of the police using force against women at Sarah Everard's vigil in London, Black Lives Matter protests or during the Women's Strike in Poland. More crucially, it raises questions about the suitability and even the ability of the law—especially criminal law[49]—to work for women given the deeply entrenched biases of the justice system and its actors, which are reflected in the failure to conceptualise, prosecute, punish and redress the harms suffered by women and the ignorance of their experiences.[50]

---

[46] Grant (2021).

[47] See, for example, Donaldson (2020).

[48] Boyd (1997); Chinkin (1999).

[49] See, for example: Bibbings and Nicolson (2000); Kotiswaran (2014); Cowan (2019).

[50] Barker and Jurasz (2021c, p. 795).

As the Scottish poet Tom Leonard[51] said:

And their judges spoke with one dialect,
But the condemned spoke with many voices.

And the prisons were full of many voices,
But never the dialect of the judges.

And the judges said:
"No one is above the Law."

Given the long history of law's gender bias and the marginalisation of women's voices and their experiences, it is hardly surprising that women's trust in the justice system and in the police, especially following Sarah Everard's murder, is rapidly declining.[52] However, the rise of the human rights-based approach to VAW, especially the articulation of due diligence obligations with respect to combatting VAW (discussed in Sect. 1.1.2.1), helped clarify the scope of positive duties to protect women from violence and establish accountability where these duties are not met—including by the police force. For example, the UK Supreme Court clarified in *Commissioner of Police of the Metropolis (Appellant) v. DSD and Another (Respondents)*,[53] a case involving the 'black cab rapist,' John Worboys, that the police have a positive duty under Article 3 of the Human Rights Act 1998 (prohibition of torture or inhuman or degrading treatment or punishment) to investigate crimes which involve serious violence to the individual—here, allegations of rape and sexual assault. Furthermore, the judgement sums up a number of structural problems with regard to policing of VAW: institutional disregard for written policies concerning recognising and dealing with cases of VAW (here, drug-induced rape), failure to treat women's/claimants' complaints with sufficient gravity and care and internal/institutional pressure to write off certain types of cases involving VAW.[54]

---

[51] Leonard (1995, p. 17).

[52] End Violence Against Women (2021).

[53] [2018] UKSC 11.

[54] Ibid., para. 140.

These factors combine to contribute to the legitimisation of VAW, which further reinforces the created hierarchies of VAW (and, what follows, hierarchies of harm)[55] which prioritise certain acts of VAW over others or attribute it a higher degree of importance. This can be observed not only in how the law is applied, how women are treated by the criminal justice systems and the manner in which reported cases of VAW are handled, but also within the legislative process. The manner and time efficiency with which laws concerning VAW are created and enter into force is in itself reflective of aforementioned hierarchies. For instance, the legislative expediency of incorporating image-based sexual abuse into the law across the UK[56] compared with the lethargy of addressing online text-based abuse[57] is illustrative of this dynamic.[58] This is despite the hypervisibility of text-based abuse, as well as not dissimilar harms (online and offline) associated with both image-based and non-image-based abuse,[59] including cultural harms,[60] emotional distress, violation of privacy and reputational harms. The legislative dualism between these two forms of online and technologically facilitated abuse has a real and tangible impact on women who are subjected to text-based abuse, leaving them without appropriate and effective avenues of redress. Furthermore, such legislative gaps make women and their experiences of text-based (sexual) abuse invisible within the legal system (or, the 'formal' record), contributing to the erasure of the full narrative of online violence against women (OVAW)[61] from the legal system and normalisation of such abusive behaviours.[62]

---

[55] Barker and Jurasz (2021d, p. 251).

[56] England and Wales: Criminal Justice and Courts Act 2015, s. 33. Scotland: Abusive Behaviour and Sexual Harm Act 2016, s. 2 (asp 22). Northern Ireland: Justice Act (Northern Ireland) 2016, s. 51.

[57] Barker and Jurasz (2022, forthcoming).

[58] Barker and Jurasz (2021d, p. 251).

[59] For a comprehensive overview of harms arising in relation to text-based (sexual abuse), see Barker and Jurasz (2021d, pp. 256–258).

[60] McGlynn and Rackley (2017).

[61] For discussion of OVAW, see Chap. 6.

[62] Barker and Jurasz (2021d, p. 251).

1.2.1 Violence Against Women: What's in a Name?

In general, VAW is defined differently amongst law and policy documents as well as across various disciplines. More contemporary definitions of VAW—especially those that draw on international law/international human rights approaches to VAW—tend to capture it as gender-based, occurring in private and public life, and focus on a number of types and impacts of such violence, beyond acts sexual in nature and those associated with women's physicality. For example, the Council of Europe Convention on preventing and combating violence against women and domestic violence (the Istanbul Convention),[63] which is generally acknowledged as a modern and progressive treaty on VAW and domestic violence,[64] defines 'violence against women' as

> a violation of human rights and a form of discrimination against women and shall mean all acts of gender-based violence that result in, or are likely to result in, physical, sexual, psychological or economic harm or suffering to women, including threats of such acts, coercion or arbitrary deprivation of liberty, whether occurring in public or in private life.[65]

As such, it draws heavily on the two early definitions of VAW in international law, which pre-date Devolution in Scotland—namely the definition of VAW in General Recommendation 19 of the Committee on Elimination of All Forms of Discrimination Against Women (CEDAW Committee) that captures VAW as gender-based violence and "a form of discrimination that seriously inhibits women's ability to enjoy rights and freedoms on a basis of equality with men,"[66] as well as Article 1 of the Declaration on the Elimination of Violence Against Women:

> any act of gender-based violence that results in, or is likely to result in, physical, sexual or psychological harm or suffering to women, including

[63] Council of Europe Convention on preventing and combating violence against women and domestic violence 2011, Council of Europe Treaty Series—No. 210.

[64] Jurasz (2015).

[65] Istanbul Convention, art. 3(a).

[66] Committee on the Elimination of Discrimination against Women (1992, para. 1).

> threats of such acts, coercion or arbitrary deprivation of liberty, whether occurring in public or in private life.[67]

Depending on the disciplinary as well as sectoral focus, definitions of VAW are likely to further vary. Whilst they remain generally focused on the gender-based nature of violence and underlying human rights aspects, their focus, typology and emphasis may fall on different aspects of the problem. For instance, Public Health Scotland, whilst focusing on the gender-based and human rights aspects of VAW, draws attention to gender inequality as a root cause of VAW as well as multiple risk factors (for example, financial dependency, insecure immigration, poverty) which exacerbate the likelihood of experiencing such violence.[68]

The conceptually broader definitions of VAW engage not only with its typology but also with the root causes, such as gender inequality, gender stereotypes or structural violence.[69] The *Equally Safe* definition of VAW reflects such an approach by focusing on the social angle especially, viewing it as a form of violence that is rooted in social norms, structures and unequal power relations between men and women:

> Gender based violence is a function of gender inequality, and an abuse of male power and privilege. It takes the form of actions that result in physical, sexual and psychological harm or suffering to women and children, or affront to their human dignity, including threats of such acts, coercion or arbitrary deprivation of liberty, whether occurring in public or private life. It is men who predominantly carry out such violence, and women who are predominantly the victims of such violence. By referring to violence as "gender based" this definition highlights the need to understand violence within the context of women's and girl's subordinate status in society. Such violence cannot be understood, therefore, in isolation from the norms, social structure and gender roles within the community, which greatly influence women's vulnerability to violence.[70]

---

[67] Declaration on the Elimination of Violence against Women, UNGA Res 48/104 (20 December 1993), art 1; reaffirmed by the UN General Assembly in the 2006 resolution on violence against women: Intensification of efforts to eliminate all forms of violence against women, Res 61/143 (19 December 2006) UN Doc. A/RES/61/143, para. 3.

[68] Public Health Scotland (2021).

[69] Galtung (1969).

[70] Scottish Government and COSLA (2018, p. 10), updated from 2016.

Equally Safe provides a positive example of a progressive definition of VAW not least because legal and policy definitions relatively rarely engage with its structural and root causes. At an international level, the CEDAW Committee acknowledged the central role of prejudice, patriarchal attitudes[71] and gender stereotypes in furthering VAW and as its root causes.[72] These practices, if unaddressed, reinforce and perpetuate interconnected cycles of discrimination, inequality and violence which "is a critical obstacle to the achievement of substantive equality between women and men and to the enjoyment by women of their human rights and fundamental freedoms."[73]

Despite being increasingly debated as a factor fuelling violence and VAW specifically,[74] misogyny does not generally feature as a root cause in legal and policy definitions of VAW (discussed at 1.2.2.). Writing about domestic violence in India, Nigam observes that patriarchy and misogyny are not only interconnected but also rooted in the "old practices which facilitated patriarchy to reign [...] despite the constitutional guarantees of equality and justice."[75] This is accompanied and strengthened by the various portrayals of misogyny embodied in "privileges; discrimination; sexual assaults; belittling of women, commodification and objectification of women; and denial of basic rights to women, including suppression of their right to survive, and their right to life."[76] In contrast, Kelly notes that whilst misogyny exists, it does not provide "an adequate explanation or theoretical framework for understanding *all* violence against women, especially when we examine the intersections with race/ethnicity, age, disability and sexuality."[77]

VAW is both a cause and an effect of gender inequality, frequently reinforced by discriminatory social norms and attitudes, gender stereotypes, discriminatory laws and institutionalised discrimination and

---

[71] Committee on the Elimination of Discrimination against Women (2017, para. 30(a)).

[72] Ibid., para. 26.

[73] Ibid., para. 10.

[74] For example, the link between misogyny and violence has been raised in a response to the Plymouth shootings in 2021, see Rawlinson (2021).

[75] Nigam (2021, p. 4).

[76] Ibid.

[77] Kelly (n.d.: https://www.troubleandstrife.org/new-articles/the-trouble-with-hate/).

violence within the justice system. These practices and attitudes have a profound impact on the strategies and efforts to address VAW, especially in Scotland. Deprioritisation of VAW, especially within messaging from key actors within the justice system, is undermining efforts to overcome the societal and attitudinal barriers to reporting, redressing and tackling VAW. For example, 2018 statements by Cressida Dick, the Metropolitan Police Commissioner, and Sara Thornton, the chairwoman of the National Police Chiefs Council, calling for forces to focus on "core policing," instead of focusing on dealing with reports of misogyny,[78] unhelpfully positioned the issue of misogyny and VAW as less important (or real) than other violent crime, and did so prominently. Similarly, ridiculing women's concerns over their public safety by advising women to be "streetwise"[79] or "shout or wave down a bus"[80] if in danger is symptomatic of the prevailing dismissive attitudes towards VAW and women's experiences. Nicola Sturgeon publicly voiced strong critique of these comments, stating that "[t]he problem is male violence, not women's 'failure' to find ever more inventive ways to protect ourselves against it,"[81] which, whilst powerful to start with, was somewhat undermined by a much milder critique[82] of Police Scotland's failure to consider women's public safety during COP26. Furthermore, turning a blind eye to the acts of VAW perpetrated by actors within the criminal justice system (e.g., the police as shown in Sarah Everard's case), tolerating sexist and misogynistic attitudes towards women demonstrated by these actors,[83] ignoring the issue of women's public safety (e.g., by Police Scotland during COP26)[84] and, last but not least, disbelieving women's experiences of violence and not investigating the reports of violence with due diligence and care (e.g., the Worboys case) are powerful yet disappointing reminders of the persistent structural obstacles in the battle to combat VAW.

---

[78] Quinn (2018).

[79] BBC News (2021).

[80] Middleton (2021).

[81] Twitter (2021: @NicolaSturgeon, 1 October 2021, 3:10pm).

[82] Grant (2021).

[83] Syal (2021).

[84] Carrell (2021).

The manner in which incidents of VAW are reported in the media and publicly reacted to is also telling of pervasive and deeply entrenched problematic social attitudes towards such forms of violence. Victim blaming and increasing demands being put on women doing "safety work"[85] to protect themselves from violence are (too) frequently the point of focus in such reporting. As illustrated by aftermath of recent murders of Ashling Murphy and Sabina Nessa, the overarching narrative was one focusing on what women were doing at the time—'just going for a run' or 'just going to the pub.' Although perhaps well intentioned, this approach has been rightly criticised[86] for carrying the implication, however slight, that the extreme violence the women fell victims to would have been any less tragic had they been doing something else or less ordinary. Similarly, the public commitments made by politicians (such as the call for a zero-tolerance policy towards VAW in Ireland)[87] surrounding such 'extraordinary' events of VAW are generally short-lived and rarely carry a substantive law and policy change which could have, in principle, long-term impact. We critiqued this elsewhere (and in a different context) as VAW suffering from "slick campaigns"[88] and peaks of high-publicity annual events (e.g., International Women's Day or International Day on Elimination of All Forms of Violence Against Women) which, although significant for raising awareness about VAW, do not translate into sustained efforts to prevent and combat VAW (Fig. 1.1).

Cultures and practices of misogyny, patriarchy and inequality evolve into cultures of violence—both the everyday and the extraordinary (e.g. VAW in conflict). The two are mutually reinforcing, creating a fertile ground for VAW in its various forms and spaces. These may range from everyday transgressions which are too frequently mislabelled as 'minor' and the impact of which is underplayed (e.g., verbal abuse, online text-based abuse on social media or sexist comments in the workplace) to 'extraordinary' acts of VAW which shake the 'public conscience,'[89] such as

[85] Kelly (2012, pp. xvii–xxvi).

[86] Instagram (2022: laura_bates__); Petter (2022).

[87] Government of Ireland (2022).

[88] Barker and Jurasz (2020e).

[89] Barker and Jurasz (2019b, p. 120).

Fig. 1.1 Instagram post by Laura Bates, 13 January 2022

the killing of the Labour MP Jo Cox in June 2016; the kidnapping, rape and murder of Sarah Everard in March 2021; the murder of Sabina Nessa in September 2021; and the murder of Ashling Murphy in January 2022. Nonetheless, the everyday and the extraordinary events of VAW intertwine, creating a "continuum of violence"[90] experienced by women.

Importantly, VAW is not a uniform experience for all women[91]—as such, policy responses need to reflect the specificity of acts of VAW. As Vera-Grey observes, the "hierarchical structures interact and intersect with gender inequality," and their "manifestation differs according to other markers of a woman's or a girl's social location,"[92] including, for

[90] The idea of 'continuum of violence' was articulated by Liz Kelly in 1988, in relation to sexual violence against women. Continuum of sexual violence is understood by Kelly as twofold: first, as 'a continuous series of elements or events that pass into one another and which cannot be easily distinguished' and second, as a 'basic common character' behind various forms and incidents of violence, connecting what might otherwise be perceived as disparate phenomena. See Kelly (1988, p. 76).

[91] For a critique of essentialism in relation to VAW see, for example: Harris (1990); Crenshaw (1991); Montoya and Rolandsen Agustín (2013).

[92] Vera-Grey (2017, pp. 127–136).

example, their race, class, sexual orientation and geopolitical location.[93] A similar observation is made by Smith in relation to misogyny, which she describes as wearing "many guises, [revealing] itself in different forms which are dictated by class, wealth, education, race, religion, and other factors, but its chief characteristic is its pervasiveness."[94] Furthermore, various hierarchies arise in relation to VAW and towards women who suffer it, for example hierarchies of worth,[95] harms,[96] seriousness[97] and hierarchies of acts of VAW within the law.[98] These ultimately lead to a structure whereby some acts of VAW are prioritised, especially within the law, whereas others are shifted towards the margins, as seen in relation to creating laws capturing image-based versus text-based abuse. Cumulatively, these factors have in turn a differential impact on women subjected to violence, including the avenues of redress available and their treatment within the legal/justice system.

1.2.2 Violence Against Women, Hate and Misogyny: Law and Language

> Misogyny is so ingrained, so normalised within our society, so structural within our institutions it needs some radical action to tackle it. Conference, I can therefore confirm that in our consultation on Hate Crime I will ask a specific question on whether to make hate motivated by misogynistic harassment an offence, just as hate based on religion and race is. We will send a signal that Scotland has zero tolerance for hatred directed to women.[99]

The term 'misogyny' made a relatively recent arrival to international law and policy level, as well as in the UK and Scotland specifically. In recent years, there has been a noticeable rise in recognising and drawing links between the issues of VAW, misogyny and hate (although not always

[93] Park (2012).
[94] Smith (1989, pp. xviii–xix).
[95] Vera-Grey (2017, pp. 127–136).
[96] Barker and Jurasz (2019b, pp. 87 and 93).
[97] Kelly (n.d.: https://www.troubleandstrife.org/new-articles/the-trouble-with-hate/).
[98] Barker and Jurasz (2021d, p. 251).
[99] Yousaf (2018).

as a triad), in academic, campaigning, policy and even law reform contexts. However, it is notable that none of the international law and/or policy definitions of VAW explicitly refer to misogyny as a root cause/factor of violence, nor explicitly link it to hate crime/hate speech. The same generally applies in the UK and in Scotland, albeit in the case of the latter, the proposal to introduce the offence of misogynistic harassment[100] has prompted a closer and more formal examination of the links between misogyny and VAW—not least as a part of the remit of work carried out by the Working Group on Misogyny and Criminal Justice in Scotland.[101]

Misogyny and VAW

Interestingly, mentions of 'misogyny' or 'misogynistic' arise primarily in policy documents related to OVAW, online abuse and online hate speech, as well as in literature in these fields,[102] rather than in relation to VAW generally. For example, in 2016, the Parliamentary Assembly of the Council of Europe referred to misogyny when recognising that

> Hate speech is not limited to racism and xenophobia: it may also take the form of sexism, antisemitism, Islamophobia, misogyny, homophobia, and other forms of hate speech directed against specific groups or individuals.[103]

In 2017, the UN Special Rapporteur for cultural rights, Karima Bennoune, warned about the "multidirectional global avalanche of misogyny to which we must have an urgent global feminist riposte,"[104] whereas the (then) UN Special Rapporteur on violence against women, its causes and consequences, Dubravka Šimonović, noted the increase in

---

[100] Engender (2019b).

[101] Scottish Government (2021b).

[102] Jane (2017); Vickery and Everbach (2018); Barker and Jurasz (2019b).

[103] Council of Europe Parliamentary Assembly (2016, para. 2). The position taken in this report expanded the definition encapsulated in Council of Europe Committee of Ministers (1997) which does not include misogyny. The previous position was confirmed in *Gündüz v. Turkey* App. No. 35071/97 (ECtHR, 14 June 2004), para. 22.

[104] UN General Assembly (2017, para. 95).

sexist and misogynistic behaviours directed at women and girls online—albeit not elaborating about the scope of or distinction between the two:

> Despite the benefits and empowering potential of the Internet and ICT, women and girls across the world have increasingly voiced their concern at harmful, sexist, misogynistic and violent content and behaviour online.[105]

The UN Secretary General, António Guterres, has also commented on the "rising rates of violence and misogyny that women and girls face in every society,"[106] referred to "violent misogyny [that] has thrived in the shadow of the pandemic"[107] and framed misogyny as "a common feature of violent extremism."[108]

In the UK context, the rise of 'misogyny' language largely resulted from calls for introducing 'misogyny hate crime' into the law, including creating a standalone offence of misogyny. The Nottingham Citizens' (the local branch of Citizens UK) *No Place for Hate* report (2014) was instrumental in bringing this issue to a public and policy debate, soon prompting considerations of law reform to that effect. The study, which investigated the reporting of hate crimes in Nottingham, found that 38% of women who reported hate crime linked it explicitly to their gender, although the latter is not a protected characteristic under the English hate crime framework.[109] This finding led the Citizens Hate Crime Commission to recommend that

> Nottinghamshire Police should work with Nottingham Women's Centre and other groups specialising in gender equality to monitor crimes and incidents motivated by misogynistic intent ... [and] ensure there are processes in place to pick up the wider spectrum of misogynistic offences that women experience.[110]

---

[105] United Nations Human Rights Council (2018).

[106] UN Women (2021).

[107] Guterres (2021b).

[108] United Nations (2020, p. 7).

[109] Nottingham Citizens (2014).

[110] Ibid., p. 30.

In 2016, Nottinghamshire Police adopted this recommendation, becoming the first police force in the UK to recognise misogyny as hate crime in their recording practices. The reported success[111] of the pilot led other police forces in England (North Yorkshire Police,[112] Northamptonshire Police[113]) to record *misogyny* as hate crime, whilst others decided to record *gender* (Avon and Somerset Police)[114] or *sex* motivated crimes (West Yorkshire Police)[115] instead. However, as we argue elsewhere, the inconsistencies in the approach towards recording or 'flagging' misogyny and/or gender hate incidents (rather than crimes given the legal impossibility to do so currently) are highly problematic. Not only does the decision to record or flag misogyny as a hate incident have no grounding in the existing hate crime framework in any of the devolved jurisdictions of the UK but

> [f]ocusing on misogyny looks at much more narrow and specific motivations as opposed to gender which, although is most commonly suggested as including women, could just as well include crimes committed against persons who do not identify as cisgender.[116]

Moreover, the recording/flagging of misogyny and/or gender as perceived motivation for committing reported crimes does not (and, legally, cannot at this point) result in prosecution as a hate crime because there exists no legal basis to warrant such an approach—neither misogyny nor gender is a protected characteristic for the purposes of hate crime legislation (in neither Scotland nor England). As such, despite progressive appearances, the recording/flagging of such incidents by selected police forces does little more than gather data on women's perceptions of factors that motivate crimes committed against them, which could, optimistically speaking, contribute to informing wider efforts aimed at reforming hate crime frameworks across the UK.[117]

[111] Mullany and Trickett (2018).
[112] North Yorkshire Police, Fire & Crime Commissioner (2017).
[113] Cohen and Hymas (2020).
[114] Ashcroft (2017).
[115] Jacques (2021).
[116] Barker and Jurasz (2021b, p. 82).
[117] Ibid., p. 83.

The growing popularity of 'misogyny' in public debate, campaigning and, increasingly, in the context of hate crime law reforms is contrasted with the apparent lack of its definitional certainty. To put it simply, there is no legal definition[118] of misogyny, nor any legislation making it a stand-alone offence in any of the UK jurisdictions (correct as of February 2022). It is notable in this context that one of the tasks of the Working Group on Misogyny and Criminal Justice in Scotland, chaired by Baroness Kennedy QC, is to "develop an agreed working definition of misogyny".[119] That said, Scotland and England take somewhat divergent approaches to incorporating misogyny within the legal framework, especially that related to hate crime. In Scotland, the Hate Crime and Public Order (Scotland) Act 2021 (asp 14) (HCPOA 2021) did not make any explicit provisions with regard to misogyny—as such, it does not feature as a protected characteristic or anything else in the legislation. Instead, a pathway of exploring a stand-alone offence of misogynistic harassment has been favoured, albeit little substantive development followed after some initial enthusiasm. In contrast, the Law Commission of England and Wales recommended not to add sex and/or gender as protected characteristics under hate crime legislation[120] and remained silent on drawing a substantive distinction between terms 'sex,' 'gender' and 'misogyny.' This approach, however, has been subverted by the House of Lords who voted in favour of a two-part amendment, which would allow the courts to consider at the sentencing stage whether sex or gender was an aggravating factor in the commission of the offence.[121]

Where definitions of misogyny were proposed, these varied drastically, especially depending on the discipline in which the authors work. For instance, Ging and Siapera (media studies) use

> the broader concept of misogyny, which may not involve violence but almost always entails some form of harm; either directly in the form of psychological, professional, reputational, or, in some cases, physical harm;

[118] Barker and Jurasz (2020a); Barker and Jurasz (2020e).

[119] Scottish Government (2021b).

[120] Law Commission (2021, para. 5.380).

[121] Police, Crime, Sentencing and Courts HL Bill (2021–22) 95, cl. 73.

or indirectly, in the sense that it makes the internet a less equal, less safe, or less inclusive space for women and girls.[122]

In contrast, Barker and Jurasz (law) take a working definition of misogyny to be "the manifestation of hostility towards women because they are women," whereas Johnston and True (politics and international relations) see it "as both fear and hatred of women and/or the feminine."[123] Feminist philosopher Manne thinks of misogyny as

> a system that serves to enforce and police gendered norms and expectations to which groups of girls and women are subject under historically patriarchal orders, given the intersection between patriarchal forces with other systemic forms of domination and disadvantage, oppression and vulnerability.[124]

In 2016, Nottinghamshire Police arrived at a policy definition of misogyny as "incidents against women that are motivated by the attitude of men towards women, and includes behaviour targeted at women by men simply because they are women,"[125] which, somewhat surprisingly given the hate crime context, does not entail notions of hate and/or prejudice and/or hostility. This fragmentation of approaches to defining misogyny is further reinforced by various (mis)understandings of the term by politicians,[126] campaigners[127] and, as a result, the general public.[128]

However, as Pinson Wrisley writes, "there is a significant difference in something being functional and something being accurate, meaningful or appropriately utilised."[129] This rings particularly true where legal

---

122 Ging and Siapera (2018).

123 Johnston and True (2019).

124 Manne (2017, p. 1).

125 Nottinghamshire Police, 'Hate Crime Policy' (2016).

126 Dathan (2021). This approach is also evidenced in the House of Lords debate of the Police, Crime, Sentencing and Courts Bill: see HL Deb 17 January 2022, vol 817, cols. 1328–1486.

127 Barker and Jurasz (2020e).

128 Mullany and Trickett's 2018 evaluation of the pilot study on misogyny hate crime revealed that many of the participants were not familiar with the policy and that they did not fully understand the concept of misogyny hate crime. See Mullany and Trickett (2018).

129 Pinson Wrisley (2021, p. 4).

categories and legal meanings are concerned, which ultimately determine whether a particular act is to fall under legal regulation or not.[130] Misogyny remains undertheorised in feminist theory, similarly to, once, patriarchy.[131] In general, misogyny is not addressed within legal theory (or feminist legal theory) either, with very few examples of law literature embarking upon the discussion of the (im)possibility of the legal regulation of misogyny,[132] despite a wealth of legal, socio-legal and feminist legal theory literature on the subjects of VAW and/or gender-based violence; law and gender; sex and/or gender discrimination. Furthermore, the interchangeable use of the term 'misogyny' with 'sexism' and/or as equivalents of 'VAW' or 'GBV' leads to a significant state of confusion as to the individual meanings of these terms but also, specifically, their *legal* meaning and implications for their operation within the law.[133] As Chalmers and Leverick argue, fair labelling is significant, especially in the context of criminal offences, on both macro and micro levels, including in areas of criminal law which may be "less well understood by the general public."[134] In such cases, fair labelling not only carries the symbolic function of accurately recognising the criminal act and its consequences, but also has the benefit of accurately conveying the essential nature of wrongdoing, particularly to those operating outside the criminal justice system (i.e. where no assumption of legal knowledge can be made).[135]

The need for fair labelling is illustrated by the UK-wide experience of reforming 'hate crime,'[136] which also saw calls for making misogyny a stand-alone offence, and/or to incorporate it as a protected characteristic under hate crime legislation. However, the misconceptions about the practicality of incorporating 'misogyny' into law, combined with occasional misunderstandings of the scope of the hate crime framework and its operation, proved especially problematic in the context of campaigning.

[130] Barker and Jurasz (2020b, pp. 56–57); Barker and Jurasz (2021c, pp. 794–795).

[131] Walby (1990).

[132] See, for example, Barker and Jurasz (2019b).

[133] Barker and Jurasz (2020b, pp. 56–57); Pinson Wrisley (2021, pp. 16–17).

[134] Chalmers and Leverick (2008, p. 222).

[135] Ibid., p. 238.

[136] Law Commission (2021); Scottish Government (2018); Hate Crime and Public Order (Scotland) Act 2021 (asp 14); Department of Justice (2020).

Conflation of terminology (women/sex/gender/misogyny/VAW) in those campaigns, to an extent reinforced by some media coverage, resulted in mixed messaging as to scope, possibility and, importantly, the *legal* effects of the proposed reform. This was specifically so in relation to calls for adding 'misogyny' as a protected characteristic; given that 'misogyny' is not a demographic characteristic (as opposed to, for example, race, sex or gender), it was rather difficult to envisage it becoming a protected characteristic embedded in law.[137] Arguably, it led to misinformation of the general public as to (i) the substance and scope of the proposed reform (e.g., what is the effect of having a 'protected characteristic' under hate crime laws) and (ii) the potential effects of it (e.g., not every crime committed against a woman would automatically be misogynistic nor a hate crime unless a specific legal threshold—yet to be determined—is met).[138]

Hate Speech, Hate Crime and VAW

In recent years, there has been a noticeable tendency to recognise the impact of hate crime and hate speech on the realisation of women's rights as well as to capture gender-based hate crimes within policy and proposals for law reform. For instance, in October 2021, the Report of the UN Special Rapporteur on the promotion and protection of the right to freedom opinion and expression, Irene Khan, recognised hate speech as a method of silencing women and limiting their participation in public and political life[139] whilst also noting that "sexism and misogyny are dominant factors in gendered censorship."[140] Similarly, in November 2021, the European Commission announced its intention to "propose to extend the list of 'EU crimes' to cover hate speech and hate crime [as] [t]his will allow the EU to be able to criminalise gender-based hate speech and hate crime."[141]

[137] For further discussion of this point, see Chap. 4.

[138] For a critique of campaigning for 'misogyny hate crime' across the UK, see: Barker and Jurasz (2020e); Barker and Jurasz (2021b, pp. 82–84).

[139] UN General Assembly (2021, paras. 15, 24, and 102).

[140] United Nations (2021).

[141] European Commission (2021).

However, from a legal perspective, there is a significant distinction between categories of 'hate crime' and 'hate speech,' which has, in turn, (legal) implications for capturing acts of VAW under either one of these concepts. An act of VAW may amount to a hate crime if (1) it is currently captured in law as a criminal offence and (2) it is committed in relation to existing protected characteristics.

In Scottish contexts, this alone presents difficulties for a number of reasons. Firstly, VAW is not defined (in Scotland nor generally in the UK) with reference to hate crime and vice versa; this means that these concepts are not linked within law and policy, and it is a matter of dispute whether they ought to be.[142] Secondly, even if a specific act of VAW is indeed captured in Scots criminal law, at present it is not legally possible to treat gender as an aggravation for prejudice given the absence of 'gender' amongst the protected characteristics under the HCPOA 2021. Instead, the Act provides for a special category of "variations in sex characteristics,"[143] which hardly provides for conceptual or legal clarity,[144] not to mention its departure from the recommendation of Lord Bracadale's Review of Hate Crime Legislation in Scotland.[145] Even if one focuses on the purely symbolic aspect of the recognition of VAW within the hate crime framework, the net result of doing so—at least from the legal perspective—remains unsatisfactory. The lack of gender as a protected characteristic makes the symbolic recognition of gender as a factor motivating prejudice impossible to capture. This stands in contrast with situations where a criminal act of VAW is committed with prejudice due to other legally recognised factors such as race, nationality, age, disability

[142] Note: the position taken in this book is that viewing VAW solely through the lens of hate crime frameworks presents a number of difficulties, not only from legal, policy, and victim support perspectives but, most importantly, on a conceptual level. However, it is recognised that, in some specific cases of VAW, hate based on the victim's gender can be an important factor and having a modern hate crime framework recognising this dynamic would allow for capturing such cases. Nonetheless, this cannot be uniformly applied to *all* cases of VAW by default as it would incorrectly position the phenomenon of VAW, the motivations of the perpetrators for committing it and experiences of the victims. Furthermore, a narrow approach of viewing VAW through a singular lens of hate crime would have significant and detrimental law and policy implications, including on justice and redress available to women.

[143] Hate Crime and Public Order (Scotland) Act 2021, s. 1(2)(g) (asp 14).

[144] Barker and Jurasz (2020c).

[145] Scottish Government (2018, para. 4.50). For further discussion of this point, see Chap. 4.

or transgender identity (amongst others).[146] This disparity is amplified in cases involving intersecting factors in prejudice, for example, the gender of the victim *and* their religion. Whilst the latter will be given legal recognition, the former remains invisible in the official—legal—record due to (1) the absence of gender as protected characteristic under Scots Law and (2) the recording of only a single characteristic with regard to the "malice or ill will" towards the victim at the time of committing the offence. The current legal impossibility of capturing multiple intersecting protected characteristics deepens the problem of invisibility of gender as a basis for prejudice.

In contrast, hate speech is a broader term which can encompass, for example, "expressions which spread, incite, promote or justify hatred"[147] based on a specific characteristic. As such, it does not require an underlying act which is a crime (unlike in cases of hate crime), and although in some instances hate speech acts may lead to the person being prosecuted, not all hate speech acts amount to a hate crime. In general, restrictions on 'free speech' or freedom of expression and opinion are relatively rare and carefully balanced, both at international and domestic levels. International law protects freedom of opinion and expression,[148] but also places positive obligations on States which limit it. For instance, Article 20(2) of the International Covenant on Civil and Political Rights states that "any advocacy of national, racial or religious hatred that constitutes incitement to discrimination, hostility or violence shall be prohibited by law." Nonetheless, there is an absence of a treaty-based (or legally binding) definition of hate crime and/or hate speech. As such, approaches to it tend to vary and are often disputed, both in national and international fora. The UN Strategy and Plan of Action on Hate Speech adopted a broad, gender-inclusive and open-ended definition of hate speech, seeing it as

[146] For a full list of protected characteristics under Scots Law, see Hate Crime and Public Order (Scotland) Act 2021, s. 1(2)(a) – (g) (asp 14).

[147] Council of Europe (n.d.: https://rm.coe.int/CoERMPublicCommonSearchServices/DisplayDCTMContent?documentId=0900001680651592).

[148] International Covenant on Civil and Political Rights (adopted 16 December 1966, entered into force 23 March 1976) 999 UNTS 171 (ICCPR), art. 19.

> any kind of communication in speech, writing or behaviour, that attacks or uses pejorative or discriminatory language with reference to a person or a group on the basis of who they are, in other words, based on their religion, ethnicity, nationality, race, colour, descent, gender or other identity factor.[149]

Equally, the UN Committee on the Elimination of Racial Discrimination understands hate speech as "a form of other-directed speech which rejects the core human rights principles of human dignity and equality and seeks to degrade the standing of individuals and groups in the estimation of society."[150] Whilst the scope of this Recommendation focuses on racist hate speech, the notion of the rejection of human dignity and equality rings true for cases involving gender, especially where race and gender intersect in the context of hate speech/hate crime. That said, as noted by the Committee of Ministers of the Council of Europe,

> [w]hile racist hate speech is recognised as contrary to European and international human rights standards, the same is not always true of sexist or misogynist hate speech, and current policies and legislation at all levels have not been able to adequately address the issue.[151]

In recognition of this problem, the Committee of Ministers drew a link between hate speech and VAW in the landmark Recommendation on Preventing and Combatting Sexism,[152] which is the first instrument to include an internationally agreed definition of sexism. It recognises that "sexist behaviour such as, in particular, sexist hate speech, may escalate to or incite overtly offensive and threatening acts, including sexual abuse or violence, rape or potentially lethal action,"[153] therefore demonstrating the potential causality between hate speech (here: sexist hate speech) and VAW.

---

[149] United Nations (2019, p. 2).

[150] Committee on the Elimination of Racial Discrimination (2013, para. 10).

[151] Council of Europe Committee of Ministers (2019, p. 8).

[152] Ibid.

[153] Ibid., Appendix to Recommendation CM/Rec(2019)1 (Guidelines for preventing and combating sexism: measures for implementation).

The UN CEDAW Committee also increasingly recognises the links between hate speech/hate crime, discrimination of women and VAW. The Committee recommended specific actions to combat hate speech against women to a number of States, including the need to "strengthen measures to tackle hate speech against ethnic minority and other women and girls in the media, including on Internet discussion boards and in social media,"[154] criminalise hate speech, especially when directed against women human rights defenders,[155] and "address the use of misogynistic language, hate speech against LBTI women (and) punish hate crimes against LBTI women."[156]

However, the unqualified linking of VAW and hate crime is also disputed. Whilst for some it offers an avenue for capturing hate towards women as a driver behind committing (some) acts of VAW,[157] and therefore enabling symbolic recognition[158] of this suggested dynamic, others remain sceptical about the benefits of making such associations. Kelly specifically notes the unhelpful direction of subsuming VAW under the hate crime framework, emphasising the limitations in furthering understandings of why certain traditional practices leading to VAW persist—such as female genital mutilation or forced marriage.[159] In particular, the campaigns proposing to include misogyny within hate crime frameworks in Scotland (and elsewhere in the UK) have been criticised as promoting a short-sighted approach towards tackling VAW, especially at the potential expense of a more holistic consideration and implementation of frameworks to prevent and combat VAW.[160] In their submission to the Scottish Government consultation on hate crime legislation in Scotland, Engender expressed strong concerns

[154] Committee on the Elimination of Discrimination against Women (2014, para. 15).

[155] Committee on the Elimination of Discrimination against Women (2021b, paras. 21–22).

[156] Committee on the Elimination of Discrimination against Women (2021a, paras. 23(c) and 47(c)).

[157] Maher et al. (2015, p. 182); Angelari (1994).

[158] Barker and Jurasz (2019b, p. 104); Brooks (2021).

[159] Kelly (n.d.: https://www.troubleandstrife.org/new-articles/the-trouble-with-hate/).

[160] Barker and Jurasz (2021b, p. 93); Gill and Mason-Bish (2013).

about the possibility of an ineffectual hate crime to institutionally entrench and systematise indifference to misogyny" as well as "arguments that suggest that the symbolic or communicative quality of criminalising gendered hate crime is sufficient to respond to the reality of women's experience.[161]

The organisation relied on experiences from New Jersey where between 1999 and 2008 only four gender-bias incidents were recorded in comparison with, for instance, 3521 race-bias incidents.[162] For Engender, this suggested that gender-based hate crime remains "under-investigated and under-prosecuted compared with hate crime targeting other protected groups," and its introduction will likely result in opposite effects to the ones intended—that is, that "misogyny is less harmful and less proscribed than other forms of hate crime,"[163] reinforcing the "notion that harassment of women is tolerated by society."[164]

However, there appears to be a significant gap in the law in relation to the recognition of harmful effects of misogynistic and/or gender-based and/or sexist hate speech. This is particularly the case where incitement to VAW is concerned. Whilst offences of stirring up hatred, however controversial to some,[165] have been introduced in Scotland through introduction of Section 4 of the HCPOA 2021, the characteristics covered within it mirror those in Section 1(2), therefore excluding gender. There is therefore an opportunity for Scots Law to bridge the existing legislative gap by legally recognising 'incitement to violence against women' as a separate offence.

1.2.3 Violence Against Women: International Influences on the Scottish Voices

Scotland positions itself as a country open to others—a place that is inclusive, engaged on the global scene and plays an active part in the international community, be it at a European or an international level.

---

[161] Engender (2020, p. 11).

[162] Ibid., p. 8.

[163] Ibid., p. 11.

[164] Ibid., p. 11.

[165] Joyce (2021).

This is explicitly recognised in Scotland's International Framework 2017,[166] which boldly states: "[i]nternationalising Scotland benefits us all."[167] As Scotland's foreign affairs remain a reserved matter,[168] the Scottish Government is in a good position to ensure that international laws, policies and standards on VAW are adequately reflected in Scots Law and policy. Whilst Scotland cannot ratify international treaties, it has a responsibility under schedule 5, paragraph 7 to the Scotland Act 1998 to fulfil the UK's international obligations.

There are many examples, even just in recent years, of Scotland's international outlook. Scotland voted overwhelmingly (62%)[169] against the UK's withdrawal from the European Union in the Brexit referendum and remains committed to protecting and strengthening its place in Europe[170] as one of the four strategic objectives set out in the International Framework. This is further reinforced by the adoption of the UK Withdrawal from the European Union (Continuity) (Scotland) Act 2021 (asp 4), which came into force on 31 January 2021 and, in a rather unique and progressive manner, enables Scottish ministers to make provisions in secondary legislation to allow for Scots Law to 'keep pace'[171] with EU law in devolved areas of competence. Furthermore, Scotland's role in advancing gender equality was also recognised in 2019 when the First Minister, Nicola Sturgeon, was appointed as the inaugural #HeForShe Global Advocate by UN Women, with the Scottish Government becoming signatories to the UN Women's global solidarity movement for gender equality, which engages men and boys as advocates for equality.[172] Scotland's commitment to the Sustainable Development Goals (SDGs), which include, but are not limited to, gender equality is also notable. Not only are the SDGs reflected across numerous policies, progress towards

---

[166] Scottish Government (2017).

[167] Ibid.

[168] As a result of the Devolution settlement, certain matters are reserved to the UK Parliament, i.e. they remain the responsibility of the UK Parliament rather than the Scottish Parliament.

[169] BBC News (2016).

[170] Scottish Government (2017), p. 9.

[171] UK Withdrawal from the European Union (Continuity) (Scotland) Act 2021, s. 1(1) (asp 4).

[172] Scottish Government (2020e, p. 64).

their achievement[173] is regularly assessed, demonstrating Scotland's commitment to—in particular—introducing laws and policies which align with SDG 5 Gender Equality.[174]

In addition, the Scottish National Party (SNP) manifesto for the 2021 Scottish Parliament election reaffirmed the commitment to the global positioning of Scotland, pledging to adopt a feminist foreign policy as well as undertaking to incorporate UN human rights treaties, including CEDAW, into Scots Law.[175] The latter was also recommended in March 2021 by the National Taskforce for Human Rights,[176] followed by the unanimous passing of the United Nations Convention of the Rights of the Child (Incorporation) (Scotland) Bill 2020. However, following the UK Supreme Court judgement in October 2021, some aspects of the Bill were held to be outside the powers of the Scottish Parliament, and therefore the Bill could not proceed to become law in its current form.[177] As this undoubtedly frustrating development demonstrates, Scotland's progressivism, international outlook and resilience are somewhat held back by Westminster, at the expense of preventing a more contemporary, responsive, rights-based framework from developing in Scotland—one which could have positive impacts on future generations.

CEDAW remains the focal point in terms of setting international law standards concerning non-discrimination of women, including through GBV. Although CEDAW is not, per se, an anti-violence treaty, throughout the years since its adoption, the UN Committee on Elimination of Discrimination Against Women (a body that oversees States' compliance with CEDAW) has clarified the applicability of CEDAW to VAW, including the obligations of States with respect to protecting women from violence.[178] There has been a significant level of support in Scotland towards

[173] Scottish Government (2020e).

[174] Ibid., pp. 64–74.

[175] Scottish National Party (2021).

[176] Scottish Government (2021c, p. 27).

[177] *Reference by the Attorney General and the Advocate General for Scotland – United Nations Convention on the Rights of the Child (Incorporation) (Scotland) Bill; Reference by the Attorney General and the Advocate General for Scotland – European Charter of Local Self-Government (Incorporation) (Scotland) Bill* [2021] UKSC 42.

[178] See, in particular, Committee on the Elimination of Discrimination against Women (1992); Committee on the Elimination of Discrimination against Women (2017).

the incorporation of CEDAW into Scots Law.[179] This support included information campaigns, such as 'Incorporation Fortnight,'[180] which focused on incorporating UN human rights treaties and a new human rights law for Scotland. This is further exemplified by the commitments to standards set out in CEDAW, but also the use of CEDAW as a tool for standard-setting within Scottish policy on VAW and women's rights. For example, CEDAW features prominently within *Equally Safe*, which expresses commitment to the benchmarks it sets, in addition to adopting a human-rights-based approach to defining and tackling VAW.[181] Equally, the reports and recommendations of the First Minister's National Advisory Council on Women and Girls (NACWG)[182] have consistently relied on CEDAW, as well as on other international instruments, such as the Istanbul Convention, with NACWG supporting its domestic incorporation.

The human-rights-based approach to law and policy-making on VAW in Scotland is imperative as it allows the development of responses to VAW, which are not only aligned with international standards and best practice but also build upon them. This is exemplified by the process of creation as well as substantive provisions of the Domestic Abuse (Scotland) Act 2018 (asp 5). For example, part 2 of schedule 3 to the Domestic Abuse Act 2021 extends the extra-territorial jurisdiction of the Scottish criminal courts. In doing so, it echoes the standards adopted in the Istanbul Convention.[183] Importantly, looking to CEDAW and other UN human rights treaties to operationalise law and policy on VAW enabled Scotland to bring experience of Scottish women to an international arena,

---

[179] Scottish Government (2021d); Engender, Zero Tolerance, Rape Crisis Scotland, Close the Gap, and Scottish Women's Aid (2019: https://www.engender.org.uk/content/publications/5-organisations-CEDAW-incorporation-paper.pdf); Engender (2018).

[180] Human Rights Consortium Scotland (2021); Engender (2021).

[181] Scottish Government and COSLA (2020, p. 17).

[182] One Scotland (n.d.: https://onescotland.org/equality-themes/advisory-council-women-girls/); First Minister's National Advisory Council on Women and Girls (2018); First Minister's National Advisory Council on Women and Girls (2019); First Minister's National Advisory Council on Women and Girls (2020); First Minister's National Advisory Council on Women and Girls (2021).

[183] Jurasz (2015).

conquering somewhat the dominant narrative of 'Britishness'[184] which frequently disguises an English perspective on various social issues. Monitoring and reporting mechanisms carried out by the CEDAW Committee (as well as other UN human rights treaty bodies) facilitated this through the submission of shadow reports by Scottish NGOs on official State/UK reports concerning compliance with CEDAW. As such, in every reporting period, the State (here, the UK) presents the CEDAW Committee with a State report, which is then accompanied by a number of shadow reports from civil society organisations from across the UK, giving the Committee an opportunity to carry out an objective assessment of State compliance with matters under their mandate. Furthermore, CEDAW is an important advocacy and litigation tool which can provide avenues for State accountability for VAW, not least through the use of the individual complaint procedure enabled through the Optional Protocol to CEDAW.[185]

The readiness to apply these standards by the domestic courts in Scotland remains to be seen. The success of this approach, as Fredman suggested, may rely on the visibility of CEDAW, its Optional Protocol and the work of the CEDAW Committee, as well as appropriate legal education and training of judicial officers.[186] Likewise, the impact of incorporating UN human rights treaties in Scotland cannot be assessed with certainty at this stage. Assuming successful progress with regard to incorporation, the effects of this step are likely dependent on several other factors, including "domestication of a number of international norms such as progressive realisation, minimum core obligations as well as substantive equality, the latter of which engages with a reserved matter."[187] However, the promise of the incorporation of CEDAW into the new human rights framework for Scotland could potentially pave the way to

[184] For a critique of the concept of 'Britishness' and its role in reinforcing 'blindness' to Scottish experiences, especially those of women in Scotland, see Breitenbach et al. (1998, pp. 49–60).

[185] The Optional Protocol to CEDAW enables individual communication procedure which allows individuals to bring claims alleging violations of CEDAW by the State party before the CEDAW Committee (typically, after domestic remedies are exhausted). See Optional Protocol to the Convention on the Elimination of All Forms of Discrimination against Women, UNGA Res 54/4 (15 October 1999) UN Doc. A/RES/54/4.

[186] Fredman (2013, p. 516).

[187] Boyle and Busby (2021, p. 13).

a more cohesive and integrated approach to addressing VAW in law, and before the courts, as well as better human rights protections in Scotland—especially after Brexit.[188]

1.3 Violence Against Women in Scotland: From 'Reclaim the Night' to #MeToo

Tackling VAW has certainly become a firm policy priority in post-Devolution Scotland, but, rather unsurprisingly, the problem itself has always existed in Scottish society—not unlike in other countries, regions or nations. Writing in 1978, Evelyn Hunter powerfully commented on the status of women in Scotland and their legal rights at that time, specifically noting the entrenched inferior legal status of women in Scotland as opposed to England and Wales:

> I have already discussed the narrow puritanism that saw women as the source of evil and harshly repressed all sexual sins. Its influence remains with us today in the strains of orthodoxy and prudery in our national "character", in spite of the so-called sexual revolution. An acceptance of women's inferior status is shared by Orangemen and Roman Catholics together, despite their opposition to each other. We waited years for our divorce laws to change in line with those of England and Wales, and even now divorce is more complicated and costly in Scotland. […] The recent laws helping battered women, rape victims, and women's rights to the marital home do not apply here, limited though they are for women in England and Wales. It is commonly believed that these laws have not been passed for Scotland because the British Parliament has not allocated parliamentary time to make essential legislation for what they consider a mere region of the country.[189]

Hunter also boldly called out the social and political resistance to challenging the status quo of women in Scotland:

---

[188] Scottish Government (2020f): the Report outlines a number of impacts on women, including in relation to VAW (see pp. 49–50).

[189] Hunter (1979, pp. 11–12).

> Apart from the parliamentary disinterest, resistance to change is also to blame for the slowness of legislative reform for Scotland. When divorce legislation was first drafted it was blocked for some time by a Scottish MP. When divorce reform did get through, the legal profession in Scotland prevented divorce procedures from becoming as simple as in England. The Housing (Homeless Persons) Act almost failed to apply to Scotland because of the opposition of the Scottish local authorities. And what changes in the law can rape victims expect from members of a Scottish Assembly, considering the deep-rooted notion that women have asked to be assaulted?[190]

The timing of Hunter's account of women's legal rights in Scotland is significant, as, critical as it is, it looks with some hope towards the (then planned) Scottish Assembly (see Chap. 2) to provide the opportunity to put women's rights and matters affecting women in Scotland on the political and law reform agenda. Whilst sceptical of the progressive and transformative potential of the (then proposed) Scottish Assembly, Hunter nonetheless saw it as a space for public discussion of these issues and an opportunity for the Women's Liberation Movement in Scotland to campaign for changes in the law and raise awareness of the continuing oppression of women in Scotland by women in Scotland.[191] For Hunter, the agency of Scottish women in bringing about these changes was crucial as she refreshingly, yet poignantly, notes that "we cannot expect our English sisters to do so for us, ignorant as many of them seem of the difficulties we face."[192]

That said, there was a degree of cross-fertilisation of ideas and solidarity across the Women's Liberation Movements in the UK, as women were brought together by common goals and outrage at their treatment, especially before and within the law. Rape and sexual violence, impunity for domestic violence fuelled by regressive social and institutional attitudes towards it, access to abortion and women's reproductive rights, women's equal pay and women's public safety have been the key themes of women's liberation which united women across the nations of the UK.[193] The

[190] Ibid., p. 12.

[191] Ibid.

[192] Ibid.

[193] Browne (2014); Hunter (1979, app. 6: The Seven Demands of the Women's Liberation Movement); Treasure (n.d.: https://www.bl.uk/spare-rib/articles/violence-against-women).

united voices of women across the UK were particularly strongly felt in the late 1970s when women took to the streets in Leeds (and then other parts of the UK, including in Edinburgh, Glasgow and Aberdeen)[194] in 'Reclaim the Night' marches to protest over the advice given to women after Peter Sutcliffe (the Yorkshire Ripper) murders to 'stay at home' and 'avoid walking alone at night.' As Browne writes, the preferred chant on these marches was, "however we dress, and wherever we go, yes means yes and no means no."[195] Although the Reclaim the Night march in Leeds in 1977 is often identified as a focal point of the Reclaim the Night movement, similar events had been held in Scotland before:

> [a] precursor to the marches in Scotland had occurred in 1976 at an event called Witching the Meadows, held on Halloween. A group of women gathered on the Meadows in Edinburgh, dressed like witches and hexed a section of the park known to be particularly dangerous. They also hung an effigy of a rapist from a tree with a sign around its neck, which read 'an end to rape'. A year later at a Radical Feminist Conference in Edinburgh some participants decided to spill out on to the streets and 'take back the night', protesting against the fear women felt when walking the streets alone. In doing so they inaugurated the first RTN march in Britain.[196]

Nonetheless, the North-South/Scotland-England divide, its impact on law and policy reform in Scotland and its reflection in social attitudes have been important yet often overlooked elements in shaping legal and policy responses to VAW and the position of women in Scotland more generally. Breitenbach, Brown and Myers (1998)[197] identify English cultural and political hegemony as a key factor in obscuring Scottish women's experiences which leads to their marginalisation within (feminist) research, therefore creating a gap which in turn is reflected within law and policy-making, especially on matters concerning women. The detrimental and often discriminatory ripple effects of this gap have been also playing out in everyday experiences of Scottish women and have been

[194] Waterson (2021).
[195] Browne (2014, p. 166).
[196] Ibid.
[197] Breitenbach et al. (1998, p. 59).

further exacerbated by discrimination due to other characteristics such as age, class, race, disability, sexuality or religion.[198] The lived experiences of this dynamic—particularly the "triple oppression [of] race, gender and class"[199]—were highlighted in late 1980s by Arshad and McCrum (1989) who wrote about the oppression and marginalisation of black[200] women in Scotland. They posed an important question—which continues to be relevant in contemporary Scotland:

> when we use the term 'Scottish', to whom are we referring—a white Scotland or multi-racial Scotland? It is a matter of the speaker's perception of what is the norm. Who do we therefore mean when we use the term 'woman'? Today, the political struggle for equality in Scotland has produced women's committees, women-only events, women officers within trade unions, women representatives on committees and so on, but how many of these represent the voices of black Scottish women?[201]

However, as Arshad and McCrum note, the issue facing black women in Scotland was not one of visibility (or lack thereof) but rather the selective areas in which black women's lives and experiences are positioned and how they are contextualised in a manner "acceptable to a society operating within a racist framework."[202] This, in turn, had an effect on meeting the needs of black, Asian and Minority Ethnic (BAME) women. For example, the lack of appropriate support for black and minority ethnic women in Scotland was particularly challenging for BAME women who faced violence, especially in the domestic/intimate-partner context. The creation of Shakti Women's Aid[203] in 1986—the first refuge for BAME women, children and young people who experienced domestic/intimate-partner abuse—was instrumental in providing a much-needed support and a stepping stone in closing the gap in provision of support

[198] Brown et al. (1994, p. 78).

[199] Arshad and McCrum (1989, p. 207).

[200] Arshad and McCrum clarified that the term 'black' in the paper has broad application: "We have chosen the word 'black' to refer to all people of colour who are discriminated against by racist structures and attitudes within Scotland's white dominated culture" (Ibid., p. 225).

[201] Arshad and McCrum (1989, pp. 208–209).

[202] Arshad and McCrum (1989, p. 210).

[203] Shakti Women's Aid (n.d.: https://shaktiedinburgh.co.uk/).

services to BAME women in Scotland. The significance and early impact of Shakti Women's Aid work was described by Sachidharan as allowing "black women to define their own terms in fighting racism and sexism, which would not have been possible in the mainstream women's aid movement."[204] This struggle continues to be significant in contemporary Scotland, as powerfully conveyed by Folorunso:

> The conversation, or shared experience of being black in Scotland, is often one of loneliness. We have had to work very hard to find communities and spaces where we can truly be ourselves. For a long time, we feel unseen, unheard and ignored and unsafe. Often entering spaces as the "only one" or one of a few, acts of racism and a multitude of micro-aggressions experienced become part of our norm. When we have needed it, solidarity has been nowhere to be seen, and allies quiet.[205]

While issues facing BAME women in Scotland cannot go unnoticed, they form part of the bigger societal challenges of inequalities which continue to persist in Scotland.

1.3.1 Post-Devolution Scotland and VAW: #GenerationEqual?

The tensions within the Women's Liberation Movement (both across the North-South/Scotland-England divide as well as within Scotland) are an important part of the sociopolitical history of women's rights in Scotland as well as the struggle to end VAW. They are a testament to the becoming and inherent evolution of the women's movement in Scotland which, whilst "differed in some significant ways," also "evolved and developed and so did the women involved in it."[206]

Fortunately, much has changed since with regard to laws and policies applicable to women in Scotland, including noticeable influences of

[204] Pramila Sachidharan, 'Separate Refuges for Black Women: Ghettos or Power Houses' in *Leeds Black Women's Newsletter*, Issue No. 1, January 1987, quoted in Arshad and McCrum (1989, p. 217).

[205] Folorunso (2020).

[206] Browne 2014, p. 18.

international law (see Sect. 1.2.3) on the advancement of women's rights and setting standards on protecting women from GBV. Moreover, post-Devolution Scotland has emerged as a leader amongst the UK's four nations in pioneering a progressive approach towards tackling VAW. It would be incorrect to attribute this progress entirely to the Devolution settlement—to do would erase the activism and work of women in Scotland who have fought and campaigned to tackle VAW. However, there has been a noticeable impetus to tackle VAW through law and policy in Scotland since the late 1990s and early 2000s, which certainly coincides with Scotland rising and developing as a devolved nation and becoming bold, ambitious but also pragmatic about making VAW and "gender inequality a historical curiosity."[207] Whether the achieved successes and progress made with respect to these goals is due to careful design or geopolitical serendipity is debatable (see Chap. 2). That is far from saying that Scotland has eradicated VAW once and for all or that it is free of GBV and intersectional discrimination—far from it. Nonetheless, the progress in Scotland—both in terms of law and policy—concerning addressing VAW, identifying opportunities for law reform and working towards ending women's inequalities and VAW in a number of areas (including, e.g., tackling period poverty[208] or introducing domestic abuse legislation which covers economically abusive behaviours[209]) is notable.

In 1998, the Scottish Partnership on Domestic Abuse was established, which later became the National Group to Address Violence Against Women. In 2007, the First Minister signed the Women's Coalition Statement of Intent, committing the Scottish Government to continue its work on preventing and combatting VAW and to adopt a broader definition of gender-based violence.[210] This commitment was reflected in the publication of *Safer Lives: Changed Lives. A Shared Approach to Tackling Violence Against Women in Scotland*[211]—a key policy document which provided a "shared understanding and approach which will guide the

[207] First Minister's National Advisory Council on Women and Girls (2020).

[208] Period Products (Free Provision) (Scotland) Act 2021 (asp 1); Rocks (2020).

[209] Domestic Abuse (Scotland) Act 2018 (asp 5).

[210] The Women's Coalition is a coalition formed in Scotland by Engender, Scottish Women's Aid, Rape Crisis Scotland, The Women's Support Project and Zero Tolerance.

[211] Scottish Government and COSLA (2009).

work of all partners to tackle violence against women in Scotland."[212] Importantly, the document also positioned addressing VAW in the context of the Gender Equality Duty and the National Performance Framework by recognising that working to address the causes and consequences of VAW is necessary to achieve several of the national outcomes.[213] This important step has set the foundations for the later landmark policies, such as *Equally Safe*.[214]

However, importantly, steps taken to address VAW in Scotland also go beyond commitments confined in the policy documents. Various measures have been actioned to operationalise them or otherwise enable their progressive realisation, such as the Scottish Government's Delivering Equally Safe funding programme which provides financial support to third-sector organisations and public bodies whose work contributes "to the objectives, priorities and outcomes of the Equally Safe Strategy."[215] In 2017, the NACWG[216] was established to advise and support the First Minister on matters of tackling gender inequality in Scotland, and "by proving a challenging voice to the First Minister and her team, where there are gaps in the work being undertaken to address gender inequality or where progress is not effecting real change."[217] The creation of NACWG is an example of progressive outlook in Scottish governance, which has not found an equivalent (thus far) at a UK Government level. NACWG, whose initial three-year strategy came to an end in 2021, produced annual reports and recommendations as well as worked to raise awareness about gender equality issues in Scotland. Although the scope of work of the group was much broader than just gender inequality in relation to VAW, NACWG made a number of recommendations which would help tackle VAW and support women and girls experiencing such violence, including recommendations to incorporate CEDAW into Scots Law, criminalise serious misogynistic harassment and create a world-leading process for

[212] Ibid., p. 3.

[213] Ibid., p. 4.

[214] Scottish Government and COSLA (2014).

[215] Inspiring Scotland (n.d.: https://www.inspiringscotland.org.uk/what-we-do/our-funds/equally-safe/delivering-equally-safe-fund/).

[216] One Scotland (n.d.: https://onescotland.org/equality-themes/advisory-council-women-girls/).

[217] First Minister's National Advisory Council on Women and Girls (2021, p. 6).

complainers[218] of sexual violence.[219] Furthermore, the NACWG made progressive recommendations to the Scottish Government to improve Scotland's 'gender architecture,' highlighting in particular the absence of diverse voices contributing to its design and work.[220] Gender architecture is understood in this context as "the structures that are designed to advance women's equality and rights—like ministries, regulators, equality laws, duties, indicators, policy processes and any accountability mechanisms,"[221] making it a core element in ensuring effective, cross-sectoral work to advance gender equality.

Effective and intersectional gender architecture also has positive influences on tackling VAW, which, at a legal level, can be illustrated by the legislative progressivism in Scotland in relation to VAW. For instance, the Domestic Abuse (Scotland) Act 2018 (asp 5) and the Gender Representation on Public Boards (Scotland) Act 2018 (asp 4) are amongst laws widely acknowledged for their conceptual openness, also recognised at an international level by the UN Committee on Elimination of All Forms of Discrimination Against Women.[222] The Domestic Abuse (Scotland) Act 2018 (asp 5) in particular has been described as "'gold standard' law [...] because it emerged from a process that drew on significant expertise about domestic abuse,"[223] therefore capturing and reflecting women's lived experiences of domestic abuse. In addition, the Abusive Behaviour and Sexual Harm (Scotland) Act 2016 (asp 22) marked a significant step towards modernising the law in Scotland on abusive behaviour and sexual harm as well as being the first piece of legislation in the UK to introduce provisions concerning image-based sexual abuse.[224] Furthermore, the bold suggestion from Engender to create an offence of

[218] In Scots criminal law, complainer is the alleged victim named in a charge. Complainers in sexual offences cases do not have an automatic right to anonymity in Scots Law. For a critique of this issue, see Stevenson-McCabe et al. (2021, p. 5).

[219] First Minister's National Advisory Council on Women and Girls (2018).

[220] First Minister's National Advisory Council on Women and Girls (2020, p. 5).

[221] Ibid., p. 12.

[222] Committee on the Elimination of Discrimination against Women (2019, para. 4(g)).

[223] Engender (2020, p. 7).

[224] Abusive Behaviour and Sexual Harm (Scotland) Act 2016, s. 2 (asp 22); Rackley (2018, pp. 637–643).

misogynistic harassment[225] to tackle widespread and common harassment of women—whilst not without problems[226] (see Chap. 5)—ought to be commended for its creative and innovative outlook to tackle contemporary challenges facing women in Scotland and elsewhere on a daily basis. These examples, whilst not exhaustive and not uniformly applicable to all areas (see, e.g., our critique of the HCPOA 2021 in Chap. 4), promise some rays of hope with regard to legislating on VAW and gender equality in Scotland.

1.3.2 Scotland and VAW Today: #MeToo, #TimesUp and #ReclaimTheseStreets (Again)

VAW remains a societal challenge in today's Scotland, which cannot be read and interpreted in isolation from other global and national events. In an increasingly interconnected world, which is adequately described as a 'global village,' international developments and phenomena travel across the geopolitical boundaries and designations, having ripple effects on matters of local or regional concern. The same applies to advocacy, policies and strategies concerning VAW. The influence of international law and policy developments on shaping the approach towards tackling VAW in Scotland is one example of this dynamic. However, the same applies to the effects of sociopolitical events and movements that, largely thanks to the growth and popularity of the Internet, are amplified across the world.

One of the most significant of such events in recent years has been the rise of the #MeToo movement. The #MeToo movement,[227] founded by Tarana Burke in 2006 and subsequently popularised through the use of

---

[225] Scottish Government (2018, para. 4.45); Engender (2019b).

[226] Barker and Jurasz (2020a); Barker and Jurasz (2021a).

[227] Boyle draws a distinction between 'Me Too movement' as started by Tarana Burke and '#MeToo movement' which was popularised by Alyssa Milano in 2017 using the #MeToo hashtag on Twitter. According to Boyle, "for Burke, Me Too was an intersectional demand for support and recognition for young women of colour who had experienced sexual abuse, as well as statement of solidarity. Burke's version of Me Too was *not* initially visible in Milano's tweet, but Milano *did* subsequently acknowledge Burke's work, largely as a result of Black feminists amplifying Burke's voice online". See Boyle (2019, p. 5).

the hashtag #MeToo in a tweet by the US actress Alyssa Milano, has changed the narrative about women's experiences of harassment and violence worldwide. Using predominantly social media, women started to openly speak out about their experiences of violence, especially sexual harassment, protesting its commonplace, everyday occurrence, and lack of accountability. In doing so, #MeToo has shown on an unprecedented scale that "violence against women, both online and offline, has been normalised across the world and across various geographical, demographic, professional, and contextual backgrounds."[228]

In Scotland, #MeToo has sparked a debate about sexual harassment of women in a number of professions and contexts. For instance, a survey by Women in Journalism Scotland in 2018 has shown that 1 in 10 women working in Scottish media had been sexually assaulted at work, while 48% had experienced lewd or sexist behaviour on more than three occasions and 59% had lewd or sexist language used in their presence.[229] In the wake of #MeToo, actress Maureen Beattie established the Safe Spaces campaign[230] to challenge (sexual) harassment and bullying as well as provide avenues for the victims to get support and to report such behaviours. Drawing on this momentum, women in the entertainment industry in Scotland also took steps to raise awareness and speak about commonplace sexual harassment in the sector, including by putting together and circulating a list of "powerful and abusive men in the industry to avoid."[231]

However, Scotland has also had its "failed #MeToo moment,"[232] centred around the sexual harassment and other sexual offences allegations against the former First Minister Alex Salmond. Salmond's case,[233] which following a trial in 2020 ended in his acquittal on 13 charges of rape, sexual assault, indecent assault and attempt to rape, has brutally (re)opened public debate about the power that abusers—especially men who are in prominent professional positions—ultimately exercise over

[228] Barker and Jurasz (2019a, p. 102).

[229] Gender Equal Media Scotland (2018).

[230] Equity (n.d.: https://www.equity.org.uk/getting-involved/campaigns/safe-spaces/).

[231] Webster (2021).

[232] Ditum (2021).

[233] *HM Advocate v. Salmond* [2021] HCJ 1 (court order as amended).

Fig. 1.2 A tweet from Emma Ritch, 3 March 2021

their victims. It also demonstrated deeply entrenched, sexist attitudes which, on this occasion, played out in the form of Salmond alleging breaches of ministerial conduct by the First Minster, Nicola Sturgeon, calling her testimony "simply untrue."[234] This was later reinforced by a request to Sturgeon by Murdo Fraser, a Tory MSP, to apologise for Salmond's alleged actions (Fig. 1.2).[235]

However, irrespective of the relative success of #MeToo in raising public awareness about sexual harassment, for women in contemporary Scotland, harassment and violence, especially in public spaces, is a lasting, real and everyday concern. In March 2021, a ScotPulse survey (carried out on behalf of Scotland Tonight) revealed that 59% of women in Scotland, that is, nearly 3 in 5 women, have experienced sexual harassment or assault. A total of 46% of women said that harassment or assault happened in hospitality venues (rising to 72% within the 18–34-year-old demographic), whereas one in four women said they were harassed on the street. Alarmingly, two in three women (68%) reported that they do not feel safe walking home at night, and an overwhelming 97% of surveyed women confirmed that they take measures to try to reduce any risk of harassment whilst in public spaces. These findings concerning women's safety in Scotland are particularly chilling given the timing of the survey, which took place soon after Sarah Everard's murder. They also highlight

[234] Andrews (2021).

[235] Nutt (2021).

the amount of 'safety work'[236] that women continue to do to keep themselves safe and to prevent violence from happening, often trading their freedom for safety[237] and changing their behaviours. What is more, how bitterly frustrating and disappointing it is that women's public safety remains a significant issue over four decades since the Reclaim the Night marches of 1970s!

As Scotland awaits the future fate of the proposed misogynistic harassment offence and looks forward to the report of Baroness Kennedy QC's Working Group, one pressing question comes to mind: what, if at all, can the law do to address the pandemic of VAW that women in Scotland (and elsewhere) still experience every day?

1.4 Conclusion: Combatting VAW in Scotland: A Promising Future Or Sisyphean Task?

The influence of global and political events on the work towards combating VAW in Scotland is significant. For instance, the implications of the UK's withdrawal from the EU for combatting VAW and for gender equality have been raised by key women's organisations,[238] including by the Scottish Human Rights Commission,[239] highlighting mostly the perils but also some potential opportunities for growth.[240] Similarly, the politicisation of gender and rise of anti-genderism across Europe[241] have also contributed to polarisation amongst feminists and women's groups, especially around the sex/gender divide,[242] gender recognition and its reflections within the law and policy.

[236] Kelly (2012, pp. xvii–xxvi).

[237] Vera-Grey (2018). This issue is further discussed in Chap. 5.

[238] Scottish Women's Convention (2017); Women's Budget Group (2018); Engender (2019a).

[239] Scottish Human Rights Commission (2018).

[240] Wilson (2019); Walby (2020).

[241] Kuhar and Paternotte (2017); Krizsán and Roggeband (2021).

[242] First Minister's National Advisory Council on Women and Girls (2021, p. 12).

With VAW happening every day, across various spaces and contexts, it is not unreasonable to look towards the law for direction/indicators that this pervasive problem is recognised. In a modern progressive justice system, these issues need to be comprehensively captured. However, it is important to have laws that are designed for women, work for women and draw upon women's lived experiences of violence—not just "add women and stir."[243] The reform of hate crime legislation in Scotland, whilst significant, is incidental to the joint law and policy efforts to address and combat VAW in Scotland. Whilst some aspects of the hate crime framework may have application to acts of VAW, hate crime is not, nor should it be, the default framework through which to view VAW. The important aspect of addressing VAW is strengthening of the legal system and functioning of its institutions, including the eradication of structural violence and structural discrimination within them. Part of this shift would be to ensure that the law recognises various forms of VAW, including those that have traditionally been excluded from judicial and statutory recognition. Furthermore, greater recognition of the factors and behaviours leading to VAW is necessary, including the notion of 'incitement to VAW' which has escaped legislative consideration (unlike, for instance, incitement to terrorism or prostitution).

This cannot be achieved just through legislative progressivism—institutional and attitudinal changes need to follow in order to address known structural and institutional obstacles that prevent accountability and redress for VAW. The societal approach to VAW needs to change too, especially with regard to the indifference and/or acceptance of everyday/not extraordinary acts of violence that women are subjected to. Otherwise, the law and the legal system continue to legitimise VAW, maintaining the continuum of it for future generations, and in the process reducing the 2030 SDG of Gender Equality to a utopian dream.

[243] The reference to 'add and stir' is borrowed from literature critiquing gender mainstreaming. See, for example, Chinkin (1997, p. 18).

References

Andrews, Kieran. 2021. Nicola Sturgeon is accused of 'untruths' by Alex Salmond. *The Times*, January 9.

Angelari, Marguerite. 1994. Hate Crime Statutes: A Promising Tool for Fighting Violence Against Women. *American University Journal of Gender, Social Policy & the Law* 2 (1): 63–105.

Arshad, Rowena, and Mukami McCrum. 1989. Black Woman, White Scotland (A Comment on the Position of Black Women with particular reference to Scotland). *Scottish Government Yearbook*: 207–227.

Ashcroft, Esme. 2017. Cat-calling and Wolf-Whistling Now Classed as Gender-Hate Crimes by Avon and Somerset Police. *Bristol Post*, October 16. https://www.bristolpost.co.uk/news/bristol-news/gender-hate-now-recognised-crime-635194?utm_content=bufferf8757&utm_medium=social&utm_source=twitter.com&utm_campaign=buffer. Accessed 10 February 2022.

Barker, Kim, and Olga Jurasz. 2019a. Online Misogyny: A Challenge for Digital Feminism? *Journal of International Affairs* 72 (2): 95–114.

———. 2019b. *Online Misogyny as a Hate Crime: A Challenge for Legal Regulation?* London: Routledge.

———. 2020a. Misogynistic Harassment: Advancing Scots Criminal Law? University of Stirling Public Policy Blog. https://policyblog.stir.ac.uk/2020/01/27/misogynistic-harassment-advancing-scots-criminal-law/. Accessed 10 February 2022.

———. 2020b. Online Violence Against Women as an Obstacle to Gender Equality: A Critical View from Europe. *European Equality Law Review* 1: 47–60.

———. 2020c. Scots Hate Crime Bill: A Missed (Gender) Opportunity? University of Stirling Public Policy Blog. https://policyblog.stir.ac.uk/2020/05/01/scots-hate-crime-bill-a-missed-gender-opportunity/. Accessed 10 February 2022.

———. 2020d. Submission of Evidence on COVID-19 and the Increase of Domestic Violence Against Women to the UN Special Rapporteur on Violence Against Women, Its Causes and Consequences, Dr Dubravka Šimonović. Open Research Online. http://oro.open.ac.uk/78667/. Accessed 10 February 2022.

———. 2020e. Why Misogyny and Hate Crime Reforms Need More Than Slick Campaigns. *The Conversation*, March 26. https://theconversation.com/why-misogyny-and-hate-crime-reforms-need-more-than-slick-campaigns-134265. Accessed 10 February 2022.

———. 2021a. Misogynistic Harassment: A Stumbling Block for Scots Hate Crime Reform? *Juridical Review* 1: 1–17.

———. 2021b. Online Misogyny as a Hate Crime: #TimesUp. In *Misogyny as Hate Crime*, ed. Irene Zempi and Jo Smith, 79–98. London: Routledge.

———. 2021c. Sexual Violence in the Digital Age: A Criminal Law Conundrum? *German Law Journal* 22 (5): 784–799.

———. 2021d. Text-Based (Sexual) Abuse and Online Violence Against Women: Toward Law Reform? In *The Emerald Handbook of Technology-Facilitated Violence and Abuse*, ed. Jane Bailey, Asher Flynn, and Nicola Henry, 247–264. Bingley: Emerald Publishing.

Barker, Kim and Olga Jurasz. 2022, forthcoming. Online Text-Based (Sexual) Abuse. In *Comprehensive Guide to Gender-Based Violence*, eds. Parveen Ali and Michaela M. Rogers. New York: Springer.

———. 2023, forthcoming. Women, Violence and Protest in Times of COVID-19. In *Law, Humanities and the Covid Crisis*, ed. Carl Stychin. London: University of London Press.

BBC News. 2016. EU Referendum: Results. *BBC News*, Archived. https://www.bbc.co.uk/news/politics/eu_referendum/results. Accessed 10 February 2022.

———. 2020. Domestic Abuse Charged Reach Four Year High. *BBC News*, September 8. https://www.bbc.co.uk/news/uk-scotland-54071027. Accessed 10 February 2022.

———. 2021. Sarah Everard Murder: Police Boss Philip Allott Urged to Quit Over Comments. *BBC News*, October 1. https://www.bbc.co.uk/news/uk-england-york-north-yorkshire-58762029. Accessed 10 February 2022.

Bibbings, Lois, and Donald Nicolson. 2000. *Feminist Perspectives on Criminal Law*. London: Cavendish Publishing.

Boyd, Susan B., ed. 1997. *Challenging the Public/Private Divide: Feminism, Law, and Public Policy*. Toronto: University of Toronto Press.

Boyle, Karen. 2019. *#MeToo, Weinstein and Feminism*. London: Palgrave Macmillan.

Boyle, Katie, and Nicole Busby. 2021. Human Rights and Devolution: Devolution as a Vehicle for Human Rights Protection and Progress. Human Rights Consortium Scotland. https://hrcscotland.org/wp-content/uploads/2021/09/Final-Devolution-and-Human-Rights-Dev-as-a-vehicle-for-HR-protection-and-progress-Sept-2021.pdf. Accessed 10 February 2022.

Breitenbach, Esther, Alice Brown, and Fiona Myers. 1998. Understanding Women in Scotland. *Feminist Review* 58 (1): 44–65.

Brooks, Libby. 2021. Scottish Misogyny Law Must Protect All Women, Says Helena Kennedy. *The Guardian*, February 22. https://www.theguardian.com/law/2021/feb/22/ill-set-no-limits-on-which-women-to-protect-from-hate-says-helena-kennedy. Accessed 10 February 2022.

Brown, Alice, Fiona Myers, and Esther Breitenbach. 1994. Researching Women in Scotland: Problems and Opportunities. *Scottish Affairs* 8 (1): 71–85.

Browne, Sarah. 2014. *The Women's Liberation Movement in Scotland*. Manchester: Manchester University Press.

Bussey, Katrine. 2021. Police Scotland Criticised for 'problematic attitude' to Allegations of Sexual Violence Against Women. *The Scotsman*, November 3. https://www.scotsman.com/news/crime/police-scotland-criticised-for-problematic-attitude-to-allegations-of-sexual-violence-against-women-3442349. Accessed 10 February 2022.

Carrell, Severin. 2021. Police Scotland Apologises to Women in Glasgow After Streets Blocked Off. *The Guardian*, November 2. https://www.theguardian.com/uk-news/2021/nov/02/police-scotland-apologises-to-women-in-glasgow-after-streets-blocked-off. Accessed 10 February 2022.

Chalmers, James, and Fiona Leverick. 2008. Fair Labelling in Criminal Law. *Modern Law Review* 71 (2): 217–246.

Chinkin, Christine. 1997. Feminist Interventions into International Law. *Adelaide Law Review* 19 (1): 13–24.

———. 1999. A Critique of the Public/Private Dimension. *European Journal of International Law* 10 (2): 387–395.

Cohen, Claire, and Charles Hymas. 2020. Treat Misogyny as a Hate Crime, Say MPs, as They Lay Amendment to Change Law. *The Telegraph*, June 10. https://www.telegraph.co.uk/politics/2020/06/10/treat-misogyny-hate-crime-say-mps-lay-amendment-change-law/. Accessed 10 February 2022.

Committee on the Elimination of Discrimination Against Women. 1992. General Recommendation No. 19: Violence Against Women. UN Doc. A/47/38. https://tbinternet.ohchr.org/Treaties/CEDAW/Shared%20Documents/1_Global/INT_CEDAW_GEC_3731_E.pdf. Accessed 10 February 2022.

———. 2014. Concluding Observations on the Seventh Periodic Report of Finland. UN Doc. CEDAW/C/FIN/CO/7. https://digitallibrary.un.org/record/768414?ln=en. Accessed 10 February 2022.

———. 2017. General Recommendation No. 35 on Gender-Based Violence Against Women, Updating General Recommendation No. 19. UN Doc. CEDAW/C/CG/35. https://digitallibrary.un.org/record/1305057. Accessed 10 February 2022.

———. 2019. Concluding Observations on the Eighth Periodic Report of the United Kingdom of Great Britain and Northern Ireland. UN Doc. CEDAW/C/GBR/CO/8. https://digitallibrary.un.org/record/3801131. Accessed 10 February 2022.

———. 2021a. Concluding Observations on the Ninth Periodic Report of the Russian Federation. UN Doc. CEDAW/C/RUS/CO 9. https://www.ecoi.net/en/file/local/2064360/N2135183.pdf. Accessed 10 February 2022.

———. 2021b. Concluding Observations on the Sixth Periodic Report of Maldives. UN Doc. CEDAW/C/MDV/CO/6. https://www.ecoi.net/en/file/local/2064359/N2135159.pdf. Accessed 10 February 2022.

Committee on the Elimination of Racial Discrimination. 2013. General Recommendation No. 35: Combating Racist Hate Speech. UN Doc. CERD/C/GC/35. https://docstore.ohchr.org/SelfServices/FilesHandler.ashx?enc=6QkG1d%2fPPRiCAqhKb7yhssyNNtgI51ma08CMa6o7Bglz8iG4SuOjovEP%2bcqr8joDoVEbW%2bQ1MoWdOTNEV99v6FZp9aSSA1nZya6gtpTo2JUBMI0%2boOmjAwk%2b2xJW%2bC8e. Accessed 10 February 2022.

Council of Europe. n.d. Combating Sexist Hate Speech. Council of Europe Gender Equality Strategy. https://rm.coe.int/CoERMPublicCommonSearchServices/DisplayDCTMContent?documentId=0900001680651592. Accessed 10 February 2022.

Council of Europe Committee of Ministers. 1997. Recommendation No. R (97) 20 of the Committee of Ministers to Member States on "Hate Speech". Adopted by the Committee of Ministers on 30 October 1997 at the 607th Meeting of the Ministers' Deputies. https://rm.coe.int/CoERMPublicCommonSearchServices/DisplayDCTMContent?documentId=0900001680505d5b. Accessed 10 February 2022.

———. 2019. Recommendation CM/Rec(2019)1 of the Committee of Ministers to Member States on Preventing and Combating Sexism. Adopted by the Committee of Ministers on 27 March 2019 at the 1342nd Meeting of the Ministers' Deputies. https://rm.coe.int/CoERMPublicCommonSearchServices/DisplayDCTMContent?documentId=090000168093b26a. Accessed 10 February 2022.

Council of Europe Parliamentary Assembly. 2016. Ending Cyberdiscrimination and Online Hate. Committee on Equality and Non-Discrimination: Rapporteur Marit Maij, Doc. 14217. https://pace.coe.int/pdf/dead9c9335176c398b7e2a6b38ac7c923569027ec7ea32b548ad2d95a9457a30/doc.%2014217.pdf. Accessed 10 February 2022.

Cowan, Sharon. 2019. Sense and Sensibilities? A Feminist Critique of Legal Interventions Against Sexual Violence. *Edinburgh Law Review* 23 (1): 22–51.

Crenshaw, Kimberle. 1991. Mapping the Margins: Intersectionality, Identity Politics, and Violence Against Women of Color. *Stanford Law Review* 43 (6): 1241–1299.

Crown Office & Prosecutor Fiscal Service. 2021. Domestic Abuse and Stalking Charges in Scotland, 2020–21. https://www.copfs.gov.uk/media-site-news-from-copfs/1976-domestic-abuse-and-stalking-charges-in-scotland-2020-21. Accessed 10 February 2022.

Crown Prosecution Service. 2012. Violence Against Women Strategy and Action Plans. https://www.cps.gov.uk/publication/violence-against-women-strategy-and-action-plans. Accessed 10 February 2022.

Dathan, Matthew. 2021. Dominic Raab's Misogyny Remark on BBC Breakfast 'insults women'. *The Times*, October 7. https://www.thetimes.co.uk/article/dominic-raab-gets-himself-in-a-muddle-over-misogyny-9l8zlr8wv. Accessed 10 February 2022.

Department of Health, Department of Justice, and The Executive Office. 2022. New Strategies: Domestic and Sexual Abuse (DoH, DoJ); Violence Against Women and Girls (TEO) | Call for Views. https://www.health-ni.gov.uk/sites/default/files/consultations/health/doh-das-abuse-call-views-new-strategies.pdf. Accessed 10 February 2022.

Department of Justice. 2020. Hate Crime Legislation in Northern Ireland: Independent Review: Executive Summary. Hate Crime Review Team. https://www.justice-ni.gov.uk/sites/default/files/publications/justice/hate-crime-review.pdf. Accessed 10 February 2022.

Ditum, Sarah. 2021. Scotland's Failed #MeToo moment. *UnHerd*, March 10. https://unherd.com/2021/03/scotlands-failed-metoo-moment/. Accessed 10 February 2022.

Dodd, Vikram. 2021. Met Officers Guilty of Misconduct After Sharing Photos of Murdered Sisters. *The Guardian*, 24 November. https://www.theguardian.com/uk-news/2021/nov/24/met-officers-sacked-sharing-whatsapp-photos-murdered-sisters. Accessed 10 February 2022.

Dodd, Vikram, and Haroon Siddique. 2021. Sarah Everard Murder: Wayne Couzens Given Whole-Life Sentence. *The Guardian*, September 30. https://www.theguardian.com/uk-news/2021/sep/30/sarah-everard-murder-wayne-couzens-whole-life-sentence. Accessed 10 February 2022.

Donaldson, Anni. 2020. Domestic Abuse, Culture and Scottish History. Scottish Women's Aid. https://womensaid.scot/domestic-abuse-culture-and-scottish-history/. Accessed 10 February 2022.

End Violence Against Women. 2021. Almost Half of Women Have Less Trust in Police Following Sarah Everard Murder. https://www.endviolenceagainstwomen.org.uk/almost-half-of-women-have-less-trust-in-police-following-sarah-everard-murder/. Accessed 10 February 2022.

Engender. 2015. What's Next? Women's Equality in Scotland 20 Years After the Beijing Platform for Action. https://www.engender.org.uk/content/publications/EngenderBeijing20.pdf. Accessed 10 February 2022.

———. 2018. CEDAW: How Can Women's Rights Be Better Realised in Scotland? https://www.engender.org.uk/content/publications/CEDAW-incorporation-paper.pdf. Accessed 10 February 2022.

———. 2019a. Engender Joins Forces with Over 85 Civil Society Organisations to Express Concerns About No-Deal. https://www.engender.org.uk/news/blog/engender-joins-forces-with-over-85-civil-society-organisations-to-express-concerns-about-n/. Accessed 10 February 2022.

———. 2019b. Making Women Safer in Scotland: The Case for a Standalone Misogyny Offence. https://www.engender.org.uk/content/publications/Making-Women-Safer-in-Scotland%2D%2D-the-case-for-astandalone-misogyny-offence.pdf. Accessed 10 February 2022.

———. 2020. Engender Submission of Evidence to the Scottish Parliament Justice Committee call for Views on the Hate Crime and Public Order (Scotland) Bill. https://www.engender.org.uk/content/publications/Engender-submission-of-evidence-on-Hate-Crime-and-Public-Order-Scotland-Bill-.pdf. Accessed 10 February 2022.

———. 2021. Incorporating CEDAW – What a New Human Rights Bill Could Do for Women in Scotland. https://www.engender.org.uk/news/blog/incorporating-cedaw%2D%2D-what-a-new-human-rights-bill-could-do-for-women-in-scotland/. Accessed 10 February 2022.

Engender, Zero Tolerance, Rape Crisis Scotland, Close the Gap, and Scottish Women's Aid. n.d. Incorporating CEDAW into Scots Law. https://www.engender.org.uk/content/publications/5-organisations-CEDAW-incorporation-paper.pdf. Accessed 10 February 2022.

Equity. n.d. Safe Spaces. https://www.equity.org.uk/getting-involved/campaigns/safe-spaces/. Accessed 10 February 2022.

European Commission. 2021. Stop Violence Against Women: Statement by the European Commission and the High Representative. https://ec.europa.eu/commission/presscorner/detail/en/statement_21_6211. Accessed 10 February 2022.

European Union Agency for Fundamental Rights. 2014. *Violence Against Women: An EU-Wide Survey. Main Results*. Luxembourg: Publications Office of the European Union. https://fra.europa.eu/sites/default/files/fra_uploads/fra-2014-vaw-survey-main-results-apr14_en.pdf. Accessed 10 February 2022.

First Minister's National Advisory Council on Women and Girls. 2018. 2018 First Report and Recommendations. https://onescotland.org/wp-content/uploads/2021/03/2018report.pdf. Accessed 10 February 2022.

———. 2019. 2019 Report and Recommendations. https://onescotland.org/wp-content/uploads/2020/01/NACWG-2019-Report-and-Recommendations.pdf. Accessed 10 February 2022.

———. 2020. 2020 Report and Recommendations. https://onescotland.org/wp-content/uploads/2021/01/562006_SCT1120576152-002_NACWG.pdf. Accessed 10 February 2022.

———. 2021. Next Steps Report 2021. https://onescotland.org/wp-content/uploads/2021/03/590637_SCT0321216300-001_p1.pdf. Accessed 10 February 2022.

Folorunso, Tomiwa. 2020. Police Brutality Against Black People Isn't Shocking Or Surprising. *The National*, June 7. https://www.thenational.scot/news/18501323.police-brutality-black-people-isnt-shocking-surprising/. Accessed 10 February 2022.

Fredman, Sandra. 2013. The CEDAW in the UK. In *Women's Human Rights: CEDAW in International, Regional and National Law*, ed. Anne Hellum and Henriette Sinding Aasen, 511–530. Cambridge: Cambridge University Press.

Galtung, Johan. 1969. Violence, Peace, and Peace Research. *Journal of Peace Research* 6 (3): 167–191.

Gayle, Damien. 2022. Met Apologises to Woman for 'sexist, derogatory' Language in Strip-Search. *The Guardian*, January 24. https://www.theguardian.com/uk-news/2022/jan/24/met-apologises-to-academic-for-sexist-derogatory-language. Accessed 10 February 2022.

Gender Equal Media Scotland. 2018. Women in Journalism Scotland Survey Reveals a Third of Woman Working in the Scottish Media Saying They Have Been Sexually Harassed. https://www.genderequalmedia.scot/news/blog/women-in-journalism-scotland-survey-reveals-a-third-of-woman-working-in-the-scottish-media/. Accessed 10 February 2022.

Gill, Aisha K., and Hannah Mason-Bish. 2013. Addressing Violence Against Women as a Form of Hate Crime: Limitations and Possibilities. *Feminist Review* 105 (1): 1–20. https://doi.org/10.1057/fr.2013.17.

Ging, Debbie, and Eugenia Siapera. 2018. Special Issue on Online Misogyny. *Feminist Media Studies* 18 (4): 515–524.

Government of Ireland. 2022. Dáil Statement by the Taoiseach, Micheál Martin on Violence Against Women. Department of the Taoiseach: Press Release. https://www.gov.ie/en/press-release/53368-dail-statement-by-the-taoiseach-micheal-martin-td-on-violence-against-women/. Accessed 10 February 2022.

Graham-Harrison, Emma. 2021. Police Clash with Mourners at Sarah Everard Vigil in London. *The Guardian*, March 13. https://www.theguardian.com/uk-news/2021/mar/13/as-the-sun-set-they-came-in-solidarity-and-to-pay-tribute-to-sarah-everard. Accessed 10 February 2022.

Grant, Alistair. 2021. COP26 Anger as Women Forced to Walk Through 'pitch-black' Kelvingrove Park. *The Herald*, November 2. https://www.heraldscotland.com/politics/19688144.cop26-anger-women-forced-walk-pitch-black-kelvingrove-park/. Accessed 10 February 2022.

Gunka, Charlotte, and Maria Snitsar. 2020. The Shame Or the Shining: Covid-19's Trap of Domestic Violence in France and Russia. International Bar Association. https://www.ibanet.org/Article/NewDetail.aspx?ArticleUid=74b42fab-a8ba-4edd-8543-d97c2496c32f#1. Accessed 10 February 2022.

Guterres, António. 2021a. A Crisis with a Woman's Face. United Nations. https://www.un.org/sg/en/content/sg/articles/2021-03-04/crisis-womans-face. Accessed 10 February 2022.

———. 2021b. A Global Model to Tackle Violence Against Women. United Nations. https://www.un.org/sg/en/content/sg/articles/2021-06-28/global-model-tackle-violence-against-women. Accessed 10 February 2022.

Hamilton, Fiona. 2021. Sarah Everard Murder: Killer and police shared abusive messages. *The Times*, October 1. https://www.thetimes.co.uk/article/sarah-everard-murder-killer-and-police-shared-abusive-messages-5bpkj5wsk. Accessed 10 February 2022.

Harris, Angela. 1990. Race and Essentialism in Feminist Legal Theory. *Stanford Law Review* 42 (3): 581–616.

HM Inspectorate of Constabulary in Scotland. 2021. Thematic Inspection of Hate Crime. https://www.hmics.scot/sites/default/files/publications/HMICS%20Thematic%20Inspection%20of%20Hate%20Crime%202021.pdf. Accessed 10 February 2022.

Human Rights Consortium Scotland. 2021. Human Rights Incorporation Fortnight 2021, 30th August–10th September. https://hrcscotland.org/2021/08/18/human-rights-incorporation-fortnight-2021-30th-august-10th-september/. Accessed 10 February 2022.

Hunter, Eveline. 1979. *Scottish Woman's Place: A Practical Guide and Critical Comment on Women's Rights in Scotland*. Billings & Sons Ltd.

Independent Office for Police Conduct. 2021. IOPC Warns Officers About Inappropriate Social Media Use. https://www.policeconduct.gov.uk/news/iopc-warns-officers-about-inappropriate-social-media-use. Accessed 10 February 2022.

Inspiring Scotland. n.d. Delivering Equally Safe. https://www.inspiringscotland.org.uk/what-we-do/our-funds/equally-safe/delivering-equally-safe-fund/. Accessed 10 February 2022.

Instagram. 2022. laura_bates__. https://www.instagram.com/p/CYr31VLLCNv/. Accessed 10 February 2022

Jacques, Paul. 2021. Misogyny to Be Recorded by West Yorkshire Officers to Tackle Gendered Hostility. *Police Professional*, December 1. https://www.policeprofessional.com/news/misogyny-to-be-recorded-by-west-yorkshire-officers-to-tackle-gendered-hostility/. Accessed 10 February 2022.

Jane, Emma. 2017. *Misogyny Online: A Short (and Brutish) History*. London: SAGE Publications.

Johnston, Melissa, and Jacqui True. 2019. Misogyny & Violent Extremism: Implications for Preventing Violent Extremism. Monash University and UN Women. https://asiapacific.unwomen.org/sites/default/files/Field%20Office%20ESEAsia/Docs/Publications/2019/10/ap-Policy-Brief_VE_and_VAW_v6_compressed.pdf. Accessed 10 February 2022.

Joyce, Helen. 2021. Scotland's New Hate Crime Act Will Have a Chilling Effect on Free Speech. *The Economist*, November 8. https://www.economist.com/the-world-ahead/2021/11/08/scotlands-new-hate-crime-act-will-have-a-chilling-effect-on-free-speech. Accessed 10 February 2022.

Jurasz, Olga. 2015. The Istanbul Convention: A New Chapter in Preventing and Combating Violence Against Women. *Australian Law Journal* 89 (9): 619–627.

Kelly, Liz. 1988. *Surviving Sexual Violence*. London: Polity Press.

———. 2012. Standing the Test of Time? Reflections on the Concept of the Continuum of Sexual Violence. In *Handbook on Sexual Violence*, ed. Jennifer Brown and Sandra Walklate, xvii–xxvi. London: Routledge.

———. n.d. The Trouble with "Hate". *Trouble & Strife*. https://www.troubleandstrife.org/new-articles/the-trouble-with-hate/. Accessed 10 February 2022.

Kotiswaran, Prabha. 2014. Feminist Approaches to Criminal Law. In *Oxford Handbook of Criminal Law*, ed. Markus D. Dubber and Tatjana Hörnle, 59–83. Oxford: Oxford University Press.

Krizsán, Andrea, and Conny Roggeband. 2021. *Politicizing Gender and Democracy in the Context of the Istanbul Convention*. London: Palgrave Macmillan.

Kuhar, Roman, and David Paternotte, eds. 2017. *Anti-Gender Campaigns in Europe: Mobilizing Against Equality*. London: Rowman & Littlefield International.

Law Commission. 2021. Hate Crime Laws: Final Report. Law Com No 402. https://s3-eu-west-2.amazonaws.com/lawcom-prod-storage-11jsxou24uy7q/uploads/2021/12/Hate-crime-report-accessible.pdf. Accessed 10 February 2022.

Leonard, Tom. 1995. *Reports from the Present: Selected Work 1982–1994*. London: Jonathan Cape.

Mackie, Rachel. 2021. Don't Be That Guy: Police Scotland Launches New Campaign to Tackle Male Sexual Entitlement. *The Scotsman*, October 13. https://www.scotsman.com/news/crime/dont-be-that-guy-police-scotland-launches-new-campaign-to-tackle-male-sexual-entitlement-3418268. Accessed 10 February 2022.

Maher, Jane Maree, Jude McCulloch, and Gail Mason. 2015. Punishing Gendered Violence as Hate Crime: Aggravated Sentences as a Means of Recognising Hate as Motivation for Violent Crimes Against Women. *Australian Feminist Law Journal* 41 (1): 177–193.

Manne, Kate. 2017. *Down Girl: The Logic of Misogyny*. Oxford: Oxford University Press.

McGlynn, Claire, and Erika Rackley. 2017. Image-Based Sexual Abuse. *Oxford Journal of Legal Studies* 37 (3): 534–561.

Middleton, Joe. 2021. Met Police Issues Advice to Women to 'shout or wave a bus down' If They Don't Trust a Male Officer. *The Independent*, October 1. https://www.independent.co.uk/news/uk/home-news/met-police-sarah-everard-couzens-b1930331.html. Accessed 10 February 2022.

Montoya, Celeste, and Lise Rolandsen Agustín. 2013. The Othering of Domestic Violence: The EU and Cultural Framings of Violence Against Women. *Social Politics: International Studies in Gender, State & Society* 20 (4): 534–557.

Mullany, Louise, and Loretta Trickett. 2018. Misogyny Hate Crime Evaluation Report. Nottingham Women's Centre. https://www.nottinghamwomenscentre.com/misogyny-evaluation-report. Accessed 10 February 2022.

Nigam, Shalu. 2021. *Domestic Violence Law in India: Myth and Misogyny*. London: Routledge.

North Yorkshire Police, Fire & Crime Commissioner. 2017. Misogyny Recognised as a Hate Crime in North Yorkshire. https://www.northyorkshire-pfcc.gov.uk/news/misogyny-recognised-hate-crime-north-yorkshire/. Accessed 10 February 2022.

Nottingham Citizens. 2014. *No Place for Hate*. Citizens UK.

Nutt, Kathleen. 2021. Fury Over 'sexist' Request to Nicola Sturgeon to Apologise for Alex Salmond. *The National*, March 3. https://www.thenational.scot/news/19133691.fury-tory-msps-request-nicola-sturgeon-apologise-alex-salmond/. Accessed 10 February 2022.

Office for National Statistics. 2020. Domestic Abuse During the Coronavirus (COVID-19) Pandemic, England and Wales: November 2020. https://www.ons.gov.uk/peoplepopulationandcommunity/crimeandjustice/articles/domesticabuseduringthecoronaviruscovid19pandemicenglandandwales/november2020#calls-for-service-for-domestic-abuse-incidents. Accessed 10 February 2022.

One Scotland. n.d. First Minister's National Advisory Council on Women and Girls. Scottish Government. https://onescotland.org/equality-themes/advisory-council-women-girls/. Accessed 10 February 2022.

Park, Hijin. 2012. Interracial Violence, Western Racialized Masculinities, and the Geopolitics of Violence Against Women. *Social & Legal Studies* 21 (4): 491–509. https://doi.org/10.1177/0964663912443919.

Petter, Olivia. 2022. Ashling Murphy Was 'just going for a run' When She Was Killed, But That Doesn't Matter. *The Independent*, January 14. https://www.independent.co.uk/life-style/women/ashling-murphy-going-for-run-victim-blaming-b1993315.html. Accessed 10 February 2022.

Pinson Wrisley, Samantha. 2021. Feminist Theory and the Problem of Misogyny. *Feminist Theory* 1: 1–20. https://doi.org/10.1177/14647001211039365.

Plan International. 2020. Free to Be Online? Girls' and Young Women's Experiences of Online Harassment. https://plan-international.org/publications/freetobeonline. Accessed 10 February 2022.

Price, Hannah. 2020. Coronavirus: 'Revenge porn' Surge Hits Helpline. *BBC News*, April 25. https://www.bbc.co.uk/news/stories-52413994. Accessed 10 February 2022.

Priestley, Catherine. 2021. Northumbria Police Officer Sacked Over Sexual Photos on Twitter and Instagram. *The Northern Echo*, December 23. https://www.thenorthernecho.co.uk/news/19804849.northumbria-police-officer-sacked-sexual-photos-twitter-instagram/. Accessed 10 February 2022.

Public Health Scotland. 2021. Overview of Gender Based Violence. http://www.healthscotland.scot/health-topics/gender-based-violence/gender-based-violence-overview/overview-of-gender-based-violence. Accessed 10 February 2022.

Quinn, Ben. 2018. Met Police Chief Backs Call to Focus on Violent Crime Not Misogyny. *The Guardian*, November 2. https://www.theguardian.com/uk-news/2018/nov/02/metropolitan-police-chief-cressida-dick-backs-call-focus-violent-crime-misogyny. Accessed 10 February 2022.

Rackley, Erika. 2018. Section 2 of the Abusive Behaviour and Sexual Harm (Scotland) Act 2016. In *Women's Legal Landmarks: Celebrating the History of Women and Law in the UK and Ireland*, ed. Erika Rackley and Rosemary Auchmuty, 637–643. London: Hart Publishing.

Rape Crisis Scotland. 2021. Rape Crisis Scotland Calls for Action as New Figures Show Further Fall in Convictions for Rape. https://www.rapecrisisscotland.org.uk/news/news/rape-crisis-scotland-calls-for-action-as-new-figures-show-further-fall-in-convictions-for-/. Accessed 10 February 2022.

Rawlinson, Kevin. 2021. Plymouth Shooting: Police Urged to Take Misogyny More Seriously. *The Guardian*, August 14. https://www.theguardian.com/uk-news/2021/aug/14/plymouth-shootings-police-urged-to-take-misogyny-more-seriously. Accessed 10 February 2022.

Rocks, Chelsea. 2020. What Is Period Poverty? Why Sanitary Products Are Now Free in Scotland – And Where They Are Available. *The Scotsman*, November 25. https://www.scotsman.com/health/what-period-poverty-why-sanitary-products-are-now-free-scotland-and-where-they-are-available-3046216. Accessed 10 February 2022.

Scottish Government. 2017. Scotland's International Framework 2017. https://www.gov.scot/publications/scotlands-international-framework-9781788514033/. Accessed 10 February 2022.

———. 2018. Independent Review of Hate Crime Legislation in Scotland: Final Report. https://www.gov.scot/binaries/content/documents/govscot/publications/progress-report/2018/05/independent-review-hate-crime-legislation-scotland-final-report/documents/00535892-pdf/00535892-pdf/govscot%3Adocument/00535892.pdf. Accessed 10 February 2022.

———. 2020a. Abortion – Covid-19 – Approval For Mifepristone To Be Taken At Home And Other Contingency Measures. https://www.sehd.scot.nhs.uk/cmo/CMO(2020)09.pdf. Accessed 10 February 2022.

———. 2020b. Budget Increase to Tackle Violence Against Women. https://www.gov.scot/news/budget-increase-to-tackle-violence-against-women/. Accessed 10 February 2022.

———. 2020c. Domestic Abuse and Other Forms of Violence Against Women and Girls (VAWG) during COVID-19 Lockdown for the Period 30/3/20–22/05/20. https://www.gov.scot/binaries/content/documents/govscot/publications/research-and-analysis/2020/06/domestic-abuse-forms-violence-against-women-girls-vawg-during-covid-19-lockdown-period-30-3-20-22-05-202/documents/domestic-abuse-forms-violence-against-wom. Accessed 10 February 2022.
———. 2020d. Preventing and Eradicating Violence Against Women and Girls. https://www.gov.scot/news/preventing-and-eradicating-violence-against-women-and-girls/. Accessed 10 February 2022.
———. 2020e. Scotland and the Sustainable Development Goals: A National Review to Drive Action. https://www.gov.scot/publications/scotland-sustainable-development-goals-national-review-drive-action/. Accessed 10 February 2022.
———. 2020f. Social and Equality Impacts of Brexit. A Report for the Scottish Government by Dr Eve Hepburn. https://www.gov.scot/publications/social-equality-impacts-brexit/documents/. Accessed 10 February 2022.
———. 2021a. Domestic Abuse Recorded by the Police in Scotland, 2020–2021. https://www.gov.scot/news/domestic-abuse-recorded-by-the-police-in-scotland-2020-21/. Accessed 10 February 2022.
———. 2021b. Misogyny and Criminal Justice in Scotland Working Group: Remit. https://www.gov.scot/publications/misogyny-and-criminal-justice-in-scotland-working-group-remit/. Accessed 10 February 2022.
———. 2021c. National Taskforce for Human Rights Leadership Report. https://www.gov.scot/binaries/content/documents/govscot/publications/independent-report/2021/03/national-taskforce-human-rights-leadership-report/documents/national-taskforce-human-rights-leadership-report/national-taskforce-human-rights-leadership-report. Accessed 10 February 2022.
———. 2021d. Next Step Towards Scottish Human Rights Bill. https://www.gov.scot/news/next-step-towards-scottish-human-rights-bill/. Accessed 10 February 2022.
———. 2021e. Tackling gender-based violence. https://www.gov.scot/news/tackling-gender-based-violence/. Accessed 10 February 2022.
Scottish Government, and COSLA. 2009. Safer Lives: Changed Lives. A Shared Approach to Tackling Violence Against Women in Scotland. https://www.safershetland.com/assets/files/resources-and-publications/Safer%20lives%20Changed%20lives%202009.pdf. Accessed 10 February 2022.

Scottish Government, and COSLA. 2014. Equally Safe: Scotland's Strategy for Preventing and Eradicating Violence Against Women and Girls. https://www.webarchive.org.uk/wayback/archive/20180517142036mp_/http://www.gov.scot/Resource/0045/00454152.pdf. Accessed 10 February 2022.

Scottish Government, and COSLA. 2018. Equally Safe: Scotland's Strategy for Preventing and Eradicating Violence Against Women and Girls. https://www.gov.scot/publications/equally-safe-scotlands-strategy-prevent-eradicate-violence-against-women-girls/documents/. Accessed 10 February 2022.

Scottish Government, and COSLA. 2020. Equally Safe: Year Three Update Report. https://www.gov.scot/binaries/content/documents/govscot/publications/progress-report/2020/11/equally-safe-final-report/documents/equally-safe-year-three-update-report-november-2020/equally-safe-year-three-update-report-november-2020/govscot%3Adocument/equ. Accessed 10 February 2022.

Scottish Human Rights Commission. 2018. The Scottish Human Rights Commission Submission to the United Nation's Committee on the Elimination of All Forms of Discrimination Against Women. https://tbinternet.ohchr.org/Treaties/CEDAW/Shared%20Documents/GBR/INT_CEDAW_IFL_GBR_31376_E.pdf. Accessed 10 February 2022.

Scottish National Party. 2021. SNP 2021 Manifesto: Scotland's Future, Scotland's Choice. https://www.snp.org/manifesto/. Accessed 10 February 2022.

Scottish Women's Convention. 2017. The Impact of Brexit on Women in Scotland. https://www.scottishwomensconvention.org/files/brexit-event-report.pdf. Accessed 10 February 2022.

Shakti Women's Aid. n.d.. https://shaktiedinburgh.co.uk/. Accessed 10 February 2022.

Smith, Joan. 1989. *Misogynies*. London: Faber & Faber.

Stevenson-McCabe, Seonaid, Annabel Mackay, and Faiza Ashfaq. 2021. Opinion: Campaign for Complainer Anonymity. *The Journal of the Law Society of Scotland* 66 (6): 5. https://www.lawscot.org.uk/members/journal/issues/vol-66-issue-06/opinion-campaign-for-complainer-anonymity/. Accessed 10 February 2022.

Syal, Rajeev. 2021. Evidence of 'vulgar and sexist' WhatsApp Texts Ignored, Says ex-Met Detective. *The Guardian*, October 3. https://www.theguardian.com/uk-news/2021/oct/03/vulgar-and-sexist-whatsapp-evidence-ignored-says-ex-met-detective. Accessed 10 February 2022.

Treasure, Aimee. n.d. Violence Against Women. British Library: Spare Rib. https://www.bl.uk/spare-rib/articles/violence-against-women. Accessed 10 February 2022.

Twitter. 2021. @NicolaSturgeon, 1 October 2021, 3:10pm. https://twitter.com/NicolaSturgeon/status/1443941345295491072. Accessed 10 February 2022.

UK Government Equalities Office and UN Women. 2020. Beijing+25 National Report: The Response of the Government of the United Kingdom to the UN Questionnaire on the Implementation of the Beijing Declaration and Platform for Action (1995). https://www.unwomen.org/sites/default/files/Headquarters/Attachments/Sections/CSW/64/National-reviews/United_Kingdom.pdf. Accessed 10 February 2022.

UN General Assembly. 2017. Report of the Special Rapporteur in the Field of Cultural Rights. UN Doc. A/72/155: Special Rapporteur Karima Bennoune. https://documents-dds-ny.un.org/doc/UNDOC/GEN/N17/216/94/PDF/N1721694.pdf?OpenElement. Accessed 10 February 2022.

———. 2021. *Report of the Special Rapporteur on the Promotion and Protection of the Right to Freedom of Opinion and Expression*. Special Rapporteur Irene Khan.

UN Women. 2020. Message from UN Secretary-General António Guterres on the International Day for the Elimination of Violence against Women. https://www.unwomen.org/en/news/stories/2020/11/statement-secretary-general-on-the-international-day-for-the-elimination-of-violence-against-women. Accessed 10 February 2022.

———. 2021. Remarks by Secretary-General António Guterres at the UN Security Council Open Debate on Women, Peace and Security. https://www.unwomen.org/en/news/stories/2021/10/speech-sg-guterres-security-council-open-debate-on-women-peace-and-security. Accessed 10 February 2022.

———. n.d. The Shadow Pandemic: Violence Against Women During COVID-19. https://www.unwomen.org/en/news/in-focus/in-focus-gender-equality-in-covid-19-response/violence-against-women-during-covid-19. Accessed 10 February 2022.

United Nations. 2019. United Nations Strategy and Plan of Action on Hate Speech. https://www.un.org/en/genocideprevention/documents/UN%20Strategy%20and%20Plan%20of%20Action%20on%20Hate%20Speech%2018%20June%20SYNOPSIS.pdf. Accessed 10 February 2022.

———. 2020. The Highest Aspiration: A Call to Action for Human Rights. https://www.un.org/sg/sites/www.un.org.sg/files/atoms/files/The_Highest_Asperation_A_Call_To_Action_For_Human_Right_English.pdf. Accessed 10 February 2022.

———. 2021. 'Sexism and misogyny' Heightened; Women's Freedoms Supressed. *UN News*. https://news.un.org/en/story/2021/10/1103382. Accessed 10 February 2022.

United Nations Human Rights Council. 2018. Report of the Special Rapporteur on Violence Against Women, Its Causes and Consequences on Online Violence Against Women and Girls from a Human Rights Perspective. UN Doc. A/HRC/38/47. https://digitallibrary.un.org/record/1641160. Accessed 10 February 2022.

United Nations Population Fund. 2020. Impact of the COVID-19 Pandemic on Family Planning and Ending Gender-Based Violence, Female Genital Mutilation and Child Marriage. Interim Technical Note: Information as of 27 April 2020. https://www.unfpa.org/sites/default/files/resource-pdf/COVID-19_impact_brief_for_UNFPA_24_April_2020_1.pdf. Accessed 10 February 2022.

Vera-Grey, Fiona. 2017. Outlook: Girlhood, Agency, and Embodied Space for Action. In *Nordic Girlhoods: New Perspectives and Outlooks*, ed. Bodil Formark, Heta Mulari, and Myry Voipio, 127–136. London: Palgrave Macmillan.

———. 2018. *The Right Amount of Panic: How Women Trade Freedom for Safety*. Bristol: Policy Press.

Vickery, Jacqueline Ryan, and Tracy Everbach, eds. 2018. *Mediating Misogyny: Gender, Technology, and Harassment*. London: Palgrave Macmillan.

Walby, Sylvia. 1990. *Theorizing Patriarchy*. Oxford: Blackwell.

———. 2020. Gender, Violence and Brexit. *Northern Ireland Legal Quarterly* 70 (1): 17–33.

Waterson, Kirstie. 2021. Reclaiming the Night: How Aberdeen Women Took a Stand Against Violence in the 1970s. *The Press and Journal*, March 18. https://www.pressandjournal.co.uk/fp/education/higher-education/2974330/reclaiming-the-night-how-aberdeen-women-took-a-stand-against-violence-in-the-1970s/. Accessed 10 February 2022.

Webster, Laura. 2021. Women in Scotland's Entertainment Industry Share List of 'abusive' Men to Avoid. *The National*, May 18. https://www.thenational.scot/news/19310292.women-scotlands-entertainment-industry-share-list-abusive-men-avoid/. Accessed 10 February 2022.

WHO. 2021. Violence Against Women Prevalence Estimates, 2018. https://www.who.int/publications/i/item/9789240022256. Accessed 10 February 2022.

Wilson, Leanne. 2019. Brexit – A Risk to Women's Equality, Or an Opportunity to Reshape Gender Mainstreaming in Economic Development? *Engender*, November 1. https://www.engender.org.uk/news/blog/brexit-a-risk-or-an-opportunity-to-reshape-gender-mainstreaming-in-economic-development/. Accessed 10 February 2022.

Women's Aid. 2019. Women's Aid Report Says £393 Million a Year Is Needed to Fund Domestic Abuse Services in England. https://www.womensaid.org.uk/womens-aid-report-says-393-million-a-year-is-needed-to-fund-domestic-abuse-services-in-england/. Accessed 10 February 2022.

Women's Budget Group. 2018. Exploring the Economic Impact of Brexit on Women. https://wbg.org.uk/wp-content/uploads/2018/03/Economic-Impact-of-Brexit-on-women-briefing-FINAL-for-print.pdf. Accessed 10 February 2022.

World Wide Web Foundation. 2020. There's a Pandemic of Online Violence Against Women and Girls. https://webfoundation.org/2020/07/theres-a-pandemic-of-online-violence-against-women-and-girls/. Accessed 10 February 2022

Yousaf, Humza. 2018. Justice Secretary Humza Yousaf's Speech to SNP Conference. SNP: News, October 7. https://www.snp.org/justice-secretary-humza-yousafs-speech-to-snp-conference/. Accessed 10 February 2022.

2

(D)Evolved Policy-Making: Women and Scotland

2.1 Introduction: The Scottish Constitutional Settlement (And Women?)

One of the things I pledged when I became First Minister, the first woman to have the privilege of holding this office, was that I'd do everything I could to improve opportunities for women and girls—that's a commitment that I take seriously that's extremely close to my heart and it's what the government that I lead has tried to do. We've taken a range of measures to challenge gender stereotypes, help women's voices to be heard and to tackle violence against women and girls.

However, we know we need to do much more to eradicate persistent inequalities that many women and girls still face in their daily lives.[1] (Nicola Sturgeon, First Minister of Scotland, January 2019)

As First Minister, I want to ensure that Scotland leads the way, that the generations of women and girls that come after me grow up with equal opportunities in a truly equal society. (Nicola Sturgeon, First Minister of Scotland, January 2020.)[2]

[1] Scottish Government (2019).

[2] Scottish Government (2020a).

K. Barker, O. Jurasz, *Violence Against Women, Hate and Law*, Palgrave Hate Studies,
https://doi.org/10.1007/978-3-030-99375-7_2

There is no law—neither common nor statute—that addresses conduct evincing prejudice relating to or motivated by gender in Scots Law. It represents a lacuna in the domestic legal system, particularly in light of the upsurge in violence against women (VAW) that has become prominent during the Covid-19 pandemic,[3] and which represents something of an epidemic[4] in its own right across Scottish society. In what is claimed to be a nation with a progressive policy agenda driven to 'do things differently,' it is unfortunate that behaviours relating to gender prejudice and stemming from structural inequalities in society have not (yet) been addressed in Scotland.

With its unconventional constitutional settlement, Devolved powers and ever-present questions over independence and legitimacy of governance, there are labels of either progressive governance and policy-making[5] or stagnation and greater inequality in Scotland.[6] These debates, together with the evolution of the Scottish administration, both pre- and post-devolution, are intrinsic to the understanding of how women's rights, equality, gender and violence against women and girls (VAWG) policies (and law) have unfolded. Discussed in a vacuum, and without the context of contemporary Scottish society, it is difficult to fully appreciate the advances in Scotland for mechanisms addressing VAWG, and recent policy discussions relating to VAW, hate crime, GBV and women's rights more widely. This sociopolitical and policy background, therefore, while not a strictly legal examination, provides important context for an assessment of measures to address the evolution of women's rights and their legal protections in Scotland (see Chap. 1). The hope and promise offered by the re-establishment of a Parliament in Scotland could have been a critical turning point in enshrining protections for women's rights in law. The prevailing question posed here is to what extent has this potential become reality for women in Scotland.

This chapter will explore the development of Scottish policy through selected examples specifically addressing issues affecting women, but also

[3] Women's Aid (2020); World Health Organisation (2020).

[4] Davidson (2020).

[5] Mackay (2010, pp. 370–383).

[6] Torrance (2017, p. 59); Keating (2005, p. 455).

equal opportunities. The discussion here examines the—so-called—claims of progressivism, forward-thinking policy developments and leading equality benchmarks that various iterations of Scottish political leadership have ambitiously outlined as achievements. The successive Scottish Office, Scottish Executive and latterly Scottish Government have taken turns offering up—what is said to be—a more inclusive, equal and forward-thinking society. This chapter outlines the developments in Scottish governance from the perspective of the women's movement. It charts the path from Devolution discussions in the 1970s, through the constitutional settlement debates of the 1990s, to Devolution, and to the current-day Scottish Government. It focuses on the role and evolution of politics and policy, and questions whether the post-devolution settlement has heralded a new way of doing things, and a more progressive approach for women, and their rights, in Scottish society, in Scots Law, and in Scotland.

The discussion here turns to the impact of the Devolution settlement on policy-making in the years preceding the election of the first Members of the Scottish Parliament (MSPs). The focus then shifts to Scotland's post-1999 politics to assess how the—allegedly—more inclusively designed Parliament has shaped the policy landscape in Scotland. The discussion then narrows, with attention falling on the approaches to combatting VAW that have unfolded across Scotland since, highlighting the milestones from the early 1990s onwards to assess whether there is true progressivism by design, or whether accidents of timing and fortune have led to the impression of Scotland being more forward-thinking in its approach to tackling VAW. In doing so, it charts the manner by which policy relating to women and women's rights has been developed and/or implemented, and how this has shaped social, political and legal developments in preventing and tackling VAW.

This chapter examines key developments and benchmarks that have been witnessed since the first MSPs took their seats. It explores the approach to tackling problems affecting women in Scotland between 1995 and 2021, exploring the absence of consideration of women's issues during the 1980s and 1990s, and the shift to greater prominence and consideration of policy and law as a result.[7] Consideration begins, first, with the work that shaped the early years of the Scottish Parliament, and the ways in which Devolution offered up a watershed moment for Scotland—albeit not immediately for the women's movement in Scottish society.

2.2 The (D)evolution Settlement: A Watershed Moment for Women's Opportunity in Scotland?

Charting any discussion of 'development' or 'progressivism' in Scotland struggles to ignore the influence of Devolution. Women's rights and the women's movement in Scotland do not, of course, originate with Devolution—it has a far longer and much more influential history than a discussion beginning with the Scotland Act 1998 may suggest (see Chap. 1). That said, in order to assess the significance of the changes to policy affecting gender, women and women's rights in Scotland, it is necessary to consider the lead up to, and impact of, the revised constitutional settlement that took shape in the late 1990s.

2.2.1 A Detour from Women's Rights in Scotland: Establishing a Devolution Settlement?

The history of Devolution and of the relationship between Edinburgh (Holyrood) and London (Westminster) is a protracted one, dominated by partisan politics, policy and rhetoric.[8] That there was a Devolution settlement is a resounding achievement for proponents of greater independence for Scotland. This is especially so given the turbulent developments during the 1970s which suggested that there would be an earlier devolved settlement and that such an arrangement would need further

[7] Representing a Scotland with its own Executive under the Scotland Act 1998. This Act led to the establishment of a devolved administration following on from the devolution referendum held in 1997. The Scottish Parliament was founded on 12 May 1999.

[8] Mitchell (2009, p. 137).

development before there could be a tranche of powers devolved to a Scottish Parliament which would work on a broader spectrum than either the Scottish Office or the Scottish Secretary and Lord Advocate.[9] In their October 1974 election manifesto, Labour promised to create an elected assembly in Scotland[10] and followed this in their 1979 manifesto with a reaffirmation of the "commitment to devolution for Scotland."[11] The promise of the Scotland Act 1978 and the March 1979 referendum fell short of delivering a fresh reality, and a Scottish Assembly, when the 1978 Act was repealed by Thatcher's government in June 1979[12] following the collapse of the previous government. Then Secretary of State for Scotland, George Younger MP, highlighted the limitations of the 1979 referendum, and the 40% rule contained within it when putting the Repeal Order 1979 before Parliament, stating: "legislation effecting major constitutional changes that would be almost irreversible in practice should have the support of a substantial majority of the electorate affected before being given full and final effect in law."[13]

That is not to say that Devolution was not back on the political agenda in the decade that followed. In fact, by 1987, there was something of a critical turning point—described by Lynch as "Doomsday"[14]—when the General Election returned a Conservative government in England, while in Scotland, MPs from a combination of parties favouring a Scottish Parliament were elected. With an increased appetite for Scottish Parliament-supporting elected representatives, and growing questions over the legitimacy of the governing party at Westminster to make policy for Scotland,[15] in the 1980s, Devolution was once again a political topic, but one which did not see any significant action during the Conservative rule beyond piecemeal increases in responsibilities given to the Scottish Office. While insignificant in their own right, collectively these responsibilities indirectly triggered Labour's 1987 Scotland Bill—which stood no

[9] Ibid., p. 113.
[10] Dale (2000, p. 208).
[11] Ibid., p. 230.
[12] Scotland Act 1978 (Repeal) Order 1979, SI 1979/928. Hereafter Repeal Order 1979.
[13] HC Deb 20 June 1979, vol. 968, col. 1328.
[14] Lynch (2010).
[15] Mitchell (2009, p. 127).

realistic prospect of being passed. What it did was indicate a sea change in the thinking of Labour Party policy vis-à-vis Devolution. Interestingly, this appeared not long before the Scottish Constitutional Convention (SCC) (signed by 58 of the then 72 Scottish MPs),[16] and the later agreement of Labour in October 1988 to sign the Convention. Without these incremental changes to the remit of the Scottish Office, the—inevitable—Labour agreement to the SCC may never have materialised. That it did, proved to trigger further appetite for Devolution—something the Conservative government failed to give proper attention to, dismissing it as "not of general interest" in the prelude to the 1992 General Election.[17] Within this system of political tension, and skirting around sensitive issues—such as that of Devolution—little attention was paid specifically to policy issues affecting women.

The Scottish Constitutional Convention proved useful, if for no other reason than to trigger further action after the change in government in 1997. In committing to a Scottish Parliament, the Labour Government necessarily filled some of the gaping holes in the SCC. In unveiling the future path of devolved governance, and filling those gaps, Donald Dewar MP made clear the evolution in Labour thinking (and policy) from the 1970s by stating, "Unlike in 1978, the full range of the Scottish Office's functions will be devolved."[18] Other indicators went further, suggesting that there would be a much broader range of powers devolved, "with one or two prescribed and limited exceptions."[19] These early indicators suggested there was enormous potential for Scotland to chart its own policy ambition, and to develop policies that may not necessarily be a priority at Westminster, heralding, at the very least, appetite for greater prominence to be given to women's rights. The ambition was one which promised to allow for the opportunity of considering women's issues, if little else.

In contrast to Conservative short-sightedness, the landslide General Election victory for Labour in 1997 laid the way for decisive action on devolution as a priority, with proposals for a referendum outlined within months of Labour's election victory. The resulting referendum took place

---

[16] Ibid., p. 129.

[17] Gourtsoyannis (2017).

[18] HC Deb 24 July 1997, vol. 298, col. 1046.

[19] Gay (1998, p. 6).

on 11 September 1997—less than 20 years since the 1979 devolution debacle, and the consequential stagnation of discussions of women's issues. Following the affirmation that Devolution was the will of the people, the Scotland Bill was tabled in the UK Parliament in January 1998, becoming law that November.[20] The overwhelming level of public support for a devolved administration saw plans laid out for the re-establishment of the Scottish Parliament.

It has been suggested that the Scottish Constitutional Convention of the 1980s formed the "blueprint"[21] for the Scottish Parliament of the late 1990s, but such a claim is dismissive of the growth in appetite for a Scotland ruled from within its own geographical borders, as well as the wider political context. The actual 'blueprint' stemmed from the Consultative Steering Group (CSG) established in 1997 in preparation for the transition to the Scottish Parliament. In that respect, the Parliament was "designed"[22] by the key stakeholders who would have to operate within it—the leading political parties in Scotland[23] (amongst others). Importantly, the composition of the CSG membership included women (a surprising development given the lack of attention paid to women and their opinions prior to the mid-1990s)[24]—a necessary measure given the appetite and ambition of a different political and working culture for—at a minimum—the new Parliament.

Devolution paved the way for *expectations*[25] of a different political culture, and a different political attitude by design.[26] Post-Devolution, the

[20] Scottish Parliament (n.d.-a. https://www.parliament.scot/about/history-of-the-scottish-parliament/the-path-to-devolution).

[21] Mitchell (2009, p. 130).

[22] Consultative Steering Group on the Scottish Parliament. 1998. Shaping Scotland's Parliament. The Scottish Office. https://www.parliament.scot/-/media/files/history/report_of_the_consultative_steering_group.pdf. Accessed 10 February 2022.

[23] Scottish Parliament (n.d.-b: https://www.parliament.scot/about/history-of-the-scottish-parliament/the-path-to-devolution).

[24] Hills (2001, p. 27).

[25] The composition of the CSG is perhaps partly responsible for the attention paid to how to make the Scottish Parliament work for women. In the CSG report, for instance, there are 28 mentions of points specific to women and how to deliver a Scottish Parliament which works for women. See Consultative Steering Group on the Scottish Parliament (1998).

[26] Originating, at least in part, from the Consultative Steering Group and its subsequent report in 1999.

Scottish Executive had been charged with new responsibilities, including the setting of policy—a marked change from the focus of policy implementation that existed as the primary responsibility of its predecessor, the Scottish Office.[27] The ideas that formulated as part of the design of the Scottish Parliament, its electoral system and its work have influenced the policy landscape and programmes of work of successive Scottish governments. Indirectly, the legal arrangements surrounding Devolution have led to a change in the landscape affecting equalities, but especially women and girls, if for no other reason than there is now a governmental body in Scotland charged with setting and implementing policy affecting women. More specifically, issues of equality were embedded into the design and operation of everyday politics in Scotland, with the recommendation that the Scottish Parliament convene an Equal Opportunities Committee as one of the mandatory committees to help ensure that "equal opportunities … be mainstreamed into the work of the Parliament"[28] and across Scottish society. This followed the power enshrined in the Scotland Act 1998 to "encourage" equal opportunities[29] (and which operated as the precursor to the public sector equality duty (PSED) now found in Section 149 of the Equality Act 2010). The Scottish Government was keen to encourage innovation in respect of equal opportunities, and "interpreted this broadly."[30] It is also significant that this was encouraged in respect of characteristics including gender,[31] more so given that gender has often been overlooked in law reform in Scotland (see Chap. 4). Despite encouragement from the Scottish Parliament, the PSED has fallen short of triggering actual change, especially for women.

2.2.2 What About Women? The Emergence of 'Women's Issues' on a National Level

The debates surrounding changes in the constitutional settlement arrangements for Scotland in the 1970s emerged after 'second-wave'

[27] Keating (2005, p. 455).
[28] Georghiou and Kidner (2007, p. 12).
[29] Scotland Act 1998, sch. 5, s. L2.
[30] Birrell (2009, p. 72).
[31] Georghiou and Kidner (2007, p. 11).

feminism. The 'second-wave'[32] of feminism built on the first, but focused on more entrenched issues, including de facto inequalities, but also sexuality, family and broader debates surrounding legal aspects of inequality. While there is little to suggest there is any correlation between the emergence of Devolution and second-wave feminism, the timing provided an opportunity for women in Scotland to challenge the social norm of women remaining "repressed," with their "achievements even more ignored."[33] The emerging prominence of feminism to include women's trade unionism (with figures suggesting that women accounted for 70% of the increase in members between 1964 and 1970)[34] along with the trend towards liberation suggested there was potential for the emergence of a more national voice for women as the 1970s passed by. This impression was solidified with moves away from the "insider politics"[35] that had been the dominant political modus operandi across Scotland. The coinciding of these events provided an opportunity for the voices of women in Scotland to be heard and was mirrored by developments in women's activism, suggesting that this momentum would be seized.

The normal scepticism and reluctance of women to get involved in frontline politics extended to almost outright hostility at the idea of engaging in parliamentary politics,[36] but there were indicators that changing feminist attitudes may see that shift too. In short, Scottish societal attitudes—Devolution or otherwise aside—made political engagement unappealing for women during the 1970s and 1980s. This hesitancy was tempered somewhat when it came to a more realistic prospect of the proposed Scottish Assembly, but generally, the overwhelming response from women to politics during this period was one of ambivalence.[37] The notions of Devolved elected bodies did not seem to strike a chord with women in Scotland either, and created—at best—a lacklustre level of engagement as a result. This was partially due to the fact that "[i]ssues of particular concern to women were not merely ignored: their existence

[32] Lear (1968).

[33] Hills (2001, p. 27).

[34] Sinclair (1996, p. 241).

[35] Innes and Randall (2006, p. 72).

[36] Ibid.

[37] Ibid.

was not recognised."[38] The silencing of women's issues was coupled with the added concern that any such Scottish Assembly (or other proposed Devolved body) "would not be sympathetic to women's rights."[39] Not only did women not have a voice, but their issues and concerns were not recognised, discussed or even acknowledged as a valid point of policy (or action). With this background, it is little wonder that discussions of women's rights in Scotland were scant, with initiatives and policies relating to women, and especially VAW, not recognised as priorities (if at all) and were non-existent (see Chap. 1).

The Thatcher years offered little more. They saw the establishment of a different pattern in steps taken to address issues facing women in Scotland. In the absence of any transparency[40] or sensitivity[41] in the setting and shaping of policy, and the lack of a national policy-setting body for Scotland (the Scottish Office and Cabinet Secretary for Scotland implemented policy set by Westminster,[42] often without any reform-minded Scottish Secretary at the helm[43]), new groups, agendas and organisations begin to form against the backdrop of a push for a Scottish identity, and Scottish perspectives for Scotland. This was also triggered to some extent by a need to redress the historical exclusion of women and women's issues from the dominant narratives in Scotland and further afield.[44] The pervasiveness of such attitudes, reflecting misogynistic habits (and society), and the general ignorance of matters affecting women reached a flash point in the early 1990s through the combination of the deregulation of the labour market, increased privatisation and the habit of "concentrating [Tory] power in the South East."[45] In some respects, feminism rediscovered its voice having been sidelined by a prolonged period of

[38] Hills (2001, p. 27).

[39] Innes and Randall (2006, p. 73).

[40] Mitchell (1998, p. 75).

[41] Brown et al. (1998, p. 97).

[42] Keating (2005, p. 455). Albeit this was likely to change under the proposed devolution arrangements discussed in the late 1990s: see Consultative Steering Group on the Scottish Parliament (1998, para. 28).

[43] Mitchell (2006, p. 161).

[44] Hills (2001, pp. 29–30).

[45] Ibid., p. 28.

Westminster Conservative government—the voices of women survived, but barely. The correlation of these factors all but ensured the exclusion of the voices of women in Scotland. The General Election of 1992 and the extension of Conservative rule served to add to the general lack of voices for women, and their issues. These factors compounded the lack of opportunities for women to engage in the political system or to enact change from within Scotland. This limitation was palpable in early 1990s Scotland, not least because women tended to engage politically at local levels rather than national ones. In the late 1980s and early 1990s, there were few such routes into national politics open—or appealing—to women in Scotland. Moreover, attempting to get feminist or women's issues covered in the Scottish media was always problematic—a challenge intrinsically linked to a society with exclusionary tendencies, or as described by Hills, "a society demonstrating its misogyny in its press, its public life, and the daily lives of women."[46]

It is then surprising—particularly to women—that the women's movement started to re-engage with politics and parliamentary discussions in the early 1990s. It did so while simultaneously forming—what would become powerful—organisations[47] to campaign for equal roles, representation and voices in a new sociopolitical system, and in a society undergoing attitudinal flux. Such mobilisation coincided—in part—with the outcry from the 1992 General Election, where issues of representation and a lack of voice were notable protests—from men in Scotland. This protest by Scottish men about the lack of *their* voice was part of a broader movement concerning the legitimacy of government for Scotland, and which raised—again—questions of a devolved body. The outcry about representation and Scottish voices for Scotland's men was something that women were able to utilise because they recognised, "wryly the protests of their male friends that they had no autonomy and were at the mercy of a small group of men for whom they had not voted and who did not have their best interests at heart."[48] With a hefty dose of irony, the trigger point for more women to engage more prominently in public life and

[46] Ibid., p. 30.

[47] Notably, Engender, Zero Tolerance, and For Women Scotland Ltd.

[48] Hills (2001, p. 30).

raise awareness of issues affecting women came about—at least partially—because of men's dissatisfaction with the representation arrangements of the male voice in Scotland. It is also a stark example of where there was recognition that changes needed to be made to allow for Scottish voices to be heard. Disappointingly, it was men's voices—showing once again that there was a habit of disregarding women's voices in favour of those of men. Amongst a society with a tendency towards the misogynistic, this is hardly surprising but shows the scale of the challenge facing women in Scotland before, and during, the 1990s.

In the early 1990s, Engender was formed, "born in passion, anger and frustration."[49] While recognising that to change the lives of women in Scotland for the better, there was—and continues to be—a need to bring together information, conduct specific gender disaggregated research and celebrate women.[50] Engender was—and is—not the only prominent women's organisation to have formed in Scotland in the late 1980s and early 1990s. Other groups, including, for example, Shakti Women's Aid (founded in 1986), were gaining traction at similar times. This also included what was (then) the Zero Tolerance Campaign. At a formative point in Scottish society—and politics—women were mobilising to address the deep dissatisfaction that stemmed from "the society that men have made and the culture they have formed."[51]

Across Scotland, elements of the women's movement were emerging, but did so without coordination and without centralisation. The individual groups were formed in cities or regions based on need (Shakti Women's Aid, Zero Tolerance Campaign), or borne out of a need to ensure women had a voice in policy developments (Engender). Indirectly, this perhaps led to the emergence of groups like Engender that have taken on national roles and are now the coordinating voices across Scotland for women (and feminist issues). The lack of representation, dialogue, attention, rights and women-specific policy-setting during the 1970s and 1980s led to a changing tide in the 1990s. In reacting, women's movements and groups found their voice and triggered a more concerted effort

[49] Ibid., p. 31.
[50] Ibid.
[51] Ibid., p. 32.

in representing and, ultimately, advocating for women's rights and interests. In this, the old adage of wanting a job done properly, so ending up doing it yourself certainly seems to have rung true for women's groups across Scotland.

The developments, evolution and trends that followed have shown that in some respects, some things have changed for the better—though perhaps more by accident than by design in the policy landscape. That said, women's rights—and issues—were not always front and centre, and the political establishment not progressive. In taking the baton of women's rights and spearheading the movement, Engender was joined in mission—and spirit—by Zero Tolerance, and in turn, other women's organisations. Collectively, this movement spearheaded change, and the emergence of women's voices at a national level in Scotland. Nonetheless, much work remained to be done—policy, attitudes and women's interests still needed significant attention, even in a society clamouring for a "new"[52] way of doing things, and a "democratic regeneration."[53] The new Scottish Parliament, with the accompanying rhetoric of newness in politics,[54] together with enhanced political representation, offered an opportunity for this momentum to translate into a resetting of policy mechanisms and political attitudes.

2.2.3 Developing Policy and Resetting Political Attitudes

With the advent of "contemporary Scottish politics"[55] starting in 1999, there was a resulting change in political infrastructure, ways of delivering policy and priorities for Scotland. There was, at the time, Mackay suggests,[56] increased optimism for a refreshed approach to gender issues, and especially gender-balanced politics that would result in a different policy landscape compared to that in England. This coincided with what

[52] Mitchell (2006, p. 153).
[53] Innes (2001, p. 249).
[54] Mitchell (2009, p. 136).
[55] Mackay (2009, p. 79).
[56] Mackay (2010, p. 370).

Mackay refers to as the "professionalisation"[57] of politics, with a wider remit to design *and* deliver policy for Scotland. With this came the shaping of the political parties such as the Scottish National Party (SNP) into more than bit-part players. The re-establishment of a Parliament for Scotland allowed what were previously volunteer-led political bodies (both political parties and women's groups) to take on a more serious role. The Devolution settlement paved the way for Scottish politics to move to the forefront of domestic debate in Scotland.[58] This is a reflection considered by Brown, McCrone and Paterson who suggest that the unfolding of devolution in the 1980s and 1990s offered potential for there to be, firstly, equality of representation for women, but secondly, influence by women across a broader sphere[59] to encourage change and ensure that things could be done differently. With this came a change in the prominence of political parties, a change in the way politics was conducted but also a change in representation and selection opportunities[60]—both generally and more specifically for women. It is perhaps notable that these changes also provided challenges for the leading actors across Scotland. For the SNP, for example, there was a distinct 'women' problem in terms of image, issues and policy evident in the initial rounds of Scottish Parliament elections—a challenge that persisted through the 2007 Parliament and the election results. Amidst suggestions of "institutional and ideological barriers,"[61] the SNP's mantra of an inclusive nationalism seemed to sit oddly. It also suggests that in the years between the re-establishment of the Scottish Parliament and the 2007 elections, the SNP focus was less on issues relating to women, equal opportunities and gender, and more on becoming a viable and appealing opposition and leading party. This appears—retrospectively at least—to be something of an oversight, given the leading work done by, for instance, the Zero Tolerance Campaign across Scotland. This inaction by the SNP is confusing in light of its ambitions to create an inclusive society, not least

[57] Mackay (2009, p. 79).
[58] Ibid., p. 80.
[59] Brown et al. (1998, p. 172).
[60] Mackay and Kenny (2009, p. 47).
[61] Ibid., p. 52.

because of the mixed message it sends out. For example, the SNP have repeatedly shied away from legislating to add protections for women to the hate crime framework (see Chaps. 3 and 4), yet have been the driving force behind other applauded legislation such as the Domestic Abuse (Scotland) Act 2018 (asp 5).

That is not to say that there were not broader gender sensitive issues on the agenda, or that they were brushed aside—as had been the case in the Scotland of the 1970s and 1980s. In some contexts, the opposite was true, with an overemphasis on elements relating to gender equality, and a keenness to deliver differently, and with a firmer balance, to politics. At the founding of the Scottish Parliament, for instance, this appetite was palpable. With the first Members of the Scottish Parliament taking office, policies, protocols, strategies and ambitions were fresh, not least because there was a greater spread of elected representatives—an almost inevitable result of a system designed to prevent any sole party having a majority.[62] The red tape that curtails ambition in other, more established, national legislatures was not (yet) in place at the time the first members took their seats at Holyrood. This freshness allowed—at least in the early years—a greater level of what Mackay refers to as "responsiveness" to the preferences of the women's movement.[63] It was also something that the rest of the UK should regard as a "benchmark" against which to measure itself because of the "strategic, gendered and integrated approach in Scotland."[64]

It is nonetheless significant—for women especially—embedded into the design of new parliament (and its processes) were gender equality concerns. It is as important that there have been clear examples of women in leadership roles, not just as First Minister (Nicola Sturgeon MSP) but others, including the former Cabinet Secretary for Health and Sport Jeane Freeman OBE. In designing parliamentary and political processes that have at their core considerations of gender and gender equity, there have been greater opportunities for women to play a role in not only frontline policy-setting, but also politics, all while representing the voices of women at the highest level in Scotland. While this indicates a

[62] Simpkins, Fiona (2019, p. 2).
[63] Mackay (2010, p. 382).
[64] Coy et al. (2007).

significant improvement for women's voices, it has not always been a positive, and comes with significant disbenefits, including violence, abuse, threats and harassment. In seeking to play a role in having a voice for women who suffer violence and abuse, women have had to put themselves in a position where they receive it. Violence against women in politics (VAWP) is not specific to Scotland nor to leaders such as Nicola Sturgeon and former party leaders Kezia Dugdale (Scottish Labour) or Ruth Davidson (Scottish Conservatives),[65] but it has become particularly prominent in recent years[66] and has been exacerbated through the rise of social media (see Chap. 6), with one in three MSPs reporting receiving hate and death threats.[67] It also coincides with the rise of digital feminism[68] and the emergence of new spaces where women's voices and participation are still to be taken seriously.

Leadership and the visibility of women in Scottish politics aside, it is particularly notable that there has been a deliberate effort to design policy-making that incorporates—and arguably relies on—consultation and participation. The CSG on the Scottish Parliament expressly consulted on things which were different to the ways in which Westminster operated. For instance, this included questions on how to involve not just civic society, but specifically "women's groups"[69]—something of a marked alteration from the overlooking of women's voices and women's issues in previous generations. It was telling that the women's movement began to mobilise and form organisations immediately prior to the development of this Parliamentary approach, suggesting that the timing was right. Perhaps obviously, their early influence can be seen in the input that women's organisations had into considerations of the new Parliament and its ways of working—one notable contributor founded in the early 1990s for precisely these reasons was Engender.[70] It was an ideal moment of timing in which to make known its existence to the newest political power in Scotland.

[65] The Sunday Post (2018); Amnesty International (2018).

[66] Scott (2021).

[67] Andrews (2021).

[68] Barker and Jurasz (2019, p. 95).

[69] Consultative Steering Group on the Scottish Parliament (1998, Annex C).

[70] Ibid., List of (Non-Confidential) Respondees to the CSG Consultation Exercise).

This "consultative style of policy making"[71] specifically builds in the expertise of women's organisations and is something which suggests there is now greater influence by women, for women, at the highest policy levels in Scotland. That said, questions over whether a select few organisations have too much influence persist, not least because of the number of committees, or consultations that civil society groups sit on as expert organisations, and the number of groups that are represented on multiple committees.[72] It is difficult to suggest that selected groups and non-governmental organisations do not have access though. It is, however, perhaps more notable given the size of Scotland that a select number of groups seem to have a lot of access—this is maybe a quirk of a system designed to ensure exactly this but under the auspices of attempting to do things differently. In trying to design a system to counteract insider politics, that is exactly what has been created. The distinction, at least with women's organisations, is that they have the position (now) to be able to exert influence—quite a turnaround from the situation of the early 1970s.

For instance, in tackling domestic violence, VAW organisations—notably Scottish Women's Aid—were designated with expert status during the policy process.[73] This indicates that the system has—by design—created a process by which there are multiple points for those advocating for women and women's rights to exert influence, but also that the system caters for this in a much greater way than is apparent in England. While this could—and perhaps should—be heralded as a successful alternative model to that in other parts of the UK, there are some significant concerns and associated disbenefits. Notably, the selected voices are those which are heard repeatedly, but more problematically routes to insider status are ultimately dependent on having the resources to be able to engage,[74] and not all potential expert or advocacy organisations are equal in that respect. While some organisations—including Engender—have developed into a body with a more formal relationship

[71] Mackay (2010, p. 369).

[72] The number of which, as of 15 February 2021, was stated to be 18 Scottish Government Advisory and Strategic Groups, with representation on a further three to follow once their respective work starts, making a total of 21. See McKelvie (2021).

[73] Mackay (2010, p. 382).

[74] Cairney and Rummery (2018, p. 545).

with the Scottish Parliament, Cairney and Rummery suggest that this level of access may be the result of a repeated contact that has built up relationships based on trust and reliability.[75] Again, this is something reminiscent of the closed circle, 'insider-ism' of a previous era—breaking through may be difficult for those who do not have the resources or links to do so. That said, there are some suggestions that post-devolution structures in Scotland lend themselves a more favourable environment for—in particular—"the voice, activism and representation of BME women,"[76] though there is still some room for improvement to overcome the 'quietness' of BME women's voices.[77] Similarly, there are emerging impressions now that Scottish women's voices are being heard, albeit at regional and international levels (rather than within the UK), through the influence of international standards on civil society organisations. The reciprocal impact on Scottish politics is evident through Scotland's willingness to engage with international standards for rights, such as the rights of the child[78] (See Chap. 1.)

In some respects, the rapidity with which there has been a shift from political outsiders with little influence to insiders exerting considerable strategic input is a significant achievement for advancing policy agendas relating to women's rights and equality. While it is progress to have representation of women's organisations and women's perspectives on strategic and advisory groups, questions persist about how representative it is to have so few organisations exerting influence across such a large number of Scottish Government groups (see Fig. 2.1). Such a rapid change also suggests two things. First, that despite the shift away from the insider politics of the 1970s and 1980s,[79] there has been a U-turn, and that is exactly the situation that now appears evident at Holyrood. It also suggests, second, that despite the significant growth of influence and 'insider-ism' that seems to have developed (and now dominates) in domestic

[75] Ibid.

[76] Casserly (2014, p. 439).

[77] Ibid.

[78] See, for example, Boyle and Busby (2021, p. 7).

[79] Innes and Randall (2006, p. 72).

Question ref. S5W-35024
Asked by: Elaine Smith, Central Scotland, Scottish Labour
Date lodged: 5 February 2021

Question

To ask the Scottish Government on which of its advisory and strategic groups is Engender represented.

Current status: Answered by Christina McKelvie on 15 February 2021

Answer

Engender is represented on the following Scottish Government advisory and strategic groups:

- Misogynistic Harassment Group
- Social Renewal Advisory Board
- Gender Index Working Group
- Women's Health Group
- Gender Equality Taskforce in Education and Learning
- Gender Pay Gap Working Group
- First Minister's Advisory Council on Women & Girls
- Joint strategic board of Equally Safe
- Gender Based Violence and Learning Disability Working Group
- The Carers Benefit Advisory Group
- The Best Start Reference Group
- Gender Equality Taskforce on Education and Learning
- National Taskforce on Human Rights civil society reference group
- Working group on Commercial Sexual Exploitation
- The Transport Equalities Forum
- The Planning Community Engagement Working Group
- Equally Safe Expert Experience Panel
- UNCEDAW Reference Group

Please note that Engender are also represented on the Trans Inclusion and Women's Rights Guidance Advisory Group, and have been invited to join the Working Group on Non-Binary Equality, which has not yet met. The work of both of these groups has been paused due to COVID-19, but is intended to restart shortly. Engender is also part of the Mental Health and Human Rights Forum, which has not met yet.

Fig. 2.1 Written Question S5W-35024 of 5 February 2021 lodged by Elaine Smith MSP, asking the Scottish Government on which of its advisory and strategic groups Engender is represented on

Scottish policy over the last 20 years, little real progress has been made on significantly altering the policy agenda for women and in substantively addressing VAW.

There have been some developments in respect of gender equality and women's issues, albeit not as much as was hoped for with the initial design of the Scottish Parliamentary processes. In the early 1990s, there was a sense of palpable optimism that progressive-looking local councils—particularly Edinburgh District Council (EDC)—would lead a broader trend of work addressing gender equality, influence the blueprint for the future Scottish Parliament and lead to the emergence of the "femocrat."[80] While these levels of influence cannot be said to have necessarily come to fruition, there have been positive indicators since early 1990s Scotland. For instance, the implementation of the Public Sector Equality Duty via the Equality Act 2010, gender representation on public boards[81] and the development of the *Equally Safe*[82] programme of work (see Chap. 1) are steps in the 'right' direction towards greater equality. The lingering doubts that remain in respect of these developments in Scotland though concern the extent to which these can be attributed to equal opportunities policies. It is unclear whether these flagship policies were influenced by the emergence of women in leadership positions in Scottish politics, or whether they unfolded irrespective of the changing role (and input) of women in politics. Certainly, during the early years of the SNP-led Executive, there are strong indicators that policies and initiatives relating to gender equality (but also VAW and hate crime) in particular were set aside due to "limited political authority and will."[83]

2.3 VAW in Scotland: No Man Has the Right?

The evolution of approaches to preventing and tackling VAW pre-date devolution, the Scottish Parliament and even discussions of women's issues being a non-feature on the political radar during the 1970s and 1980s. VAW is an issue which has been around since long before any consideration of specific policy to address it, and yet, in 2022, remains a significant problem. Attention was raised in a striking, "compelling"[84] campaign launched in Edinburgh in the early 1990s—that of Zero

[80] Mackay (2001, p. 125).

[81] Gender Representation on Public Boards (Scotland) Act 2018, s. 1(1) (asp 4).

[82] Scottish Government and COSLA (2018), updated from 2016.

[83] Fyfe et al. (2009, p. 213).

[84] Sofou (2018).

Tolerance. It was a campaign designed to challenge attitudes, shift perceptions and raise awareness of the impact of VAW.[85] In that, it built upon the feminist movement from the 1970s, and sought to challenge the continuum of men's violence against women and children. The campaign itself was a radical one, championing a number of elements, including the need to have adequate legal protection for women/survivors of violence. It was conceived of at a local level and was launched by EDC's Women's Committee in 1992. In this, EDC built upon the emergence of a desire to address issues affecting women in Scotland, and in a society approaching the new millennium—it was an ideal opportunity to capture public attention while there was momentum. It was also perfect timing, coming against a backdrop of increasing focuses on women and equality, but also with a growing social appetite to tackle such issues.[86]

The EDC Zero Tolerance Campaign (ZT Campaign) did just that. The EDC campaign arose out of its tri-annual consultation exercise, which, in 1990, identified—amongst other things—the issues of VAW[87] and women's safety[88] as two of the most pressing concerns among those surveyed. This was coupled with increasingly alarming surveys reporting that teenagers, particularly boys, were more accepting of domestic violence.[89] In combination, these led to funding for a six-month public awareness campaign designed to put the issue of VAW squarely and uncomfortably in the public eye, by placing posters prominently in locations along the streets of the Scottish capital. Four posters were conceived of by the EDC in-house women officers, working in combination with feminist designer, Franki Raffles. The depiction of domestic situations was coupled with uncomfortable messages about the impact of emotional, physical and sexual abuses and represented a "public vindication of women's experiences."[90]

The message was clear that 'No Man Has the Right' calling out abuse and violence for what it is, while advocating for a "Zero Tolerance"

[85] Mackay (2001, p. 105).
[86] Ibid., p. 113.
[87] Ibid., p. 108.
[88] McLaughlin (2017).
[89] Falchikov (1996, p. 391).
[90] Sofou (2018).

Fig. 2.2 No Man Has the Right (left) poster and Male Abuse of Power is a Crime (Right) poster from the original Zero Tolerance Campaign in Scotland

approach—VAW would not be tolerated at any cost (Fig. 2.2). The campaign stirred up a significant strength of feeling for a change in attitudes—both to broader issues affecting women and VAW. EDC's Women's Unit Campaigns Officer, Evelyn Gillian, was instrumental in the campaign and identified that:

> the problem of women's safety was actually a problem of men's violence and abuse of power…[We] had the analysis, the determination and the boldness needed to cut the crap, name the issue and develop a groundbreaking strategy for progressive social change.[91]

The ZT Campaign was so successful that it had, by 1995, run in South Australia, in 12 Scottish councils,[92] 7 English councils and in the

[91] McLaughlin (2017).

[92] Sofou (2018).

Association of London Authorities.[93] The ZT Campaign, which later led to the establishment of the charity of the same name, almost unprecedently triggered widespread support and attention far beyond Edinburgh. It also led—perhaps most significantly—to EDC lobbying the Convention of Scottish Local Authorities (CoSLA) to "call for a co-ordinated national, regional and local anti-violence campaign."[94] In turn, this would influence—though much later—the *Equally Safe*[95] strategy developed in conjunction with the Scottish Government.

The success of the ZT Campaign was based—unusually—not on the role of national bodies or on political organs, but instead, as Mackay highlights, on a number of factors which were unusual.[96] The political, social and societal timing was fortuitous—there was a unique opportunity to capture attention with a feminist campaign on a matter of significant importance to women, at a time when there was broader social appetite for such a development. Moreover, there were a growing number of moves amongst women's organisations in Scotland which contributed to the appetite for such a campaign—networking by women in Scotland cannot be undersold in its centrality to the ZT Campaign success. There had been a gulf in anything to do with women's issues during the 1980s, with women disengaging from politics, with their issues pushed out of the public eye. That said, the campaign was so impactful because of the level of planning that went into it, the level of support garnered from key players—both political and non-political—and, crucially, retaining control over defining the issue and the materials to deliver the message.[97] It was, from the beginning, a campaign which gained support across the political spectrum, but also across the policy community, relying on insider ability to shape the campaign itself while ensuring that it was not hijacked by politicians, yet delivering one of the most successful ever local authority campaigns.[98]

---

[93] Mackay (2001, p. 105).

[94] Ibid., p. 111.

[95] Scottish Government and COSLA (2018), updated from 2016.

[96] Mackay (2001, p. 113).

[97] Ibid., p. 116.

[98] Sofou (2018).

It is, then, unfortunate that despite the brilliance and the legacy of the original campaign, the same battles are still being fought over 30 years on.[99] Perhaps more disappointing is that there has been a lack of progress made at regional and national levels to substantively tackle the issue of VAW through bespoke policy, leading to specific and comprehensive legislative measures to address the problem. Given the impact of the Zero Tolerance Campaign in the 1990s, it is a shame that Scotland has not seen fit to build on this and lead the way on issues affecting the safety of women (see Chap. 5). It is also somewhat remiss of Scottish policy organs to have not taken more direct action to build upon the foundational work of the Zero Tolerance Campaign.

Since becoming the dominant, though not majority, party at Holyrood, the SNP has made some strides in tackling issues relating to women's inequality, as well as violence against women (VAW) and the recognised "links"[100] between the two. Whether it has done enough remains a point of criticism, and one which—arguably—First Minister Nicola Sturgeon is acutely aware can only be answered in the negative.[101]

That is not to say that nothing has developed, or that there have been no significant developments for gender-focused policies to address women's issues. For instance, under the SNP, the Scottish Parliament has overseen the development of the Violence Against Women and Girls Strategy, (see Chap. 1) leading to the *Safer Lives* plan and aim of continuing Scotland's role at the "forefront of work to tackle gender-based violence."[102] This policy approach has developed incrementally into the *Equally Safe* programme of work as a collaborative partnership between the Scottish Government and CoSLA. This, together with the associated *Equally Safe Delivery Plan*,[103] is designed to tackle aspects of VAW across Scotland and make meaningful differences for those affected.

Scotland is also trying different things and trying to engage with a wider body of individuals, experts and organisations in alternative ways.

---

99 Strickland (2021).

100 Scottish Government (n.d.-b: https://www.gov.scot/policies/violence-against-women-and-girls/).

101 Scottish Government (2019).

102 Scottish Government and COSLA (2009, p. 1).

103 Scottish Government and COSLA (2017).

For instance, the First Minister has established advisory groups that report to her on issues directly related to VAW. The establishment of the First Minister's Advisory Group (FMAG) on Human Rights Leadership[104] and the National Advisory Council on Women and Girls (NACWG)[105] are just two of these groups with focused agendas, all feeding into the ways in which the Scottish Government is attempting to be more forward-thinking in addressing issues relating to women, but especially VAW. The NACWG, for instance, has a relatively open membership of individuals who contribute to 'circle'[106] meetings, which are all designed to feed in to the NACWG's annual reports to the First Minister. While this may be in some ways a political exercise, it also demonstrates a commitment to at least attempt to reach out beyond the—now—established insider groups and civil society organisations, and listen to voices beyond theirs. There is, of course, a distinct difference between 'circle' meetings and the discussions of advisory or strategic groups such as those on which, for example, Engender is a member. That said, the commitment to have a more open political system is something which seems—at least on the issue of VAW—to be one to which there remains a commitment, even if it is not a particularly progressive one. It is also reflective of a more inclusive open call for participation. This model represents the embodiment of the 'openness' that was discussed at length in plans for the Scottish Parliament.

It is possible that Scotland has also suffered from its early successes and refreshed approach, with expectations being high[107] given early initial differences being commended, to achieve "gendered-outcomes," albeit fragile ones.[108] By taking action and putting the inequality agenda at the forefront of its policies through strategies such as *Equally Safe*, it has reawakened discussions about the scale of the VAW problem, given such landmark recognition by the ZT Campaign. Early successes such as planning for an integrated programme of work[109] suggest that there was a

[104] Human Rights Leadership Scotland (n.d.: https://humanrightsleadership.scot).

[105] One Scotland (n.d.-a: https://onescotland.org/equality-themes/advisory-council-women-girls/).

[106] One Scotland. (n.d.-b: https://onescotland.org/equality-themes/advisory-council-women-girls/who-we-are-and-what-we-do/).

[107] O'Hagan (2016, p. 650).

[108] Mackay (2010, p. 383).

[109] Scottish Government and COSLA (2009).

desire—and a drive—to do things differently, though some of that ambition seems to have stalled and has recently even been the subject of some criticism for failing to live up to its promises of delivering a collaborative approach.[110]

In some respects, the scale and breadth of the problem of VAW has become much more talked about than the mechanisms implemented to attempt to tackle it. This has been compounded by the unfolding of global events well beyond the control of any national government—such as the COVID-19 pandemic,[111] or the humanitarian crises and resulting civilian displacement triggered by civil war,[112] or extreme weather events[113]—all of which have triggered different strands of the unfolding VAW epidemic. The efforts to tackle VAW and to make meaningful changes to structural inequalities have, at times, also been set back by staggering and contradictory examples of institutionalised approaches to the safety of women despite Mackay's early positivity that there has been a shift towards "a more gender-balanced politics… result[ing] in distinctive policy trajectories as compared with England."[114] For instance, Police Scotland was in 2019 backing the Fearless Glasgow drive to tackle gender-based and sexual violence across universities and further education institutions,[115] yet less than two years later, it was responsible for endangering women during the Cop26 meeting by directing them on lengthy detours through dark parks and streets in the same city.[116] These isolated but recent examples of the disconnect between the policy ambition and the practical reality for women in Scotland highlight the scale of the challenge which remains. In the words of Ruth Maguire MSP, there remains some significant work to be done to address the safety and equality of women:

---

[110] Equality and Human Rights Commission (2017, p. 3).

[111] UN Women (2020).

[112] UN Office for the Coordination of Humanitarian Affairs (2019); Whiting (2018).

[113] Thurston et al. (2021); London School of Hygiene & Tropical Medicine (2021).

[114] Mackay (2010, p. 370).

[115] Glasgow Caledonian University (2019).

[116] Sabin, Lamiat. 2021. Police apologise after Cop26 diversions force women to walk through park at night. *The Independent*, 3 November. https://www.independent.co.uk/news/uk/home-news/cop26-woman-park-night-glasgow-b1949988.html. Accessed 10 February 2022.

> Scotland is not equally safe, and four minutes is not enough time in which to do justice to all the women and girls who have been subjected to men's violence in our unequal society. In Scotland, too many women still face the burning injustice of workplace sexual harassment, pregnancy discrimination, domestic abuse, female genital mutilation, so-called honour crimes, sexual assault, rape, trafficking, stalking and prostitution. Globally, women and girls are being refused access to education and are trapped in conflicts in which rape is used as a weapon of war. The number of sex-selected abortions is rising, the number of deaths relating to pregnancy and childbirth is needlessly high, and women and girls are prevented from making deeply personal choices about their reproductive healthcare.[117]

The confusing and contradictory policy moves, played out in the shadow of the Zero Tolerance legacy, are disappointing given the momentum it had established in the 1990s. The lack of follow-up action on this at a level beyond local politics is also somewhat confusing. It raises questions about how progressive Scotland can truly claim to be on the issue of addressing VAW and suggests that the momentum has been eroded away. The Scottish Societal Attitudes Survey (SSAS) suggests that there are incremental changes in attitudes towards the acceptance of VAW in Scotland, but these are not widespread. For example, the overall proportion of people holding stereotypical views on gender roles shows a decline in 2019, compared to 2014.[118] While that is a positive step, there evidently remains a lot of work to be done on challenging societal attitudes. Across the same period, there were no recorded substantial differences in views on the "wrongness" of physical, verbal or financial abuse of women.[119] Similarly, 30 years after the landmark Zero Tolerance Campaign, evidence suggests that little has changed for women—one in ten women in Scotland has experienced rape, and one in five women in Scotland has had someone try to force them to have sex against their will, and these are just two examples.[120] These figures and the attitudes they reflect suggest, similarly to the SSAS data, that much, much more needs to be done to

[117] Meeting of the Scottish Parliament, 26 November 2020, Official Report, col. 75.

[118] Scottish Government (2020b, p. 13).

[119] Ibid.

[120] Zero Tolerance (n.d.: https://www.zerotolerance.org.uk/vaw-facts/).

address VAW in Scotland. Collectively, the data paint a depressing picture of the reality for women in Scotland and their likelihood of encountering VAW, but it also seems to suggest that progress is neither what it could have been nor what was anticipated after the developments of the 1990s.

2.4 Progressivism in Scotland: Rhetoric Or Reality?

Similar to the approach to social care,[121] the strategies and approach towards ending VAW have been portrayed in Scotland as different, progressive and more forward-thinking than that of its neighbours and counterparts. This reflects the construction in the early 2000s of Scotland as the "happening place"[122] for policy innovation. This was especially the narrative advanced in respect of social policy, though this is, firstly, misleading, secondly, nothing new[123] and, thirdly, dismissive of the work done by pre-devolution bodies, including the Scottish Office. While there is some suggestion that Scotland is progressive, it remains unclear whether this is by accident or design, or a mixture of the two. For instance, there are clear politically progressive indicators in how the Scottish Parliament has been designed procedurally. Similarly, there are some indicators that Scotland is prepared to innovate legislatively. There have also been bold policy initiatives unveiled across the course of the Scottish Parliament since 1999.

A historical consideration suggests that some progressive claims are grounded, while others are much more entrenched in what O'Hagan describes as "strong" rhetoric,[124] and while this is broadly a matter of debate in social policy circles, differences of opinion persist in respect of policy affecting women, and VAW in particular. The unfolding of Scottish Executive and Government ambition has seemed to coincide with greater law-making powers, but also with a greater societal appetite for tackling divisive issues.

[121] Rummery and McAngus (2015, p. 235).

[122] Mooney and Poole (2004, p. 459).

[123] Ibid., p. 460.

[124] O'Hagan (2016, p. 652).

Arguably the real sea change emerged in 2007 when the SNP achieved victory in the May elections[125] for the first time, beating Labour into second place. The victory—albeit narrow—shows a party that recognised the opportunity put before it by, first, Devolution,[126] and, second, a different system of representation, all while having moved on from a tumultuous number of years under leader John Swinney, when the party "turned in on itself."[127] What the outright victory allowed, at least in ambition, was for an SNP-led Scottish Parliament to implement some of its manifesto pledges. In turn, the tumultuous Swinney leadership paved the way for the rise of Nicola Sturgeon, firstly, as SNP leader, and, secondly, as First Minister. With Sturgeon becoming First Minister, there has been a clear trend from the SNP of tackling thorny political and legislative issues, but also of incrementally introducing policies to contribute to broader equalities, but especially the protection of women and the tackling of VAW. This is broadly embedded in a system which has a focus on the civic aspects of nationalism[128] that found its way into the SNP's nationalist rhetoric—something markedly different to other nationalist narratives in Europe, or even in the rest of the UK, with, for example, UK Independence Party's (UKIP's) nationalist rhetoric proving to be rather different to the SNPs (see Chap. 3).

While the 2007 Scottish election was significant politically because it marked the first time the SNP took charge, bigger changes for policy and societal developments in Scotland have unfolded since 2014. From 2014 onwards, the SNP has been in "complete command,"[129] with a much wider mandate, and importantly, experience of planning, implementing and delivering on policy. The more restricted initial SNP-led Parliaments between 2007 and 2014 were hindered by being a minority executive, but also by a devolution settlement that was anything but settled. In gaining additional powers through a revised devolution settlement post-2016, triggered by the Scottish Independence Referendum (IndyRef) in

[125] Mackay (2009, p. 86).

[126] Curtice (2009, p. 65); Mackay (2009, p. 79).

[127] Mackay (2009, p. 82).

[128] Mitchell et al. (2012, pp. 107–116); Green (2014).

[129] Torrance (2017, p. 56).

2014,[130] extra powers were granted to Scotland to exercise competence legislatively over a wider range of policy areas.[131] In some respects, the changes in policy setting have been triggered not by the SNP, but by the alterations to devolution through other policy areas. Arguably, the SNP could take credit for such progressive approaches having been the architects of the referendum that, in turn, led to the recommendation[132] that further concessions be made to Holyrood. In some ways, Scottish voices (including those of women) in Scotland have led to greater powers for Scotland. Notably, though, this is not really the reality. The 2007 SNP government struggled to deliver on its election manifesto—in no small part because of the minority nature of its control at Holyrood.

It is therefore of little surprise that there were no real radical policies addressing VAW implemented in 2007. Given the post-Devolution arrangements for the election of MSPs, and the breadth of groups in Scotland with a vested interest in flexing their political strength, it is hardly surprising that there is little real distinction to the development of policy in England.[133] In Scotland, as nice as a progressive policy agenda would be, there has been a need to govern with a healthy dose of pragmatism and the need to negotiate across groups, religions, political leaning and multiple layers of governmental control[134]—something the 2007 SNP government learnt by experience in minority rule.

The Sturgeon years, from 2014 onwards, offered greater potential and started with the suggestion of the SNP acting as a more progressive force,[135] even though the SNP lost its overall majority in 2016 under her stewardship.[136] It is also barely a surprise that in order to see a truly radical set of policies, it remains the case that there will need to be a Holyrood government with a clear majority, and a party with a truly progressive political ambition before radically different[137] policy objectives appear. The current

[130] Scottish Independence Referendum Act 2013 (asp 14).

[131] Scotland Act 2016.

[132] The Smith Commission (2014).

[133] Keating (2005, p. 461).

[134] Ibid.

[135] Maddox (2015).

[136] Stone (2016).

[137] Keating (2005, p. 462).

Fig. 2.3 Tweet from First Minister, Nicola Sturgeon, in response to a tweet by Chelsea Clinton praising Scotland's leadership on tackling period poverty and the resulting influence over other countries, including New Zealand

situation leaves itself reliant on what Keating describes as a "large degree of interdependency,"[138] with policy agendas in England and Wales. While the Sturgeon era of leadership can be credited with delivering on policies that do more to advance women's rights, and which have started to shift in a different direction to the rest of the nations of the UK—such as addressing period poverty or introducing leading legislation to tackle domestic abuse—these developments must be placed in their context, and they do not all directly address the issue of VAW (Fig. 2.3).

More targeted initiatives such as the NACWG and the FMAG have come under Sturgeon's leadership, but also in the aftermath of greater devolved powers being granted to Holyrood, which, in turn, have allowed for less policy compromise and greater policy control (even in landmark power-sharing deals with other parties).[139] In some ways, there is no real progressive policy—it is political rhetoric, posturing or compromise, whereas in other contexts, Holyrood, under Sturgeon's guidance, is doing things differently and with a clearer focus on addressing inequalities, albeit through legislative rather than policy progressivism. For instance, Scotland is comfortable pursuing international conventions to embed

[138] Ibid., p. 455.

[139] Skopeliti (2021).

rights into Scots Law that are not being considered in other areas of the rest of the UK. The challenge Scotland issued to the UK Government on the incorporation of the UN Convention on the Rights of the Child[140] is one example. Other women-specific initiatives seem set to follow this, with the SNP pledging to incorporate CEDAW into Scots Law[141] (see Chap. 1).

These indicators suggest that where Scotland is curtailed in legislative competence or is frustrated by inaction at Westminster, it is prepared to defy the UK Government and pursue alternative routes to introduce additional rights into Scots Law. There is little doubt that this is politically and legislatively creative, even if Scotland is not (yet) recognised for being legally progressive in this way. There is quite often acclaim (such as that for period poverty initiatives) for policy developments which show Scotland to be a leader on inequalities—and yet much of this stems from legislative progressivism. This may not have led to significant changes in Scottish society as yet, but in the 20 or so years since the re-establishment of the Parliament at Holyrood, there is undoubted progress, especially in areas other than women's rights, but also VAW. For instance, Scotland showed legal and social progressivism much earlier than any other country in the UK, with the smoking ban,[142] *Equally Safe*[143] and the smacking ban.[144]

These are examples of Scotland delivering on things and leading the way across the UK. Deliberately or not, Scotland is influencing legal developments beyond its borders. Similarly, in the context of VAW, legislative developments in Scotland have triggered reactions across the other devolved nations. For example, the criminalisation of voyeurism in

[140] *Reference by the Attorney General and the Advocate General for Scotland—United Nations Convention on the Rights of the Child (Incorporation) (Scotland) Bill; Reference by the Attorney General and the Advocate General for Scotland—European Charter of Local Self-Government (Incorporation) (Scotland) Bill* [2021] UKSC 42.

[141] Scottish National Party (2021).

[142] Smoking, Health and Social Care (Scotland) Act 2005 (asp 13).

[143] Scottish Government and COSLA (2018), updated from 2016.

[144] Children (Equal Protection from Assault) (Scotland) Act 2019, s. 1(1) (asp 16). Although it should be noted that there is no creation of a new offence in the 2019 Act, rather it removes the defence of reasonable chastisement previously available to those charged with assault.

Scotland[145] came before similar action in other nations of the UK, with England and Wales implementing legislation in 2019, a decade after Scotland acted.[146] The "gold-standard"[147] Domestic Abuse (Scotland) Act 2018 (asp 5) has also led to developments in other nations on a similar issue, albeit England and Wales did not enact similar legislation until 2021.[148] These developments are all examples of where Scotland is not seeking to follow, but is instead trying—if not to lead—then to do what is right for Scottish society given its history of excluding voices other than those of men. The issues that the Scottish Government has—to date—tackled also reflect the influence of those who are MSPs. Given the relative youth of the Scottish Parliament, there are very few so-called career politicians at Holyrood, unlike at Westminster. In some respects, there is lived experience in the Scottish Parliament that is directly shaping the legislative agenda in Scotland and, in turn, affecting societal attitudes across Scotland. For instance, the Cabinet Secretary for Finance and the Economy, Kate Forbes MSP, previously worked for Barclays Bank,[149] whereas Christina McKelvie MSP, the Minister for Equalities and Older People, formerly worked for Glasgow City Council in social services,[150] and these are just two examples.

The experience, perspectives and outcomes that this leads to suggest that an alternative approach to policy and politics is becoming more evident in Scotland. Not all would agree though, with Viebrock questioning whether or not there is real scope for a truly progressive Scotland while social inequalities grow,[151] whereas Scott and Wright query whether there is scope to address the lingering—and profound—shortcomings of fairness.[152] Rowson similarly questions[153] whether or not claims of

145 Sexual Offences (Scotland) Act 2009, s. 9 (asp 9).

146 Voyeurism (Offences) Act 2019, amending the Sexual Offences Act 2003 by adding a new s. 67A.

147 Friskney (2021); Brooks (2018).

148 Domestic Abuse Act 2021.

149 Nutt (2020).

150 McKelvie (n.d.: https://christina-mckelvie.org/about).

151 Viebrock (2009).

152 Scott and Wright (2012).

153 Rowson (2015).

progressiveness such as those made by the SNP[154] are really all that different to similar previous assertions made by other politicians such as Nick Clegg.[155] If it is possible to conceive of progressivism as a vision encompassing equality,[156] then arguably there is some grounding in the SNP's claims given the work done in Scotland under its leadership to implement strategies to tackle VAW and to attempt to address some elements of inequality and prejudice through hate crime reform or through protecting children via the smacking ban.

It is equally likely though, given the duration across which the SNP has made progressive claims—from 2017[157]—that both the dilemma Torrance[158] highlighted were in existence in 2017, and the rhetoric that Rummery[159] describes persist as barriers to a truly progressive approach in Scotland. It should also be noted that, historically, there has been little scope to distinguish Scottish policy from that of English policy,[160] and until greater devolved powers were handed to Holyrood, there was only very limited potential to make any kind of policy departure—a point Mooney and Poole emphasise.[161] These are not the only indicators that claims to progressivism are not always matched by reality in Scotland. Given the far from straightforward constitutional and political wrangling, and what Cairney describes as "sectoral dynamics,"[162] it is all but inevitable that there will be incoherence and disjointed policy-making—none of which are helpful in addressing VAW.

Post-1999, Scotland represents a somewhat different society to that pre-Devolution. That is in part—perhaps—due to the designed process for a new elected body but is also attributable to external factors outside of constitutional questions. That Scotland has long described itself as

154 Scottish National Party (2017); Landin (2018).

155 Clegg, Nick. 2009. The Liberal Moment. *Demos,* 18 September. http://www.demos.co.uk/files/Liberal_moment_-_EMBARGOED_18.09.09.pdf. Accessed 10 February 2022; Sparrow (2009).

156 Rowson (2015).

157 Scottish National Party (2017); Landin (2018).

158 Torrance (2017, p. 56).

159 Rummery and McAngus (2015, p. 238).

160 Keating (2005, p. 461).

161 Mooney and Poole (2004, p. 460).

162 Cairney et al. (2021, p. 414).

different and "fairer"[163] than the rest of the UK is also something that is commonly seen and heard. It is, for instance, not impossible that there is some truth in such claims. For example, the Human Rights Consortium (Scotland) has openly suggested that the current devolution frameworks allow for significant potential to do things differently compared to the UK, and enact specific protections for human rights that include social, economic, cultural or environmental rights.[164] In the context of the agenda for protecting women and addressing VAW, this is more significant because it coincides with the recommendation that Scotland incorporate the Convention on Elimination of All Forms of Discrimination Against Women.[165] Both of these potential developments indicate that there *may*[166] be some indicators emerging that Scotland, under the SNP in the 2020s, is prepared to be much more proactive than previously (see Chap. 1).

The policy initiatives with which the SNP firstly campaigned and later introduced while in power as the Scottish Government of the day have shaped Scotland. Whether these policies are truly progressive is a matter of perception—or political rhetoric—as is whether this is something attributable to the SNP or to its governing predecessors. At the very least, post-devolution policy initiatives have triggered debate, comment and a greater public awareness of the broader societal problems that continue to impede true equality in Scotland, particularly for women's equality within that. Without question, under First Minister Nicola Sturgeon, there has been a greater emphasis on addressing VAW—though whether this is directly down to her leadership and values, more women holding senior roles within the Scottish Government, or due to the constitutional developments that have unfolded post-1999 or a combination of all of these is uncertain. That there has been regular inclusion within the annual

[163] Cairney (2015).

[164] Boyle and Busby (2021, p. 7).

[165] Davidson (2021).

[166] Emphasis added. There remain unanswered questions as to whether or not implementing international conventions would be outside of the legislative competence of Holyrood. See *Reference by the Attorney General and the Advocate General for Scotland – United Nations Convention on the Rights of the Child (Incorporation) (Scotland) Bill; Reference by the Attorney General and the Advocate General for Scotland – European Charter of Local Self-Government (Incorporation) (Scotland) Bill* [2021] UKSC 42.

Programmes for Government[167] of legislative plans to address issues connected to women and to VAW is incremental evidence of a rolling programme of ambition, even if it is not always delivered.

It is, nonetheless, notable that comparative evidence from outside of Scotland (Wales and Quebec) suggests that feminists within political parties—and women more generally—are "critical"[168] in reforming party attitudes to issues affecting women and equality. This is not a new suggestion, but one that Dahlerup and Mackay[169] have advanced, indicating that without women playing leading feminist roles, it is less likely that there will be an increased focus on issues of gender. In that, while Scottish policy on women's issues and VAW may not seem to have taken leaps and bounds forward, there is clear potential for such influence to come from within the SNP as the contemporary power-holding party, and from its senior women who are in occupation of leadership roles.

2.5 Conclusion: Conquering Inequality?

All told, questions over the claims of progressivism in Scotland persist, not just in respect to women, equality, and gender, but in respect to legislation, politics and policy-making. It would be unfair to state that women and gender are ignored across all law and policy agendas in Scotland—there are some notable successes, including legislation to tackle domestic violence,[170] the 'baby box' initiative[171] and the 2021 provisions to address period poverty.[172] These are all indicators of a much broader and much more 'progressive' policy agenda than the (historical) omission of provisions for tackling VAW suggests. To what extent it is the result of 'joined up thinking' rather than an accident is difficult to say,

[167] Scottish Government (n.d.-a: https://www.gov.scot/collections/programme-for-government/).

[168] Mackay and Kenny (2009, p. 52).

[169] Dahlerup (1988); Mackay (2001, p. 106).

[170] Domestic Abuse (Scotland) Act 2018 (asp 5).

[171] Ipsos MORI Scotland. 2021. Baby Box Evaluation: Children, Education and Skills. Scottish Government. https://www.gov.scot/binaries/content/documents/govscot/publications/research-and-analysis/2021/08/baby-box-evaluation/documents/baby-box-evaluation/baby-box-evaluation/govscot%3Adocument/baby-box-evaluation.pdf. Accessed 10 February 2022.

[172] Period Products (Free Provision) (Scotland) Act 2021 (asp 1).

though it is almost certain that policies relating to gender take a back seat in any hierarchy involving economic and constitutional issues.[173] In fact, the notionally progressive approach of Scotland's Government is, to an extent, evident in its willingness to engage with notoriously difficult policy areas—for example—hate crime reform, even if it does not translate into legislative progressivism as such. There is also some evidence emerging of 'joined-up thinking' appearing in Scottish law and policy-making (something not always evident within governments or across policy areas).[174] For instance, policies such as *Equally Safe*[175] rely on a coalition of partners from across government and the third sector. Such a coalition is not enough to deliver the strategy and give effect to policy; there is also a need to fund the coalition—a realisation that has seen the Scottish Government direct resources specifically to ensure that this happens through its *Equally Safe Delivery Plan* (see Chap. 1).[176] This is one notable example of attempting to deliver legislative progressivism alongside policy progressivism in a drive to address deep-rooted societal issues. The embedding of this approach to delivering on policy issues stems from the foundations of the re-established Scottish Parliament, designed from the outset with equal opportunities as a mainstay.

The new-found willingness to engage with difficult issues has not—historically—been the case, though agreement on the reasons why is hard to come by, with the rather obvious caveat usually falling on the limitations of devolved powers, and the resultant "blame game"[177] positioning Westminster as the obstacle preventing Scotland from going further. Whether or not Westminster proves to be obstructive is far from the only thing preventing the Scottish Government from being able to do more. The expanded[178] albeit still restricted powers of the Scottish administration, together with limited resources (and budget), the evolution of devolved politics and within that, devolved party politics are arguably all factors in the unfolding of progressivism—and policy on women's issues—in Scotland. It must, though, as Breitenbach states, "be acknowl-

[173] Cairney et al. (2021, p. 418).

[174] Barker and Jurasz (2020, p. 49).

[175] Scottish Government and COSLA (2018), updated from 2016.

[176] Scottish Government and COSLA (2017).

[177] Keating (2005, p. 461); Baldini (2013, p. 141); León and Orriols (2019).

[178] Scotland Act 2016.

edged that the reduction or elimination of inequalities of gender…etc, are very hard goals to achieve"[179] and were always unlikely to be resolved by designing a parliamentary blueprint that was more innovative at embedding gender equality. Breitenbach's statement summarises the scale of the (ongoing) challenge that is *still* before the Scottish Government. There are indications of shifts in societal attitudes appearing, particularly as equality issues gain traction—even if the recognition is of the scale of the challenge, rather than substantive change.

Irrespective of who can be credited with leading the charge in seeking to tackle women's equality, the long-standing issues of inequality are complicated and interconnected and overlap with other areas of policy. That compounds other difficulties in tackling them, not least because it requires 'buy-in' from several different departments[180] and levels of government, both within and beyond Scotland, to encapsulate all relevant responsibilities. Above all else, that fragmentation makes it all but impossible to lead a concerted effort to exert the right kind of pressure, something activist groups have battled to address,[181] especially in other jurisdictions.

All told, it is then, perhaps, unsurprising that Scotland, despite its efforts to date, has not fully conquered the challenges of inequality and VAW. In that, it is not alone. What it has done is engage with (some of) the challenges posed by VAW. More recently—and perhaps bravely—it has led the way, certainly in the UK—in discussions surrounding gender, sex, misogyny and hate crime(s). It is to those that we turn next.

References

Amnesty International. 2018. Toxic Twitter – A Toxic Place for Women. https://www.amnesty.org/en/latest/research/2018/03/online-violence-against-women-chapter-1/. Accessed 10 February 2022.

Andrews, Kieran. 2021. One in Three MSPs Have Had Death Threats. *The Times*, February 15. https://www.thetimes.co.uk/article/one-in-three-msps-have-had-death-threats-m6vgq7lsb. Accessed 10 February 2022.

[179] Breitenbach (2006, p. 17).

[180] Ibid.

[181] Ibid., pp. 17–18.

Baldini, Gianfranco. 2013. Devolution and Scottish Politics Ten Years on. *Government and Opposition* 48 (1): 127–145.

Barker, Kim, and Olga Jurasz. 2019. Online Misogyny: A Challenge for Digital Feminism? *Journal of International Affairs* 72 (2): 95–114.

———. 2020. Online Violence Against Women as an Obstacle to Gender Equality: A Critical View from Europe. *European Equality Law Review* 2020 (1): 47–60.

Birrell, Derek. 2009. *The Impact of Devolution on Social Policy.* Bristol: Policy Press.

Boyle, Katie, and Nicole Busby. 2021. Human Rights and Devolution: Devolution as a Vehicle for Human Rights Protection and Progress. Human Rights Consortium Scotland. https://hrcscotland.org/wp-content/uploads/2021/09/Final-Devolution-and-Human-Rights-Dev-as-a-vehicle-for-HR-protection-and-progress-Sept-2021.pdf. Accessed 10 February 2022.

Breitenbach, Esther. 2006. Developments in Gender Equality Policies in Scotland Since Devolution. *Scottish Affairs* 56 (1): 10–21.

Brooks, Libby. 2018. Scotland Set to Pass 'gold standard' Domestic Abuse Law. *The Guardian*, February 1. https://www.theguardian.com/society/2018/feb/01/scotland-set-to-pass-gold-standard-domestic-abuse-law. Accessed 10 February 2022.

Brown, Alice, David McCrone, and Lindsay Paterson. 1998. *Politics and Society in Scotland.* 2nd ed. London: Palgrave Macmillan.

Cairney, Paul. 2015. You Talkin' to Me? *Centre on Constitutional Change*, June 26. https://www.centreonconstitutionalchange.ac.uk/opinions/you-talkin-me. Accessed 10 February 2022.

Cairney, Paul, and Kirsten Rummery. 2018. Feminising Politics to Close the Evidence-Policy Gap: The Case of Social Policy in Scotland. *Australian Journal of Public Administration* 77 (4): 542–553.

Cairney, Paul, Emily St Denny, and Sean Kippin. 2021. Policy Learning to Reduce Inequalities: The Search for a Coherent Scottish Gender Mainstreaming Policy in a Multilevel UK. *Territory, Politics & Governance* 9 (3): 412–433.

Casserly, Josephine. 2014. 'Sometimes you need to think outside their boxes': An Examination of the Voice of Black Minority Ethnic Women in Post-devolution Scotland. *Scottish Affairs* 23 (4): 419–444.

Clegg, Nick. 2009. The Liberal Moment. *Demos*, September 18. http://www.demos.co.uk/files/Liberal_moment_-_EMBARGOED_18.09.09.pdf. Accessed 10 February 2022.

Consultative Steering Group on the Scottish Parliament. 1998. Shaping Scotland's Parliament. The Scottish Office. https://www.parliament.scot/-/media/files/history/report_of_the_consultative_steering_group.pdf. Accessed 10 February 2022.

Coy, Maddy, Liz Kelly, and Jo Foord. 2007. Map of Gaps: The Postcode Lottery of Violence Against Women Support Services. End Violence Against Women. https://cwasu.org/wp-content/uploads/2010/07/MapsofGaps12007.pdf. Accessed 10 February 2022.

Curtice, John. 2009. Devolution, the SNP and the Electorate. In *The Modern SNP: From Protest to Power*, ed. Gerry Hassan, 55–67. Edinburgh: Edinburgh University Press.

Dahlerup, Drude. 1988. From a Small to a Large Minority: Women in Scandinavian Politics. *Scandinavian Political Studies* 11 (4): 275–298.

Dale, Iain, ed. 2000. *Labour Party General Election Manifestos 1900–1997*. With an Introduction by Dennis Kavanagh. London: Routledge.

Davidson, Gina. 2020. Insight: Why Violence Against Women in Scotland Is an Epidemic. *The Scotsman*, November 20. https://www.scotsman.com/news/politics/insight-why-violence-against-women-in-scotland-is-an-epidemic-3051336. Accessed 10 February 2022.

———. 2021. 'Women's Bill of Rights' Could Be Put into Scots Law After Elections. *The Scotsman*, March 12. https://www.scotsman.com/news/politics/womens-bill-of-rights-could-be-put-into-scots-law-after-elections-3163142. Accessed 10 February 2022.

Equality and Human Rights Commission. 2017. Equality and Human Rights Commission Response to the Consultation on the Equally Safe Draft Delivery Plan. https://www.equalityhumanrights.com/sites/default/files/equally_safe_draft_delivery_plan.pdf. Accessed 10 February 2022.

Falchikov, Nancy. 1996. Adolescent Attitudes to Abuse of Women: Are Wives and Nonmarital Partners Viewed Differently? *Journal of Interpersonal Violence* 11 (3): 391–401.

Friskney, Ruth. 2021. Living Up to a Gold Standard? The Implementation of the Domestic Abuse (Scotland) Act. *Improdova*, May 27. https://www.improdova.eu/blog/detail.php?we_objectID=231. Accessed 10 February 2022.

Fyfe, Gillian, Karen Johnston Miller, and Duncan McTavish. 2009. 'Muddling through' in a Devolved Polity: Implementation of Equal Opportunities Policy in Scotland. *Policy Studies* 30 (2): 203–219.

Gay, Oonagh. 1998. The *Scotland Bill*: Devolution and Scotland's Parliament. Research Paper 98/1. House of Commons Library. https://researchbriefings.files.parliament.uk/documents/RP98-1/RP98-1.pdf. Accessed 10 February 2022.

Georghiou, Nicki, and Camilla Kidner. 2007. Equal Opportunities Subject Profile. SPICe Briefing 07/50. https://external.parliament.scot/Research%20briefings%20and%20fact%20sheets/SB07-50.pdf. Accessed 10 February 2022.

Glasgow Caledonian University. 2019. GCU Hosts Launch of Fearless Glasgow. https://www.gcu.ac.uk/theuniversity/universitynews/2019-fearlessglasgow/. Accessed 10 February 2022.

Gourtsoyannis, Paris. 2017. Conservatives Thought Scottish Devolution Was 'not of general interest'. *iNews*, December 30. https://inews.co.uk/news/politics/conservatives-thought-scottish-devolution-not-general-interest-113989. Accessed 10 February 2022.

Green, Elliott. 2014. Scottish Nationalism Stands Apart from Other Secessionist Movements for Being Civic in Origin, Rather Than Ethnic. *LSE British Politics and Policy Blog*, 16 September. https://blogs.lse.ac.uk/politicsandpolicy/scottish-nationalism-stands-apart-from-other-secessionist-movements-for-being-civic-in-origin-rather-than-ethnic/. Accessed 10 February 2022.

Hills, Leslie. 2001. Why Engender? In *Women and Contemporary Scottish Politics: An Anthology*, ed. Esther Breitenbach and Fiona Mackay, 29–33. Edinburgh: Polygon.

Human Rights Leadership Scotland. n.d. First Minister's Advisory Group on Human Rights Leadership. https://humanrightsleadership.scot. Accessed 10 February 2022.

Innes, Sue. 2001. 'Quietly Thrilling': Women in the New Parliament. In *Women and Contemporary Scottish Politics: An Anthology*, ed. Esther Breitenbach and Fiona Mackay, 249–253. Edinburgh: Polygon.

Innes, Sue, and Jane Randall. 2006. Women, Gender and Politics. In *Gender in Scottish History Since 1700*, ed. Lynn Abrams, Eleanor Gordon, Deborah Simonton, and Eileen Janes Yeo, 43–83. Edinburgh: Edinburgh University Press.

Ipsos MORI Scotland. 2021. Baby Box Evaluation: Children, Education and Skills. Scottish Government. https://www.gov.scot/binaries/content/documents/govscot/publications/research-and-analysis/2021/08/baby-box-evaluation/documents/baby-box-evaluation/baby-box-evaluation/govscot%3Adocument/baby-box-evaluation.pdf. Accessed 10 February 2022.

Keating, Michael. 2005. Policy Convergence and Divergence in Scotland Under Devolution. *Regional Studies* 39 (4): 453–463.

Landin, Conrad. 2018. Scotland 'leading the world' with Progressive Policies, Says SNP Ahead of Party Conference. *iNews*, October 6. https://inews.co.uk/news/scotland/scotland-leading-the-world-with-progressive-policies-says-snp-ahead-of-party-conference-205880. Accessed 10 February 2022.

Lear, Martha Weinman. 1968. The Second Feminist Wave. *The New York Times*, March10.https://www.nytimes.com/1968/03/10/archives/the-second-feminist-wave.html. Accessed 10 February 2022.

León Sandra, and Lluís Orriols. 2019. 'It's Westminster's fault'. Political Identities and Blame Attribution in Devolved Systems. LSE British Politics and Policy Blog, April 16. https://blogs.lse.ac.uk/politicsandpolicy/blame-attribution-in-devolved-systems/. Accessed 10 February 2022.

London School of Hygiene & Tropical Medicine. 2021. Disasters Caused by Natural Hazards Linked to Increase in Triggers for Violence Against Women and Girls. https://www.lshtm.ac.uk/newsevents/news/2021/disasters-caused-natural-hazards-linked-increase-triggers-violence-against. Accessed 10 February 2022.

Lynch, Peter. 2010. Coming in from the Cold? The Thatcher Legacy, Devolution and Cameron's Conservatives in Scotland 1979–2009. *La Clé des Langues*, January 18. http://cle.ens-lyon.fr/anglais/civilisation/domaine-britannique/l-heritage-thatcherien/coming-in-from-the-cold-the-thatcher-legacy-devolution-and-cameron-s-conservatives-in-scotland-1979-2009. Accessed 10 February 2022.

Mackay, Fiona. 2001. The Case of Zero Tolerance: Women's Politics in Action? In *Women and Contemporary Scottish Politics: An Anthology*, ed. Esther Breitenbach and Fiona Mackay, 105–129. Edinburgh: Polygon.

Mackay, Colin. 2009. The SNP and the Scottish Parliament: The Start of a New Sang? In *The Modern SNP: From Protest to Power*, ed. Gerry Hassan, 79–92. Edinburgh: Edinburgh University Press.

Mackay, Fiona. 2010. Gendering Constitutional Change and Policy Outcomes: Substantive Representation and Domestic Violence Policy in Scotland. *The Policy Press* 38 (3): 369–388.

Mackay, Fiona, and Meryl Kenny. 2009. Women's Political Representation and the SNP: Gendered Paradoxes and Puzzles. In *The Modern SNP: From Protest to Power*, ed. Gerry Hassan, 42–54. Edinburgh: Edinburgh University Press.

Maddox, David. 2015. Nicola Sturgeon: SNP a 'progressive force' in UK. *The Scotsman*, January 26. https://www.scotsman.com/news/politics/nicola-sturgeon-snp-progressive-force-uk-1514397. Accessed 10 February 2022.

McKelvie, Christina. 2021. Answer to Question S5W-35024, Asked by Elaine Smith, Central Scotland, Scottish Labour, Lodged 5 February 2021. To Ask the Scottish Government on Which of Its Advisory and Strategic Groups Is Engender Represented. https://www.parliament.scot/chamber-and-committees/written-questions-and-answers/question?ref=S5W-35024. Accessed 10 February 2022.

———. n.d. About. https://christina-mckelvie.org/about. Accessed 10 February 2022.

McLaughlin, Annie. 2017. The Power of Zero: How a Bold Scotland-Based Campaign Changed the World's Thinking About Sexual Violence. *The Herald*, July 16. https://www.heraldscotland.com/opinion/15413746.power-zero-bold-scotland-based-campaign-changed-worlds-thinking-sexual-violence/. Accessed 10 February 2022.

Mitchell, James. 1998. What Could a Scottish Parliament Do? *Regional & Federal Studies* 8 (1): 68–85.

———. 2006. Evolution and Devolution: Citizenship, Institutions and Public Policy. *Publius* 36 (1): 153–168.

———. 2009. *Devolution in the UK*. Manchester: Manchester University Press.

Mitchell, James, Lynn Bennie, and Rob Johns. 2012. *The Scottish National Party: Transition to Power*. Oxford: Oxford University Press.

Mooney, Gerry, and Lynne Poole. 2004. 'A land of milk and honey?' Social Policy in Scotland After Devolution. *Critical Social Policy Ltd* 24 (4): 458–483.

Nutt, Kathleen. 2020. PROFILE: Who Is the New Finance Secretary Kate Forbes? *The National*, February 17. https://www.thenational.scot/news/18240941.profile-new-finance-secretary-kate-forbes/. Accessed 10 February 2022.

O'Hagan, Angela. 2016. Redefining Welfare in Scotland – With Or Without Women? *Critical Social Policy* 36 (4): 649–671.

One Scotland. n.d.-a First Minister's National Advisory Council on Women and Girls. Scottish Government. https://onescotland.org/equality-themes/advisory-council-women-girls/. Accessed 10 February 2022.

———. n.d.-b NACWG: Who Are We and What We Do. https://onescotland.org/equality-themes/advisory-council-women-girls/who-we-are-and-what-we-do/. Accessed 10 February 2022.

Rowson, Jonathan. 2015. What Is a 'progressive? *openDemocracy.net*, June 11. https://www.opendemocracy.net/en/opendemocracyuk/what-is-progressive/. Accessed 10 February 2022.

Rummery, Kirstein, and Craig McAngus. 2015. The Future of Social Policy in Scotland: Will Further Devolved Powers Lead to Better Social Policies for Disabled People? *The Political Quarterly* 86 (2): 234–240.

Sabin, Lamiat. 2021. Police Apologise After Cop26 Diversions Force Women to Walk Through Park at Night. *The Independent*, November 3. https://www.independent.co.uk/news/uk/home-news/cop26-woman-park-night-glasgow-b1949988.html. Accessed 10 February 2022.

Scott, Marion. 2021. One of Scotland's First MSPs Warns the Harassment of Women in Politics Has Never Been Worse and Urges and End to Hateful

Abuse. *The Sunday Post*, March 14. https://www.sundaypost.com/fp/one-of-scotlands-first-msps-warns-the-harassment-of-women-in-politics-has-never-been-worse-and-urges-an-end-to-hateful-abuse/. Accessed 10 February 2022.

Scott, Gill, and Sharon Wright. 2012. Devolution, Social Democratic Visions and Policy Reality in Scotland. *Critical Social Policy* 32 (3): 440–453.

Scottish Government. 2019. National Advisory Council on Women and Girls Report: First Minister's Speech. https://www.gov.scot/publications/national-advisory-council-on-women-and-girls-circle-event-first-ministers-speech/. Accessed 10 February 2022.

———. 2020a. First Minister Welcomes Progress on Equality. https://www.gov.scot/news/first-minister-welcomes-progress-on-equality/. Accessed 10 February 2022.

———. 2020b. Scottish Social Attitudes Survey 2019: Attitudes to Violence Against Women in Scotland. https://www.gov.scot/binaries/content/documents/govscot/publications/statistics/2020/12/scottish-social-attitudes-survey-2019-attitudes-violence-against-women-scotland/documents/scottish-social-attitudes-survey-2019-attitudes-violence-against-women-scotla. Accessed 10 February 2022.

———. n.d.-a Programme for Government. https://www.gov.scot/collections/programme-for-government/. Accessed 10 February 2022.

———. n.d.-b Violence Against Women and Girls (VAWG). https://www.gov.scot/policies/violence-against-women-and-girls/. Accessed 10 February 2022.

Scottish Government, and COSLA. 2009. Safer Lives: Changed Lives. A Shared Approach to Tackling Violence Against Women in Scotland. https://www.webarchive.org.uk/wayback/archive/20150219114447/http:/www.gov.scot/Publications/2009/06/02153519/10. Accessed 10 February 2022.

Scottish Government and COSLA. 2017. Equally Safe: A Delivery Plan for Scotland's Strategy to Prevent and Eradicate Violence Against Women and Girls. https://www.gov.scot/binaries/content/documents/govscot/publications/strategy-plan/2017/11/equally-safe-delivery-plan-scotlands-strategy-prevent-violence-against-women/documents/00528064-pdf/00528064-pdf/govscot%3Adocument/00528064.pdf. Accessed 10 February 2022.

Scottish Government, and COSLA. 2018. Equally Safe: Scotland's Strategy for Preventing and Eradicating Violence Against Women and Girls. https://www.gov.scot/publications/equally-safe-scotlands-strategy-prevent-radicate-violence-against-women-girls/documents/. Accessed 10 February 2022.

Scottish National Party. 2017. We're Leading the Way with Progressive Policies. *SNP News*, May 16. https://www.snp.org/we-re-leading-the-way-with-progressive-policies/. Accessed 10 February 2022.

———. 2021. SNP 2021 Manifesto: Scotland's Future, Scotland's Choice. https://www.snp.org/manifesto/. Accessed 10 February 2022.

Scottish Parliament. n.d.-a History of the Scottish Parliament: Referendum Results. https://www.parliament.scot/about/history-of-the-scottish-parliament/the-path-to-devolution. Accessed 10 February 2022.

———. n.d.-b History of the Scottish Parliament: The Path to Devolution. https://www.parliament.scot/about/history-of-the-scottish-parliament/the-path-to-devolution. Accessed 10 February 2022.

Simpkins, Fiona. 2019. Twenty Years of Devolution in Scotland: The End of a British Party System? *French Journal of British Studies* 24 (4): 1–17. https://doi.org/10.4000/rfcb.4938.

Sinclair, Diane M. 1996. The Importance of Gender for Participation in and Attitudes to Trade Unionism. *Industrial Relations Journal* 27 (3): 239–252.

Skopeliti, Clea. 2021. 'Historic moment': SNP and Greens Enter Power-Sharing Arrangement. *The Independent*, August 20. https://www.independent.co.uk/news/uk/politics/snp-green-party-scotland-indyref-2-b1906010.html. Accessed 10 February 2022.

Smith Commission, The. 2014. Report of the Smith Commission for Further Devolution of Powers to the Scottish Parliament. The National Archives. https://webarchive.nationalarchives.gov.uk/ukgwa/20151202171059/http://www.smith-commission.scot/smith-commission-report/. Accessed 10 February 2022.

Sofou, Maria. 2018. Zero Tolerance 1992 Campaign: A Feminist Campaign. *Zero Tolerance*, April 9. https://www.zerotolerance.org.uk/news/blog/a-feminist-campaign/. Accessed 10 February 2022.

Sparrow, Andrew. 2009. Lib Dems Claim Progressive Future from 'fundamentally flawed' Labour. *The Guardian*, September 17. https://www.theguardian.com/politics/2009/sep/17/clegg-claims-progressive-future. Accessed 10 February 2022.

Stone, Jon. 2016. SNP Loses Overall Majority in Scottish Parliament. *The Independent*, May 6. https://www.independent.co.uk/news/uk/politics/snp-loses-overall-majority-in-scottish-parliament-a7016131.html. Accessed 10 February 2022.

Strickland, Kirsty. 2021. Zero Tolerance: 30 Years on from Landmark Campaign Against Rape and Violence, Women Are Still Fighting Many of the Same Battles. *The Scotsman*, December 13. https://www.scotsman.com/news/opinion/columnists/zero-tolerance-30-years-landmark-campaign-against-rape-and-violence-women-are-still-fighting-many-same-battles-kirsty-strickland-3065691. Accessed 10 February 2022.

Sunday Post, The. 2018. Nicola Sturgeon, Ruth Davidson and Kezia Dugdale Reveal Amount of Abuse Received Online. *The Sunday Post*, March 21. https://www.sundaypost.com/fp/nicola-sturgeon-ruth-davidson-and-kezia-dugdale-reveal-amount-of-abuse-received-online/. Accessed 10 February 2022.

Thurston, Alyssa Mari, Heidi Stöckl, and Meghna Ranaganathan. 2021. Natural Hazards, Disasters and Violence Against Women and Girls: A Global Mixed Methods Systematic Review. *BMJ Global Health*. https://doi.org/10.1136/bmjgh-2020-004377. Accessed 10 February 2022.

Torrance, David. 2017. Scotland's Progressive Dilemma. *The Political Quarterly* 88 (1): 52–60.

UN Office for the Coordination of Humanitarian Affairs. 2019. Global Humanitarian Overview 2019. https://www.unocha.org/sites/unocha/files/GHO2019.pdf. Accessed 10 February 2022.

UN Women. 2020. COVID-19 and Ending Violence Against Women and Girls. https://www.unwomen.org/en/digital-library/publications/2020/04/issue-brief-covid-19-and-ending-violence-against-women-and-girls. Accessed 10 February 2022.

Viebrock, Elke. 2009. Social Policy in Scotland Since Devolution. *Social Policy & Society* 8 (3): 419–430.

Whiting, Kate. 2018. Why Do Humanitarian Crises Disproportionately Affect Women? World Economic Forum. https://www.weforum.org/agenda/2018/12/why-do-humanitarian-crises-disproportionately-affect-women/. Accessed 10 February 2022.

Women's Aid. 2020. The Impact of COVID-19 on Women and Children Experiencing Domestic Abuse, and the Life-Saving Services That Support Them. https://www.womensaid.org.uk/the-impact-of-covid-19-on-women-and-children-experiencing-domestic-abuse-and-the-life-saving-services-that-support-them/. Accessed 10 February 2022.

World Health Organisation. 2020. COVID-19 and Violence Against Women: What the Health Sector/System Can Do. https://www.who.int/reproductive-health/publications/emergencies/COVID-19-VAW-full-text.pdf. Accessed 10 February 2022.

Zero Tolerance. n.d. Violence in Scotland. https://www.zerotolerance.org.uk/vaw-facts/. Accessed 10 February 2022.

3

Scotland's History of Hate: From Public Order to Hate Crime and Back Again

3.1 Introduction: A History of Hate in Scotland

> Criminal law has always been at the heart of the anti-hate crime movement. It has provided parameters for the construction of hate crime as a social problem, the definition of its elements, the scope of its application and, arguably, it has been promoted as the key remedy to the problem.[1] (Gail Mason)

> Hate crime is abhorrent and insidious and will not be tolerated in Scotland. Targeting anyone because of a disability, their race, religion, sexuality or transgender identity—or a perception of these characteristics—is despicable.[2] (Gary Ritchie, Assistant Chief Constable of Police Scotland)

This chapter will outline the historical developments of hate crime in Scotland both immediately prior to the Devolution settlement and since the re-establishment of the Scottish Parliament at Holyrood. The discussion

[1] Mason (2014a, p. 66).

[2] Scottish Government (2021c).

K. Barker, O. Jurasz, *Violence Against Women, Hate and Law*, Palgrave Hate Studies,
https://doi.org/10.1007/978-3-030-99375-7_3

here will highlight that Scotland continues to tread a different path to the rest of the UK on hate crimes and associated issues of public policy—partially because of the different legal system, and partially because the hate crime issues experienced in Scotland have been, and continue to be, different to those experienced south of the border in England and Wales, and in Northern Ireland. The contextual and historical discussions here will outline the political, social and legislative tensions surrounding hate crime reform in Scotland, while offering an overview of a more proactive willingness to consider and discuss the challenges of embedding hate crime protections in Scots criminal law, keeping in line with societal changes and challenges.

In outlining the myriad collection of amendments made to hate crime in Scots Law, it asks the question of how Scotland has reached its current position. In doing so, it paves the way for the discussion in Chap. 4, concerning why gender has consistently been on the fringes of hate crime discussions without ever having made it into legislative provisions. The discussion here ultimately concludes that Scotland has shown a willingness to have the difficult conversations but has shied away from straying too far from safe ground when it comes to hate crime provisions. In doing so, this chapter first outlines the triggers for the establishment of the original hate crime protections before exploring the political discussions surrounding the developments of legal categories in the early 2000s. It will then, second, turn to a consideration of the piecemeal evolution of characteristics and aggravations, while considering the challenges for one of the most contentious and overlooked characteristics—gender.

3.2 Recognising 'Hate Crime'

'Hate crime' as a term is one which—despite its widespread use—does not have any formal legal status,[3] neither in Scotland nor in the UK. It is equally ambiguous for the purposes of finding a widely accepted definition—a factor mirroring its lack of formal status as a term. Perhaps unsurprisingly given the lack of consensus on the meaning and status of hate crime as a term, there is also no singular, widely accepted definition[4]

[3] Iganski and Smith (2011, p. 47).

[4] Chalmers and Leverick (2017, p. 4).

of the term in English nor in Scots Law. While there are commonly quoted definitions such as that by Perry[5] and Chakraborti and Garland,[6] an academic definition does not serve the same purpose as one operating for the purposes of a criminal conviction. In many instances, it would be (and is) undesirable and unworkable to rely on a singular conception of hate crime (if there were one), because even an agreed-upon conceptualisation of hate crime is difficult to find.[7] Even if such a conceptualisation were agreeable, it would almost certainly be one which failed to get broad-based agreement—a point clearly demonstratable when considering that differing definitions will arise dependent on the purpose, setting, sector and disciplinary context within which they operate.[8] For instance, an operational definition of hate crime for policing purposes is very different to a legal definition for prosecutorial and sentencing needs. To seek one definition to serve all purposes detracts from its usefulness, whilst posing problems in curtailing the breadth of the discussion.

Nevertheless, the definition used in this book seeks to accord to the term 'hate crime' and relies upon the understanding from Scots Law, rather than any academic definition. Hate crime is understood here to mean crimes motivated by malice or ill will towards a social group, or aggravated by prejudice(s) held by the perpetrator in relation to the victim(s). While this is the understanding adopted in this book, based on the offences encapsulated in the Hate Crime and Public Order (Scotland) Act 2021 (asp 14) (HCPOA 2021), it is subject to an important caveat, namely that hate crime as a term may be generally of little use because, as a stand-alone term, it has no legal meaning, and as a non-legal term, it is open to interpretation. This is all, in part, attributable to the recent emergence of 'hate crime' as a term—something that has a strong non-UK influence.[9] More refined phrases such as prejudice, bias or hostility may be more suitable[10] to capture the concepts that fall under the umbrella of behaviours captured through hate crime frameworks because 'hate crime'

[5] Perry (2001, p. 10).

[6] Chakraborti and Garland (2015, pp. 3–9).

[7] Schweppe (2021).

[8] Hall (2013, p. 4).

[9] Chakraborti and Garland (2015, pp. 2–3).

[10] Brax (2016, p. 233); Chakraborti and Garland (2015, p. 13).

as a term is misleading. It suggests that the crimes are crimes of hatred, whereas Chakraborti and Garland dispel this notion indicating a more accurate understanding is needed because "hate crimes are not crimes in which the offender simply *hates* the victim".[11] Instead, hate crime should be treated as something much broader, to incorporate understandings of hate crimes as violent and/or hostile acts which are based on elements of actual or perceived "difference."[12] While Scots Law refers to some of these elements—including malice, ill-will and prejudice—they fall within the term of hate crime for the purposes of the wider discussion here.

Definitional wrangling—and the challenges it presents[13]—aside, hate, hate crime, hate crime legislation and hate frameworks are terms used interchangeably, have a relatively youthful history in Scotland. In the 23 years since the first elections to the Scottish Parliament, hate crime reform has been an almost constant feature in discussions around criminal justice, equality and law reform. It is without doubt that Scotland adopts a different and distinctive approach to hate crime compared to other parts of the UK, described by Hopkins as a "proactive approach,"[14] putting Scotland in the position of a leader when addressing hate. Despite the recognised distinctiveness—which we suggest is a form of legislative progressivism—Scotland, unlike England and Wales, has entertained hate crime reforms on a repeated and regular basis since the late 1990s. This is evident, not just from the numerous reforms made to legislation, but from the most recent discussions concerning modernising hate crime[15]—conversations that began in 2016 and culminated in the HCPOA 2021. While discussions of hate crime have been a constant feature, they have not been without contention—another recurring theme throughout the infancy of the Scottish Parliament. From the legal

[11] Chakraborti and Garland (2015, p. 3).

[12] Ibid., p. 5.

[13] To take but one Scottish example, the Working Group on Hate Crime indicated in their 2004 report that their definition of hate crime is: "Crime motivated by malice or ill-will towards a social group" at paragraph 1.4, but then go on to indicate that hate crime is broader than that, and is "based on the motivation of malice or ill-will towards a social group" at para. 1.6, emphasising the importance of the motivation demonstrated by the offender. See Working Group on Hate Crime (2004, pp. 2–3).

[14] Hopkins (2009, p. 24).

[15] Scottish Government (2018b, p. 1).

articulations of transgender hostility in the early 2000s to the damaging controversy surrounding the impact on freedom of expression in the 2021 Act,[16] where hate crime has featured in Scotland, so too has outcry.

It is therefore surprising that hate crime is not more settled in Scots Law given the attention and resources dedicated to it over the last 20 years. But it is less of a surprise given that there is no single piece of legislation containing all of the relevant hate crime provisions in the UK[17]—and never has been historically. Scotland has at least attempted to modernise its hate crime provisions through its 2021 Act,[18] while England and Wales have mooted suggestions[19] that such a development may follow, though this is by no means certain.

3.3 Hate Provisions in Scots Law: A 'Different' Model

Hate crime legislation—to the extent that there is a bundle of statutory provisions—is not entirely unique in its formulation to Scots Law. It shares some features and part of its approach with its jurisdictional neighbour in England and Wales, even if there are some substantive distinctions. There are generally taken to be three models[20] for hate crime legislation:

1. Penalty enhancement provisions
2. Sentence aggravation provisions
3. Substantive criminal offences (stand-alone hate offences).

The penalty enhancement provisions operate in such a manner to mean that where there is an offence which is motivated by hatred relating to a protected characteristic, the offence will be prosecuted, and then at

[16] Nachiappan (2020).

[17] Walters et al. (2016, p. 12).

[18] Scottish Government (2021b).

[19] Law Commission (2021).

[20] Mason (2014a, p. 60).

sentencing, there will be—as in England and Wales—an 'uplift' added to reflect the hatred motivating the act. This model does not operate in Scots Law. Rather, in Scotland, sentencing aggravations exist so that where there is a criminal act and it has been aggravated, that is factored into the sentencing. This is very similar to the penalty enhancements, but with the distinction that in Scotland—unlike in England and Wales—the sentence is not uplifted specifically. It is a more holistic consideration but still takes effect at sentencing in both Scotland, and England and Wales. The third model is not related to the impact of hatred on sentencing and, instead, imposes new criminal offences. Where there are stand-alone offences, there does not need to be an underlying criminal offence which is prosecuted only for an aggravation or penalty to be added to it on the basis of hatred. As such, it is possible to have stand-alone offences of racially aggravated hatred. This is—in some respects—the most severe of the offences and sits apart from the other two models of hate crime legislation. Mason's identified trio of models does not imply that each has to operate in isolation, nor in conjunction. Many systems are a blend of one or more of the models—Scots Law is no different, with the hate crime framework in Scotland making use of two of these three, with only the penalty enhancement provisions not featuring.[21]

The hate framework in Scotland has developed partly in step with the approach adopted at Westminster, and partially with a degree of freedom to set appropriate Scots-specific policy post-1999.[22] This mixed system of influences created a legislative set of disparate provisions which historically captured a range of elements that combined to make up the hate crime framework, and which could not be located in one piece of legislation prior to the passing of the HCPOA 2021.

The legislative approach in Scotland—even before 2021—unlike in England and Wales, has been to capture a blend of different elements to produce one 'framework' of hate crime provisions. This includes:

---

[21] Chalmers and Leverick (2017, p. 7).
Perry (2001, p. 10).

[22] As devolved powers and competencies have grown since 1999, so too has Scotland's ambition and scope to tackle wider societal issues, including hate crime. See Chap. 2.

(1) statutory aggravations in respect of the protected characteristics (age, disability, race (to include colour, nationality, citizenship, ethnic or national origins), religion (or religious association), sexual orientation and transgender identity.[23]
(2) a stand-alone offence of racially aggravated harassment;[24] and
(3) offences of stirring up hatred.[25]

The development of this mixed-model through numerous pieces of legislation is partially an accident of constitutional design, part policy-driven through election pledges and government programmes of work, and part criminal justice reform influenced.

Traditionally in Scots Law, statutory aggravations are applicable to any baseline criminal offence and are used in respect of any of the historically protected characteristics of race, religion, disability, sexual orientation and transgender identity. These are part of a longer list, with characteristics of age,[26] colour,[27] nationality,[28] ethnic or national origin[29] and religious affiliation[30] now captured within the hate crime legislation in Scotland.

The messiness of the hate crime framework prior to 2021 was one of its distinctive features given that it included both statutory aggravations and protected characteristics, but was also filled with gaps, and was far from fit for dealing with modern societal challenges. As we stated in 2020, the:

> [b]ringing together of the existing provisions should also encompass addressing the shortcomings in how [the] hate crime framework operates ... it is crucial that efforts to enact a new piece of legislation are not

[23] Hate Crime and Public Order (Scotland) Act 2021, s. 1(2)(a)–(f) (asp 14). It should be noted here that there is also provision for variations in sex characteristics to be included as a protected characteristic under s. 1(2)(g), but this is subject to enactment under s. 12.

[24] Ibid., s. 3.

[25] Ibid., s. 4.

[26] Ibid., s. 1(2)(a).

[27] Ibid., s. 1(2)(c).

[28] Ibid.

[29] Ibid.

[30] Ibid., s. 1(2)(d).

drive only by consolidation but rather focus on the genuine improvement of the current legal framework concerning hate crime and its suitability for the modern times.[31]

While there has been a gradual unfolding of a different approach to hate crime legislation in Scotland, the substance is (expectedly, given the constitutional history, reassuringly) similar to that in England and Wales. For instance, the protected characteristics in Scots Law had—until the early 2000s—historically been very similar to those enshrined in the criminal law in England and Wales. The characteristics have broadened through the piecemeal developments in Scottish legislation, perhaps most notably through the HCPOA 2021, but that does not mean that the original protected characteristics did not retain their striking similarity to those captured south of the border. In fact, the original characteristics that benefitted from being captured in the hate crime provisions were identical. Both race and religion were introduced into law at the same time in England and Wales, and Scotland, admittedly pre-devolution, albeit not identically.

From following the (imposed) lead of England and Wales via the UK Government, Scotland has surpassed the protections offered through hate crime elsewhere in the UK. During the seven years of Scottish Labour's tenure leading the Scottish Executive between 1999 and 2006, piecemeal reforms were offered, followed by a refusal to act to protect further characteristics. In contrast, in the subsequent 14 years of Scottish Government leadership by the SNP, from 2007 to 2021, three significant pieces of legislation[32] and three substantial reviews or consultations took place.[33] While there is some distinction between the ambition of the SNP-led Scottish Government and the Labour-led Scottish Executive before it, the collective efforts demonstrate that Holyrood—irrespective of the controlling party—is willing to use its devolved powers to the full

[31] Barker and Jurasz (2020b, p. 2).

[32] The SNP supported the Offences (Aggravation by Prejudice) (Scotland) Bill 2003, tabled the Offensive Behaviour at Football and Threatening Communications (Scotland) Act 2012 (asp 1) and developed (protractedly) the Hate Crime and Public Order (Scotland) Act 2021 (asp 14). See Sect. 3.5.2.

[33] Scottish Government (2016b), Scottish Government (2018a) and Scottish Government (2018b).

to engage with contentious topics, and 'go it alone.' This ambition is particularly evident through Scottish leadership on issues that relate to social prejudice, irrespective of the controversy surrounding the criminalisation of social control.[34] In demonstrating such willingness, Scotland has consistently demonstrated its willingness to take a progressive approach to legislation. The unfolding history of hate crime reform in Scotland demonstrates a clear trend for additional characteristics, offences and provisions to be enacted.

3.4 Hate Crime in Scotland: An (Historical) Ever-Present Policy To-Do

The Scotland Act 1998 as a legal landmark changed the nature and scope of legislative competence in Scotland. It handed back—as has been discussed in Chap. 2—law-making powers in a number of areas. One of the areas most substantively impacted by this was that of domestic policy. In Scott's words, having "full legislative powers"[35] has had a substantial impact upon the objectives pursued by the national government, including "wide-ranging ... and far-reaching"[36] effects on Scottish criminal justice developments. While the volume (and significance) of criminal justice reform work cannot be underestimated, there is less enthusiasm about the overwhelmingly punitive[37] approach which was adopted immediately after Devolution, although this was reflective of the general growing trend in Western societies at that time,[38] something Pratt, Brown and Brown refer to as "new punitiveness."[39] This appears present—at least in Scotland—in the final legislative instruments as enacted, even if not expressly or overtly pursued as political or policy aims. Irrespective of any punitive intent, the reality for Scots Law and for hate crime within it has

[34] Husak (2004, p. 212).
[35] Scott (2011, p. 12).
[36] Eski et al. (2011, p. 1).
[37] Ibid.
[38] Hudson (2007, p. 166).
[39] Pratt et al. (2005).

been an almost ever-evolving but repetitive cycle of discussion, debate, reform proposal and legislation. With only one relatively quiet period between 2010 and 2016, hate crime reform has been a constant item for the Scottish Government of the day to address since 1999.

Before discussing the contemporary developments in Scotland, it is necessary to sketch out the developments in hate crime legislation affecting the UK as a whole, before Holyrood gained the legislative competence to take a different path. It is to that which this chapter now turns.

3.4.1 Pre-Holyrood: England Leads the (Racial) Charge?

Prior to 1999, the situation was very different for the criminal justice system in Scotland, in that matters of domestic policy and legislation were not as nuanced, and tended towards a domestic approach encapsulating Great Britain, rather than allowing for a more bespoke approach in Scotland. This is not to say that the Westminster Government did not allow for the implementation of legislation to fit to the Scots Law system—the Scottish Office existed to enable that (see Chap. 2)—but it is worthy of note that the hate crime system as it was pre-1999 was one which had less divergence and which did not reflect—as substantially—the societal differences prevalent North of the border. In some respects, the societal pressures experienced in Scotland were very different to those in England, with society in Scotland having retained misogynistic tendences,[40] compounding a system which traditionally overlooked the interests of women, a point Hunter highlights in her advocacy for Scottish women to use their hard-fought rights.[41] The bigger picture, across England and Wales, if not the whole UK, was centred not on issues specifically affecting women but on issues of racism.

Broader social attitudes aside, the situation with regards to hate crime was less distinct prior to Devolution. The hate crime landscape was much less developed across England and Wales, and Scotland. Where

[40] Hills, Leslie (2001, p. 28).

[41] Hunter (1979).

discussions of hate crime arose, they did so against a backdrop of racism, significant failings because of the racially motivated murder of Stephen Lawrence and the institutional racism problems[42] found to exist within the Metropolitan Police Service in the resulting inquiry. The issues did not arise in a vacuum surrounding Stephen Lawrence alone though—there were 25 other murders that were not treated appropriately by various arms of the criminal justice system that did not have the same level of impact as that of Stephen Lawrence. For instance, Rohit Duggal was murdered on 11 July 1992, but it was not recorded by police as being racially motivated, despite the mention at trial of racial motivations.[43] Similarly, Ruhallah Aramesh was murdered on 20 July 1992, and while this murder was recorded as racially motivated, failures led to the convicted murderers being freed or acquitted.[44] Rolan Adams was murdered, having been racially abused beforehand—his murder was only recorded as racially motivated after dithering over whether to do so.[45] Only one of the 12-strong gang that murdered Adams was sentenced for murder, with the others having their sentences later reduced to minor public order infractions.[46] Ashiq Hussain was murdered in September 1992 after helping out another who was being racially abused—the resultant sentencing saw two acquitted.[47] These are just some of the most egregious failings—both in taking the motivations seriously, but also in the handling of the investigations. To call them highlights undermines the scale of the problem and the significance of it.

Nevertheless, the debate that was triggered in the aftermath of the racist failings in policing focused on the relationship between policing and racism, not least because of the findings of the Macpherson Report.[48] It was not until the Labour General Election landslide in 1997, and the changing of the executive that anything was done, with Home Secretary Jack Straw MP announcing the establishment of an inquiry in July 1997

[42] Home Office (1999, para. 6.34).
[43] Athwal (2002).
[44] Ibid.
[45] Ibid.
[46] The Guardian (1999).
[47] Ibid.; Athwal (2002).
[48] Home Office (1999).

into Stephen Lawrence's death. While the Macpherson Report did not suggest amongst its 70 recommendations, the need for new, wholescale legislation to address racial hatred, the breadth and depth of its findings outlined the need for a wide-ranging set of changes to the criminal justice system[49]—not all of which were acted upon by the government. Sir William Macpherson did however recommend that alterations be made to legislation to address incitement to racial hatred[50] and in the process, kick-starting hate crime engagement and reform discussions. The recommended extension to legislation had not been implemented by 2009—the 10-year anniversary of the Macpherson Report,[51] albeit other legislative revisions had been made in the intervening period, with impacts across England and Wales, and Scotland.[52] Aside from the legislative amendments to racial hatred, one of the legacies of the Macpherson Report is the Public Sector Equality Duty (PSED),[53] introduced as part of the "radical rethink"[54] needed in the public sector. While not directly addressing hate crime, the PSED legacy and impact is wider—it is aimed at changing underlying approaches, rather than punishing prejudice. The extension to legislation recommended by Macpherson may not have seen immediate action but that does not mean little happened during the 1990s—quite the contrary, especially from 1997 onwards.

The Crime and Disorder Bill was published in December 1997, overtaking the publication of the Macpherson Report and its recommendations. The Bill itself was the result of the New Labour manifesto promise to "be tough on crime and tough on the causes of crime."[55] This pledge was one of the cornerstones of policy that the New Labour Government sought to act on early into their term in office. It included addressing—

[49] Home Affairs Committee (2021, p. 14).

[50] Home Office (1999, Recommendation 39).

[51] Home Affairs Committee (2009, p. 18).

[52] For instance, reports of racism in Scotland since the Macpherson Report have increased, but so too have reporting requirements. See McPhee (2015).

[53] Equality Act 2010, s. 149. The Public Sector Equality Duty (PSED) extends to all protected characteristics (age, disability, sex, gender reassignment, pregnancy and maternity, and race, religion or belief and sexual orientation) and was conceived of to integrate equality into public authorities.

[54] Equality and Human Rights Commission (2019).

[55] Dale (2000, p. 364).

what they referred to as—'Disorder'—a term featuring in the name of the Bill presented to the House of Commons in December 1997. Within the draft Bill, New Labour also included draft provisions to give effect to their manifesto commitment to "create a new offence of racial harassment and a new crime of racially motivated violence to protect ethnic minorities from intimidation."[56]

Prior to the publication of the Crime and Disorder Bill, the common law crime of breach of the peace was the legal route relied upon in Scotland to address behaviours including harassment or different types of assault.[57] This is not to say that there were no legislative provisions in Scots Law designed to address elements of criminality embodying racial prejudice. The Public Order Act (POA) 1986 contained a definition of racial hatred, as well as statutory offences which were applicable—and chargeable—in Scotland but were constrained to dealing with incidents or behaviours either likely or intended to stir up racial hatred.[58] The provisions within the POA 1986 were not quite the same as the proposed new offences put forward in the Crime and Disorder Bill (CDB) 1997.

In Scotland, in 1997, the common law crime of breach of the peace rendered the result of the crime irrelevant in its prosecution. The central element to the crime itself was the likelihood of, or actual, alarm or annoyance. As such, it was irrelevant what the result of the act was. It was also irrelevant how many times the act(s) occurred—neither of these elements were relevant to a successful prosecution. In seeking to introduce statutory offences, New Labour was—perhaps inadvertently—changing the ways in which hate crimes were to be dealt with in Scots Law. The benefits of the crime of breach of the peace at common law fall undeniably on the side of flexibility. At the time, the only constraints on sentencing or penalties were those imposed by the powers of the court (relative to its position in the hierarchy) hearing the case. Moreover, there was potentially added flexibility in not having offences of racial harassment, nor racially motivated violence (either legislatively or at common law). The absence of specific offences—such as these proposed in what is

[56] Ibid., p. 365.

[57] Thorp et al. (1998, p. 51).

[58] Public Order Act 1986, ss. 18–23.

taken to be[59] pursuit of meeting a manifesto pledge—allowed for charges and prosecutions to continue in Scotland even if the racial element of the charge was struck out, or not proved at trial. Such situations—where there were charges under specific offences—would lead to the charges failing, and the conviction not continuing. Under common law breach of the peace, however, a less specific offence could continue to be tested in front of the court. The same cannot be said for situations that would arise under the proposed CDB 1997 offences. If, for example, the essential racial elements were struck out, the prospects of conviction would also disappear.

The proposed introduction of specific statutory offences threatened to reduce the flexibility as well as some of the acknowledged uncertainty[60] previously afforded under the common law. It proposed to remove the accompanying sentencing discretion the courts enjoyed when dealing with common law breaches of the peace. Specific offences would curtail the discretion of the court when determining which factors were of relevance at sentencing. Under the common law in Scotland in 1997, a prosecutor could inform the court of a racial element to the breach of the peace. The court could then decide whether to include that as relevant in sentencing or not—but this situation and power to decide would not continue under the proposed new offences contained in the CDB 1997.

The consultation process and resulting legislative developments saw the emergence of different routes being adopted for racially motivated offences in Scotland, and in England and Wales. Distinctions in hate crime legislation were by a process of design different. For Scotland, the only offence introduced in the Crime and Disorder Act (CDA) 1998 (from the two proposed in the CDB 1997) was that of racially aggravated harassment[61]—a new statutory offence.[62] This was accompanied by the introduction of a "general statutory requirement"[63] to consider racial aggravation at sentencing, subject to the caveat that such a factor had to

[59] Chalmers and Leverick (2017, p. 19).

[60] HL Deb 17 March 1998, vol. 587, cols. 705–706; Chalmers and Leverick (2017, p. 19).

[61] Crime and Disorder Act 1998, s. 33.

[62] Criminal Law (Consolidation) (Scotland) Act 1995, s. 50A.

[63] Thorp et al. (1998, p. 54).

be proved to the court. In presenting the Bill for its second reading, Lord Williams of Mostyn stated:

> The third manifesto theme embodied in the Bill is protection against racist crime. These crimes are particularly odious, damaging... For Scotland, the Bill will provide for a new offence of racially aggravated harassment and require that a proved racist element in any crime should be taken into account by the court when sentencing.[64]

In contrast, for England and Wales, more was suggested, with both proposed offences being legislated for. New Labour went further in England, and also incorporated the *Ribbans*[65] judgement, mandating—in contrast to the general requirement in Scotland—that a proven racial element has to be considered at sentencing as an aggravating factor. This was influenced directly by the Lord Chief Justice who had added two years to the sentences of the offenders in *Ribbans* as a result of the proven racial aggravation, something not previously captured.

The different legislative enactments for Scotland reflect a nuanced, tailored approach, but one still taking hate crime seriously. This is particularly the case given that there is (still) a shared legislative definition of racial hatred across England, Wales and Scotland.[66] In the POA 1986 and the CDA 1998, the definition of racial is the same, even if the context in which the definition appears differs. For instance, in the POA, the focus falls on racial "hatred," instead of on racial "groups" which is where the CDA 1998 focuses its attention. Irrespective of this slight distinction, both pieces of legislation define hatred in the same way, placing an emphasis on, "colour, nationality ... or ethnic or national origins."[67] While there is some convergence here—and some legislative 'joined up thinking' in using shared definitions across both jurisdictions and across legislation—the same cannot have been said to have extended to other categories of hate crime, many of which were not even vaguely close to

[64] HL Deb 16 December 1997, vol. 584, cols. 534–535.

[65] *R v. Ribbans, Duggan and Ridley* (1995) 16 Cr. App. R. (S.) 698.

[66] Public Order Act 1986, s. 17.

[67] Ibid., s. 17; Crime and Disorder Act 1998, s. 96(6).

being given legislative attention in 1998.[68] What is missing from this segment of legislative history is any discussion of women or gender—it is not implicitly mentioned, it is absent from the discussion entirely. Similarly, while the focus has fallen—understandably—on racial hatred, it is singular in its focus, zeroing in exclusively on race. There is no consideration of race plus another characteristic (or characteristics), and at this stage in the evolution of hate crime legislation, little awareness of the potential for hate crime to address overlapping characteristics.

3.5 Holyrood Draws Its Own Line: A Portmanteau of Legislative Developments

Post-Devolution hate crime reform in Scotland has taken a very different direction to that in England and Wales—not least in dominating the criminal justice reform agenda over the last 20 or so years. That said, Scotland cannot take the full credit for the initial implementations of legislative reform in the late 1990s. While these were instigated at Westminster and prompted by a political pledge, the results arguably set in motion a series of other developments which have—cumulatively—encouraged and allowed Scotland to take its own journey towards tackling hate crime. The initial foundations laid in respect of racially aggravated harassment offer some legislative routes towards addressing prejudice. The challenge with those formulations was that they focused on a very narrow set of characteristics.

As hate crime reform in Scotland has grown and developed, so too has its scope. At its heart, there is now a much greater statutory basis than there was in the late 1990s—breach of the peace is no longer the cornerstone of criminal prosecutions relating to racial harassment, nor is it the key criminal offence in addressing elements of hatred. Following the Crime and Disorder Act 1998 amendment to the Criminal Law (Consolidation) (Scotland) Act 1995, other considerations have been

[68] Barker and Jurasz (2021, p. 4).

made to the hate crime offences, to the legislative provisions and to the groups and characteristics which ought to benefit from protection:

> The development of criminal provisions to address targeted hostility of social groups is a process which, in Scotland, has seen repeated consultations, legislative amendments, and working and advisory group input. … That said, the culmination of these efforts from 2002 onwards, has resulted in a fragmented, disjointed, and—for those subjected to hatred—confusing system.[69]

It is to this expansion that the discussion now turns.

3.5.1 Sectarianism, Transgender Identities and MSPs Amendments (1999–2003)

Following the introduction of statutory provisions targeting racial bias, the discussions in Scotland shifted—almost simultaneously to England and Wales—to other characteristics. Given the problems caused by religious prejudice—but especially sectarianism—in Scotland, it is unsurprising that legislation addressing this aspect was firmly on the reform agenda.

The original discussions relating to sectarianism—both prejudice and violence—did not stem from the criminal justice system per se though. Initial considerations arose in respect of measures that could be implemented to address sectarianism in sporting events, especially at the Old Firm football matches, which were described as, "one of the most readily discernible expressions of intolerance in Scotland."[70] The proposals to take action to address sectarianism came from outside of the Scottish Executive and originated at the football clubs themselves,[71] rather than anywhere else. Little, however, was legislatively done in response to these proposals, perhaps in part because the Scottish Executive stood firm in its

[69] Ibid., p. 3.

[70] Scottish Executive (2002, p. 10).

[71] The proposals led to the Sense Over Sectarianism initiative, which marked its 20th anniversary in July 2021. See Scott (2001); Stewart (2021).

view that the law was operating without the need for reform (though this position changed with the emergence of Alex Salmond as the leader of the Scottish Government in 2011).[72] The existing common law in Scotland covered potential religious aggravation through the common law crime of breach of the peace, in much the same way as it had (prior to the CDA 1998) addressed racially aggravated harassment.

External influences conflated with domestic pressures. Discussions concerning religious bias, and as Bell describes it, "anti-discrimination,"[73] began to appear against a background of developments at European,[74] EU[75] and UK[76] levels, all of which sought to address the problem. The UK Home Secretary in October 2001 announced that the proposed Anti-terrorism, Crime and Security Bill (ATCSB) (2001) would include provisions to capture religiously aggravated hatred, and by doing so would introduce statutory offences to complement (and mirror) the racially aggravated offences introduced in the CDA 1998. While the inclusion of these proposals ultimately was removed from the ATCSB (following defeats in the House of Lords), racially aggravated offences were nonetheless introduced in England and Wales in 2001, albeit in separate legislation.

The Scottish Parliament were not obliged (legally) to follow the lead of England and enact provisions to tackle religiously aggravated hatred. That said, in debating the ATCSB at Holyrood in November 2001, the then Deputy Justice Minister, Iain Gray, indicated that the Scottish

---

[72] Davidson (2011).

[73] Bell (1999, p. 5).

[74] Convention for the Protection of Human Rights and Fundamental Freedoms (European Convention on Human Rights, as amended) (ECHR) art. 9, which provides for the freedom of religion.

[75] The Treaty of Amsterdam as a treaty introduced in pursuit of Amending the Treaty on European Union, the Treaties Establishing the European Communities and Certain Related Acts (Treaty of Amsterdam) [1997] O.J. C340/1. The Treaty of Amsterdam introduced into the (then) EC Treaty a new Article 13 which allowed the Council to take action to combat discrimination on range of grounds, including religion. EU developments also saw the introduction of an Employment Directive requiring states to make discrimination unlawful on the grounds of religion or belief (amongst other characteristics), as well as a Race Directive which also required members states to make discrimination on the basis of ethnic origin (amongst other characteristics) unlawful in a number of areas including employment, education and access to goods and services.

[76] Anti-terrorism, Crime and Security Act 2001, pt. 5.

Executive felt there was no need to amend the law to capture religious hatred—it was in sufficient working order.[77] In making this pronouncement, he nevertheless went on to commit the Scottish Executive to exploring the issue further. The Scottish Executive, having committed to establishing a working group, did so in 2002, by convening the Cross-Party Working Group on Religious Hatred (RHWG). The remit of this group was to:

> Consider the need for legislation to combat religious hatred (in particular the creation of a new category of statutory aggravations and the creation of a new offence of incitement to religious hatred) and if appropriate develop effective and workable proposals for legislation to increase the protection to religious groups in Scotland. Consider whether non-legislative action could be taken as an alternative."[78]

The Religious Hatred Working Group (RHWG) disagreed with the position of the Scottish Executive as outlined by Iain Gray in November 2001. Instead of rendering the debate on further legislation to address religious hate crime null and void, the RHWG recommended that "the current legal framework needs adjustment in order to ensure that any element of religious or sectarian hatred in any particular crime is always recorded, so that offences are prosecuted in a consistent manner."[79] It also suggested that legislation would offer "much needed clarity"[80] concerning the seriousness with which religious hatred is treated in Scotland. While the overwhelming narratives relating to religion in Scotland tend to focus on sectarianism, especially in a sporting context, there is emerging recognition of the fact that it is an issue affecting women as well. Part of the challenge with which the sectarianism narrative has dominated relates specifically to the equivalent dominance of men within it. Engender, for instance, takes issue with the overlooking of women within these discussions, arguing convincingly that there should be a "focus on gender ...

[77] Scottish Executive (2002, p. 6).

[78] Ibid.

[79] Ibid., p. 21.

[80] Ibid.

directly challenging 'toxic masculinity'"[81] within sectarianism. From the perspective of inclusion, it is important to remember that women too participate in religion, and in sport, and are affected by hatred and prejudice in respect of both of these. This is part of a broader issue that women have faced in what are perceived as masculine endeavours. It is an issue which is *as prevalent* in 2022, as it was in 2002, albeit more widely recognised in contemporary society. The furore over Raith Rovers FC signing of a player who was ruled (in civil court) to be a rapist[82] is just one recent incident that highlights the breadth of the problem. For a community football club to sign such a player signals that football clubs and football (and sport more widely) still turn something of a blind eye to issues of sexism[83] and violence against women.[84] This stands in stark contrast to the approach that football has taken to issues of, for example, the abuse of footballers.[85]

The dominant narrative at this point in the evolution of the hate crime framework in Scottish legislation was one focused on race and religion—few other characteristics were on the radar until the delivery of the RHWG 2002 Report. At that stage, it offered the "impetus"[86] for broader discussions at a Scottish Parliamentary level. These were triggered by the presentation of the Criminal Justice (Scotland) Bill (CJ(S)B) 2002. In response, a number of MSPs sought to take matters into their own hands on hate crime legislation and offered amendments to the CJ(S) Bill. Donald Gorrie MSP (Member of the Scottish Parliament) sought to make amendments to the draft legislation so as to pre-empt the draft Bill of the Scottish Executive. Gorrie's amendment was focused—much like the ATCSB provisions in England and Wales—on including statutorily capturing penalties for religious prejudice. Unlike the model introduced in the CDA 1998, Gorrie's amendment did not adopt the same approach. Instead, his proposal was to introduce a higher penalty for religious prejudice where there was an existing criminal offence rather than to

[81] Engender (2015, p. 65).
[82] Brooks (2022).
[83] See, for example, Giles (2021).
[84] Press Association (2016).
[85] BT (Hope United) (n.d.: https://www.bt.com/hopeunited).
[86] Barker and Jurasz (2021, p. 5).

introduce a new statutory offence. This was a measured response to both the Scottish Executive's November 2001 position and the RHWG's recommendations. It was also a step which offered some alignment to the law reform enacted in the late 1990s without seeking to go much further and offer a broader set of provisions to address hate crimes.

Gorrie was not alone in offering an amendment to the CJ(S)B though. Robin Harper MSP also offered amendments to the draft legislation, but in so doing, took a different approach to his colleague. The Harper amendment offered more than an increased penalty for religious prejudice. Rather, it offered a set of proposed statutory aggravations to address issues of bias that extended beyond race and religion, and encapsulated prejudice against (actual or presumed) gender, sexual orientation, disability and age.[87] Harper's position, in offering a broader set of draft provisions, was to "...extend protection"[88] and ensure that the legislation included measures recognising the potential for "malice and ill will based on the other grounds on which people most commonly face harassment and prejudice."[89]

While gender (actual or presumed) featured in Harper's significant amendment to the CJ(S)B, it did not feature much, if at all legislatively, before this point. That it was a consideration in 2002 is significant—though perhaps not as much as if the amendment had been enacted—as it is one of the few serious legislative efforts to capture characteristics that apply to what is, perhaps, not a minority group, that is, women (and/or men). It is significant for other reasons also, not least because women are rarely considered as forming part of a group on their own for the purposes of hate crime. Where other characteristics are present, these are the ones given legislative consideration. For instance, Asian women benefit from intersecting identities, that is, by being Asian and women. This potentially allows for hate crimes to be captured on the basis of an Asian characteristic (i.e. race) and resulting prejudice (given that gender is not captured within hate crimes). The same may not be said for women who do not have such intersecting identities (see Chap. 1). This means that a

[87] Meeting of the Scottish Parliament 19 February 2003, Official Report, cols. 15456-15458.

[88] Barker and Jurasz (2021, p. 5).

[89] Meeting of the Scottish Parliament 19 February 2003, Official Report, col. 15456.

crime can be committed against an Asian woman purely due to gender and not intersect with race or nationality at all. Harper's amendment would have—for the first time in Scotland (and the UK)—enabled gender to feature as an aggravation for the purposes of hate crime. It retains some significance for this reason alone.[90]

To have proposed the amendments to the CJ(S)B that Harper did was a bold act. There had been little consideration given to any characteristics beyond race (late 1990s) and religion (early 2000s) before this. To attempt to pass an amendment to a significant criminal justice bill was an ambitious move. Given that there had been little background work, research or study done into the feasibility of capturing a broader range of characteristics in the hate crime framework, the Scottish Executive did not support the amendment, and it was not accepted—unsurprisingly. Harper's actions did, however, trigger two things. First, the Scottish Executive committed[91] to convening yet another working group to explore the potential need for legislative amendments to capture a wider range of characteristics than race and religion. And, second, the Gorrie amendment, which, while less substantial in terms of legislative sections, was adopted by the Scottish Executive and made its way into the Criminal Justice (Scotland) Act 2003 (asp 7) (CJ(S)A 2003), where it featured as Section 74 (until its repeal by the HCPOA 2021) and required that courts take into account religious aggravations at sentencing. Under Section 74(2), the relevant court was required to consider an aggravation where there was ill will or malice based on the victim's membership of a religious group or a group perceived to have a religious affiliation. The wording—and operation—of this offence was very similar to the provisions introduced prior to Devolution to address racially aggravated harassment via the CDA 1998.

The Scottish Executive acted upon the RHWG recommendations, even if by accident and by MSP rather than by design and intent. Irrespective of the method by which the reform was given effect, the resulting legislation—and its significance as the first piece of hate crime

---

[90] Barker and Jurasz (2021, p. 5).

[91] Meeting of the Scottish Parliament, 19 February 2003, Official Report, col. 15467; Scottish Parliament Justice Committee (2009, para. 7).

legislation post-Devolution—cannot be understated. Above all else, the passing of the CJ(S)A 2003 demonstrated that the Scottish Executive would not shy away from legislating on hate crime but also that it was competent to do so effectively, even when provoked.

3.5.2 Hatred of Groups (2003–2009)

Invariably, following the passage of the CJ(S)A 2003, and with it, the Gorrie amendment, hate crime discussions were on the reform agenda again throughout summer 2003, and into 2004. This was because of the Scottish Executive commitment in February 2003 to convene a wider working group to explore hate crimes—a much broader task compared to the narrow remit of the Working Group on Religious Hatred that reported in May 2002. The Hate Crime Working Group (HCWG) 2004 had, as its task, "[t]o look at the current criminal justice system and consider improvements, including legislation, which might be made to deal with crimes based on hatred towards social groups"[92] (see Chaps. 4 and 5).

The HCWG 2004 undertook a much broader consideration of the situation in respect of the behaviours that can amount to a hate crime, but also to the groups that could fall within its purview, including women. The HCWG explored issues both within the traditional boundaries of hate and well beyond—considering other innovations within the Scottish criminal justice system. For instance, it paid attention to other innovations enacted shortly before it was convened—including the new victims' rights embedded in the CJ(S)A 2003. It also considered the broader contexts in which hateful acts can occur, such as antisocial behaviour. The aim of this broader exploration was to situate any recommendations firmly within their context, but also to ensure that the measures developed in response to hate crimes were, first, targeting the right crime, and, second, not generic in response.[93] In some respects, the HCWG was taking steps to ensure situations such as that with the proposed Harper

[92] Working Group on Hate Crime (2004, para. 1.2).

[93] Ibid., para. 3.10.

amendment did not arise again, but should they do so, that the Scottish Executive was not taken by surprise.

The HCWG was also acutely aware of developments elsewhere in the UK—notably in England and Wales where, once again, legislation was timetabled in close correlation to developments in Scotland. In this instance, in England and Wales, the Criminal Justice Act 2003 (CJA 2003) enacted a sentencing aggravation applicable to hatred of an actual (or presumed) disability or sexual orientation.[94] These were not the only developments putting pressure on Scotland to reciprocate with its own updated (and more inclusive) hate crime provisions—the Secretary of State for Northern Ireland announced proposals for legislation to address hate crimes in October 2003.[95] The proposed legislation for Northern Ireland was to address incitement to hatred, covering the characteristics of disability and sexual orientation—much the same as that enacted in England and Wales under the (earlier) CJA 2003. In Northern Ireland, legislation was also proposed to include an aggravation based on race, religion, disability and sexual orientation in mid-2003.[96] Interestingly, the Public Prosecution Service for Northern Ireland use the perception-based test, which originates from the Macpherson Report, as their operational definition for hate crime,[97] suggesting that while developments were welcome, they were also rather protracted given the Macpherson Report was published four years earlier.

Nevertheless, during 2003, the other home nations both acted and showed progress further than Scotland in developing their respective hate crime frameworks. This is particularly intriguing given that the Scottish Executive had the opportunity in 2002 to enact legislation that was more advanced than in England and Wales, and Northern Ireland but passed up the opportunity to do so by rejecting Harper's amendment. Speed is not the be all and end all for legislation to address hatred though—by rejecting Harper's amendment, and passing Gorrie's, the Scottish

[94] Criminal Justice Act 2003, ss. 145–146.

[95] Working Group on Hate Crime (2004, para. 3.6).

[96] The Criminal Justice (No 2) (Northern Ireland) Order 2004, SR 2004/15, art. 2.

[97] Public Prosecution Service for Northern Ireland (2010, para. 2.1.2).

Executive took an evidence-based approach to the situation peculiar and specific to Scotland. It was prepared to act, just not for the sake of it.

In some respects, the delays in adding a broader range of characteristics to Scottish hate crime did not allow for much other than inevitable legislative proposals, albeit later than in the other home nations. When the HCWG reported in September 2004, it concluded that "[h]ate-aggravated harassment and alarming and distressing behaviour is a major concern,"[98] but more pressingly that "[t]he Scottish Executive should introduce a statutory aggravation as soon as possible for crimes motivated by malice or ill-will towards an individual based on their sexual orientation, transgender identity, or disability."[99] Recommendation 1—that legislation should be forthcoming as a matter of priority—was, given the developments elsewhere, unsurprising.

Recommendation 1 went further though and suggested that the legislation when it was introduced should be drafted in such a manner as to allow the extension of its provisions to other groups in the future (by statutory instrument). Such flexibility was particularly forward-thinking at the time, and somewhat reflective of the desire to avoid revisiting hate crimes repeatedly. Strikingly, it was forward-thinking enough as a recommendation to have been acted upon almost 20 years later in the HCPOA 2021—in which the power to add characteristics has been included. This was an opportunity missed in 2004. While Recommendation 1 did not specify which groups were in consideration, the HCWG Report itself discusses the priority need to review the area of the criminal law on violence against women, but, more importantly, that it must do so with a "view to combatting"[100] it. It is therefore not impossible to believe that the HCWG Report was suggesting that there was a pressing need to legislate, but to do so in a way that would allow gender to be included at a future point. This is not necessarily a stretch, especially as the HCWG consulted on the question of which groups ought to receive special protection through the hate crime legislation. In the responses, gender

[98] Working Group on Hate Crime (2004, p. 4), Recommendation 2.

[99] Ibid., Recommendation 1.

[100] Ibid., Recommendation 3.

features as third on the list.[101] This is striking, not least because it comes third on the list after disabled people and LGBT people, but because of the prominence[102] it is given amongst a range of other characteristics that are less contentious within the remit of hate crime. Without intending to create a hierarchy of characteristics, by default, this is exactly what was implemented. We have been critical of the creation of a hierarchy within hate crime, and keen to see this changed in Scotland, particularly through the (then) HCPOA Bill 2020:[103]

> there should be no hierarchy within the protected characteristics…The categories of protected characteristics operate in recognition of the fact that there are particular vulnerabilities attached to groups of people with certain features. While there are historical and social reasons for the existing hierarchy, the only way to equalise this is to ensure that the … offences are extended to cover all protected characteristics.[104]

The creation of such a hierarchy is something far more damaging given the root causes of VAW to begin with. This is also not the first time that gender has appeared as a characteristic on the fringes of inclusion within hate crime legislation in Scotland—it was almost legislated for by something resembling an accident of timing—via Harper's amendment two years before the HCWG consultation showed support for it to be included. Again, though, Scotland fell short of taking really forward-thinking steps to address hatred, while continuing to take a different approach. Instead of recommending legislation to address violence and hostility on the grounds of disability, sexual orientation, transgender identity *and* gender, the HCWG suggested that more research be undertaken to examine the social underpinnings of violence against women—but women were the only category where this added research was felt necessary,[105] all despite the fact that VAW, domestic abuse and GBV were

[101] Ibid., para. 4.10.

[102] Barker and Jurasz (2021, pp. 4 and 14). Note the language 'disabled people' and 'LGBT people' is that used in the HCWG 2004 Report: see Working Group on Hate Crime (2004, p. 14).

[103] Barker and Jurasz (2020b, p. 1).

[104] Barker and Jurasz (2019).

[105] Barker and Jurasz (2021, p. 7).

widely known issues. The justification that 'more' research was needed is perhaps most generously described as perplexing—as is the resulting inaction.

Unexpectedly, the Scottish Executive did not follow the recommendations of the HCWG Report in 2004. This is especially notable given the developments elsewhere in the UK to enact legislation that extended the scope of hate crimes to capture characteristics and groups that the Scottish Executive refused to consider legislation for. It is less notable in the 'no' in respect of adding gender as a characteristic was universal across the UK. The Scottish Executive published its response to the HCWG Report in June 2006.[106] In that response, the position was made very clear that there was little desire or ambition to adopt many (if any) of the recommendations. This response of the Executive was not predicted, but was announced while the report of the Scottish Courts and Sentencing Commission[107] exploring consistency in sentencing was produced. There was to be—in June 2006—no statutory provision introduced for sexual orientation, transgender identity or disability—effectively meaning that capturing gender conceived of more 'broadly' was an issue in Scotland. In declining to act, the Scottish Executive completely rejected Recommendation 1 of the HCWG Report. While this was not the only rejected recommendation, it was the one with potentially the starkest consequences for a range of groups that were expecting an alternative outcome following the work of the HCWG. That no legislative action was forthcoming was not something that came as unprecedented—the Scottish Executive had earlier opportunities to address the situation but had repeatedly chosen not to. In not acting, the Scottish Executive was establishing a pattern of almost quasi-progressivism—policy claims were not delivered. In that, policy ambition could not live up to the (lack of) legislative progressivism.

Perhaps, fortunately for those affected by hate crimes, once again the MSPs stepped up to address the legislative lacuna left by the (in)action of the Scottish Executive. This time, Patrick Harvie MSP entered the fray. Unlike Donald Gorrie and Robin Harper, with their earlier efforts,

---

[106] Scottish Executive (2006, p. 4).

[107] Ibid.

Harvie was not prepared to wait for a Bill to be presented and to lodge amendments. Instead, Harvie went further and lodged a Private Member's Bill. The Sentencing of Offences Aggravated by Prejudice (Scotland) Bill (SOABPB) was lodged on 2 October 2007 and was intended to advance the recommendations of the HCWG, and in so doing, stand in marked and high-profile opposition to the position adopted by the (then Labour dominated) Scottish Executive. Harvie's SOABPB was drafted to specifically give effect to the recommendations of the HCWG. In lodging his Bill, Harvie planned to enact legislation that would mandate that "the aggravation of an offence by prejudice on the grounds of disability, sexual orientation, or transgender identity … be taken into account in sentencing."[108]

While Harvie acted to fill a gap in Scots Law and keep Scotland up to date—or at least retain some degree of equivalence with the characteristics protected elsewhere in the UK, albeit without introducing new offences—the passage of the SOAPBP benefitted from quirks of both political timing and the Holyrood election cycle. It can never be known whether Harvie's Private Members Bill would have garnered sufficient support had the Labour-led Scottish Executive in control in 2006 retained power by securing the largest number of seats at the 2007 election. The election itself played a role—at least anecdotally—in the piecemeal development of hate crime legislation in Scotland. With the narrow Labour defeat in 2007, and the election of the Scottish National Party (SNP) as the party forming the next Scottish Executive—which the SNP rebranded politically (rather than legally)[109] as the Scottish Government—with the greatest number of seats,[110] there was not only a change in approach to hate crime, but also a notable difference in support for the SOABPB. The SNP manifesto in 2007 outlined the position that a government led by them would "not promote or support legislation or policies which

[108] Harvie, Patrick. 2007. Proposed Sentencing of Offences Aggravated by Prejudice (Scotland) Bill: Statement of Reasons by Patrick Harvie MSP on Why No Further Consultation Is Required. https://archive2021.parliament.scot/S3_MembersBills/Draft%20proposals/prejudice_reasons.pdf. Accessed 10 February 2022.

[109] To make a legal change would require an alteration to the Scotland Act 1998. The legal name remained Scottish Executive. See Nicoll (2007); BBC News (2007a).

[110] BBC News (2007b).

discriminate on the grounds of race, disability, age, gender, faith or religion, social background or sexual orientation,"[111] but would instead pursue an agenda that was centred on the promotion of equality. This led to a change of political direction, and ultimately wholehearted support for Harvie's proposed Bill. The commitment in the manifesto fell short of amending Harvie's Bill to include gender beyond transgender identity though. The SNP-led Scottish Government offered its backing to the SOABPB, resulting in a change in its status to a Handout Bill.[112]

The Bill, introduced on 19 May 2008, was passed without amendments at both stages 2 and 3, and it was unanimously passed on 3 June 2009. It gained royal assent on 8 July 2009 and entered Scots Law as the Offences (Aggravation by Prejudice) (Scotland) Act 2009 (asp 8) (O(ABP) A 2009). While not particularly radical as a piece of legislation, it was long overdue in terms of bringing new characteristics into the purview of hate crime within Scots Law. It was made possible, largely through the work of the HCWG in 2004. Without the processes it undertook and the report it provided, the process of passing the O(ABP)A 2009 would have been much more protracted, largely because of the need for consultation—a point Patrick Harvie MSP made very clear in his statement of reasons when presenting the Bill in late 2007.[113]

The Act, having progressed staccato-like through the legislative processes, serves as an example to indicate that substantive responses are possible in Scotland when there is a collective will to act—something less apparent during the obstinate inaction evident in 2006. At that point, until the passage of the O(ABP)A 2009, there was little action on hate crime that offered much in the way of hope for victims or members of groups in Scotland whose characteristics featured in legislation in England and Wales, and Northern Ireland. From having the opportunity to set the pace for hate crime reform across the UK in the early 2000s through Harper's amendment, Scotland fell behind, and ultimately ended up acting almost 6 years later than England and Wales, and Northern Ireland to

[111] Scottish National Party (2007, p. 66).

[112] A Handout Bill is a Member's Bill which is sponsored and supported by the government of the day. See Ross (2009, p. 2).

[113] Harvie (2007, paras. 9–15).

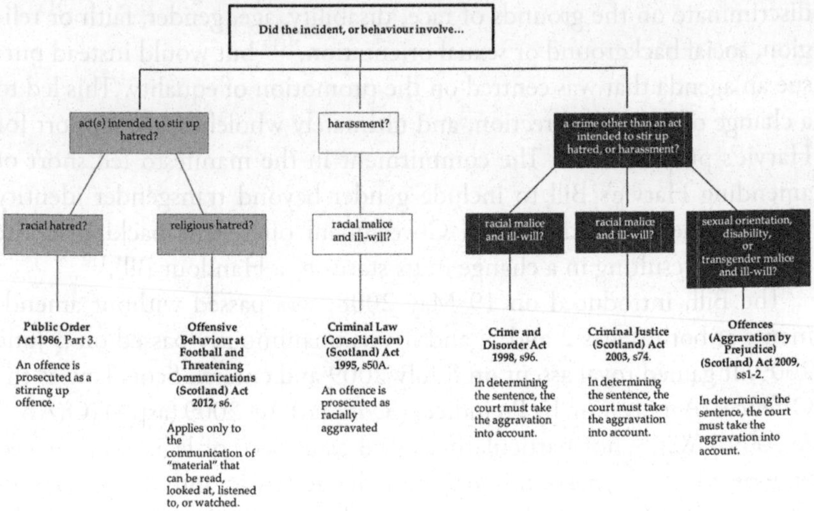

Fig. 3.1 Legislative remedies for hate crimes in Scotland prior to the Hate Crime and Public Order (Scotland) Act 2021

include transgender identity,[114] sexual orientation and disability[115] in its domestic hate crime framework (shown in Fig. 3.1).

While the new SNP Government of 2007 endorsed the recommendations made by the HCWG in its 2004 report—including in respect of those relating to gender—it did not see fit to table amendments to the O(ABP)A 2009 to capture gender within the hate crime framework either. In choosing not to act on this aspect, the Scottish Government shared the concerns voiced by both the Justice and Equality Committees about the likely creation of a hierarchy of victims' rights. In voicing such hesitation, the (then) convener of the Justice Committee, Bill Aitken MSP, indicated that there were real concerns—identified by the Equalities Committee—over widening the remit of hate crime to include characteristics related to age and gender.[116] The Equalities Committee in its 3rd Report in 2007 identified that:

[114] Offences (Aggravation by Prejudice) (Scotland) Act 2009, s. 2 (asp 8).
[115] Offences (Aggravation by Prejudice) (Scotland) Act 2009, s. 1 (asp 8).
[116] Scottish Parliament (2009).

> [t]here is, however, limited recognition of the extent of prejudice experienced by women in Scotland. Only a fifth of the public appear to believe that there is "a great deal", or "quite a lot" of prejudice against women, while almost a third think that there is none.[117]

As a result of the concerns reiterated by Aitken, neither age nor gender featured in the legislative proposals in 2009. As characteristics, they continued to be absent until the addition of age in the HCPOA 2021 (see Sect. 3.5.4).

3.5.3 Scotland Take 2(020): Hate Reform Looms (Again) (2016–2021)

Following the passage of the O(ABP)A 2009, little progress was forthcoming in respect of hate crime for what can be construed (at the time of writing) as a prolonged period. This hiatus—during which hate crime reform was, if not absent, then in occupation of a position as a lesser policy priority—spanned a considerable period in the relatively youthful history of Holyrood.

With the extension of the aggravations to transgender identity, disability and sexual orientation characteristics in 2009, hate crime moved out of the limelight and away from the legislative reform agenda—at least temporarily. Other, more dominant topics occurred instead between 2010 and 2016. For instance, the Scottish Independence Referendum (IndyRef) of 2014[118] raised constitutional questions about the future of Scotland, with wider questions about the future of the UK and Scotland within it following shortly after with the European Referendum.

The impact of IndyRef on hate crime and hate crime reform is difficult to ascertain. IndyRef has generally been recognised as "overwhelmingly civil and peaceful,"[119] with only some incidents suggesting prejudice and intolerance festered as a result. For instance, reports of homophobic

[117] Scottish Parliament (2007).

[118] Scottish Independence Referendum Act 2013 (asp 14); The Guardian (2014).

[119] Law (2015, p. 100).

abuse[120] and damage to property surfaced, but only after the announcements of the result[121] and in connection to loyalist disturbances.[122] By and large, despite the potential for discord, the Electoral Commission has heralded the conduct of the vote as one that operates as a "model for the future."[123] The same cannot be said for the referendum vote that followed in 2016, nor its effects.

The second, UK-wide vote followed IndyRef in quick succession, albeit the 2016 vote has had wider impacts on society, especially on cohesion. The EU Referendum,[124] (Brexit vote) held on 23 June 2016, triggered far greater societal division. The so-called Brexit vote fallout affected the whole of the UK and led to increased reports of intolerance and social unrest generally.[125] In some instances, it also led to claims of increased hate-related and discriminatory incidents at the UK level,[126] as indicated by Burnett,[127] although studies examining this claim suggest that this was not necessarily the case in Scotland,[128] even if it was elsewhere in the UK. In fact, some statistics show the opposite, with reports of racially aggravated crimes (including both racially aggravated harassment and conduct) between 2014–15 and 2018–19 dropping in number from 2445 to 1777, respectively,[129] after the Brexit vote in Scotland[130] (although, it should be noted that barriers to reporting hate crimes may suggest that these are low and reflect under-reporting). Gawlewicz's work shows that there has been a tendency to romanticise both the positioning of and narratives around Scotland in respect of Brexit,[131] so it is possible that the reported drop in numbers is more accurate than it may appear.

---

[120] The Herald (2014a).
[121] Duffy (2014).
[122] Law (2015, p. 100); The Herald (2014b).
[123] The Electoral Commission (2014, p. 8).
[124] European Union Referendum Act 2015.
[125] Booth (2019).
[126] Mintchev (2021, p. 124); Weaver (2016).
[127] Burnett (2017, p. 86).
[128] Hepburn (2020, p. 149); Piatkowska and Lantz (2021, p. 664).
[129] Scottish Government (2019a, p. 23).
[130] The Scotsman Newsroom (2016).
[131] Gawlewicz (2020, p. 331).

Curtice meanwhile takes a slightly different approach to Gawlewicz, noting that in Scotland, Brexit was perceived as more of an expression of English nationalism[132] than anything else. This conclusion is certainly reflected through some of the narrative positioning Brexit as a predominantly English problem and was amplified through rise of the UK Independence Party (UKIP)[133] and its deeply rooted positioning of Englishness as the central focus of Britishness[134] during the referendum campaign. Perhaps more damagingly, UKIP inexplicably ties nationalisms within the UK to the European Union as partial justifications for "bogus independence,"[135] playing on feelings of intolerance, which show in the reports of increased hate crimes across the UK more widely in the aftermath of the Brexit vote,[136] but also in the social divisions[137] that became apparent.[138] This is not the only instance of UKIP or the far-right developing damaging and divisive rhetoric surrounding women, women's rights and women's issues—other examples demonstrate the ways in which UKIP uses women and women's issues to attack minorities,[139] all while attacking women through sexist attitudes.[140] The bringing to the surface of attitudes such as those advocated for by UKIP exacerbated simmering discontent and prejudice in ways previously unseen across society. The language surrounding Brexit and Scottish independence was also damaging and divisive, with cross-jurisdictional accusations of racism coming from the rhetoric around the referendum. Scottish nationalism, for instance, was labelled as "deeply racist, with a total hatred of the English."[141] While this type of rhetoric has exacerbated prejudice and intolerance, especially when utilised for political capital, there have been

[132] Curtice (2016).

[133] Hayton (2016, p. 403).

[134] Ibid., p. 404.

[135] UK Independence Party (2010).

[136] Scottish Government (2016b, p. 4); Booth (2019).

[137] Asthana, Anushka, Quinn, Ben, and Mason, Rowena. 2016. UK votes to leave EU after dramatic night divides nation. *The Guardian*, 24 June. https://www.theguardian.com/politics/2016/jun/24/britain-votes-for-brexit-eu-referendum-david-cameron. Accessed 10 February 2022.

[138] Corbett (2016, p. 27).

[139] Murray (2015).

[140] McSmith (2014).

[141] BBC News (2013).

isolated judgements indicating that comments based on regional or national origin are encapsulated within the hate crime framework in Scotland. For instance, the use of the term "Geordie" refers to the English, and therefore fully captured within the meaning of "racial group"[142] under Section 50A(6) of the CDA 1998.

While neither Brexit nor Indyref (as two constitutional dramas) addresses specifically issues related to hate crime, they do go some way to explaining why there seems to be a 'gap' in the history of hate crime developments, at least legislatively, in Scotland between 2010 and 2016. To put it simply, there were other issues on the horizon that were more pressing—and which were deeply divisive—and the SNP Government was busy with other things. Hate crime reform unfinished though it appeared in late summer 2009 was left that way until 2016. Only after the tumultuous Brexit vote and 2016 Scottish elections did hate crime reappear—first on the SNP radar as part of its 2016 election manifesto,[143] and, second, in the Programme of Work of the SNP Scottish Government[144] duly elected in 2016.

This time, instead of committing to legislative developments, rejecting widely supported recommendations or not tabling legislation, only to be caught out by the action of MSPs, the Scottish Government adopted a different, albeit not unfamiliar, route. The Scottish Government again opted for an advisory group to be established to offer insights before acting on—what was now—an election pledge, but also strand of the Programme of Work for Government. The Independent Advisory Group on Hate Crime, Prejudice and Community Cohesion (IAG) was announced in October 2015.[145] The IAG was established at "an opportune moment to reflect on the journey Scotland ha[d] been on,"[146] given the passage of time since the 2009 amendments to strengthen the hate crime provisions. Its remit was to examine the approach to hate crime in Scotland. In its report, the IAG recommended that:

---

[142] *Moscrop v. McLintock* 2011 S.C.C.R. 621.

[143] Furby (2017).

[144] Scottish Government (2016a, p. 77).

[145] Belfast Telegraph News Headlines (2015).

[146] Scottish Government (2016b, p. 4).

> the Scottish Government should consider whether the existing criminal law provides sufficient protections for those who may be at risk of hate crime, for example, based on gender, age, or membership or other groups such as refugees and asylum seekers.[147]

This recommendation to consider the legal responses was one of the 10 recommendations made in 2016. Other recommendations highlighted the need for a "greater multi agency strategic and operational approach towards tackling hate crime, eradicating and prejudice and building community cohesion."[148] But, these suggestions are not particularly novel, nor forward-looking. Given the (missed) opportunities presented to the Scottish Executive and Scottish Governments in 2002, 2003, 2004 and 2009 to address—holistically—hate crime provisions on previous occasions, it is no surprise that the IAG made such recommendations in 2016—by this point they were long overdue.

The IAG also commented on the seemingly more contentious topic of gender within the hate crime framework, and suggested, much like the HCWG 2004, that discussions around gender as an aggravation "require[s] research and further exploration."[149] The IAG, like the Scottish Executive in 2002 and 2006, the HCWG in 2004 and the Scottish Government in 2009, all side-stepped the issue of gender as an aggravation—preferring to, again, explore further through research and advisory bodies. This was particularly evident in the Scottish Government response to the IAG Report and recommendations, when Angela Constance MSP, the (then) Cabinet Secretary for Communities, Social Security and Equalities, announced the establishment of a group to tackle across multiple agencies responses to hate crime in Scotland. This was direct action in response to the "wide ranging ... breadth and depth"[150] of the IAG recommendations. In her statement to the Scottish Parliament on 13 June 2017,[151] the Cabinet Secretary outlined the Scottish Government response in full. Rather than seeking to enact legislation, the response

[147] Ibid., p. 18.

[148] Ibid., p. 20.

[149] Ibid., p. 17.

[150] Meeting of the Scottish Parliament 13 June 2017, Official Report, col. 13.

[151] Ibid.

focused on bringing cross-sectoral groups together, but also involved commissioning further research to explore the issue of hate crime widely. This included the appointment of Lord Bracadale to lead the Independent Review of Hate Crime Legislation (Bracadale Review) announced on 26 January 2017[152]—all part of the follow-up to the IAG Report. In commenting on the response of the Scottish Government to the IAG Report, The Minister for Community Safety and Legal Affairs, Annabelle Ewing MSP stated,

> The need for robust legislation to tackle hate crime is as great as ever, which is why I am announcing today that the Scottish Government has commissioned an independent review of hate crime legislation. The review will be led by one of the most senior members of the Scottish judiciary—Lord Bracadale. He will make recommendations on how we can ensure that the hate crime legislation that is applied to protect Scottish communities is fit for purpose in the 21st century….
>
> Lord Bracadale's considerations will include whether the current mix of statutory aggravations, common law powers and specific hate crime offences is the most appropriate criminal law approach to take; whether new categories of hate crime should be created for characteristics that are not currently covered in existing legislation, such as age and gender; whether existing legislation can be simplified, rationalised and harmonised; and how any identified gaps, anomalies and inconsistencies can be addressed. Lord Bracadale will also consider whether we need to change or amend the current legislative framework and whether it guarantees that human rights and equality, including the right to freedom of speech, are protected…
>
> The current legislation that relates to hate crime has developed piecemeal over decades. The review presents us with an opportunity to take stock and to look at all the legislation holistically.[153]

The establishment of the Bracadale Review suggested that while there remained a commitment to address, in some form, hate crime, there was a lack of decisiveness on how, or how best, to do so, especially as it was the third type of review in relatively quick succession since 2006. The

[152] Meeting of the Scottish Parliament, 26 January 2017, Official Report, col. 49.

[153] Ibid.

Bracadale Review, in exploring a wide range of elements of hate crime, took a slightly different approach to others before it. The associated research report that informed the work of the Bracadale Review identified that there were two characteristics that were absent from Scots Law, but which made notable and/or numerous appearances in other jurisdictions—age and "sex/gender."[154] Given that Lord Bracadale "set out to undertake a wide examination of ideas and options in his comprehensive review,"[155] it was refreshing to see questions of extending the list of protected characteristics embraced, rather than pushed aside for being too difficult, too contentious or too uncertain. In particular, the suggestion that the "most effective way" to address hate crime is to capture hostility based on identity was notable.[156] The approach outlined in the final report from Lord Bracadale was not all positive nor forward-looking, however. The overwhelming suggestion was to extend the (then) current model of statutory aggravations rather than new offences, ostensibly on the basis of consistency. The embrace by the Bracadale Review of contentious topics—at least for discussion—was not one that extended to the Scottish Government though. In its response to the publication of the Bracadale Report, Communities Minister, Annabelle Ewing, suggested that there remained a division within the government itself. There was seemingly widespread support for an amendment to hate crime legislation, but this did not extend as readily to considerations of proposals for new stand-alone offences, especially contentious ones.[157]

The Scottish Government did not legislate in response to the Bracadale Review. Instead, it undertook further steps to inform what to do next. In doing so, it launched a public consultation of its own, rather than relying on the independent one undertaken by Lord Bracadale. In launching the One Scotland Consultation (One Scotland) on 14 November 2018, (then) Cabinet Secretary for Communities, Humza Yousaf, and (then) Cabinet Secretary for Justice and Local Government, Aileen Campbell MSP, stated, "[w]e are committed to taking this opportunity to shape our

[154] Chalmers and Leverick (2017, p. 55).

[155] Barker and Jurasz (2021, p. 12).

[156] Scottish Government (2018a, p. 43).

[157] Meeting of the Scottish Parliament, 07 June 2018, Official Report, cols. 59–63.

legislation so that it is fit for 21st century Scotland, and most importantly, affords sufficient protection for those that need it."[158] This commitment and the measured approach to build a consensus while allowing the most people to have an input into the future of hate crime provisions in Scotland is laudable, even if it compounded an already protracted process. The results of the One Scotland consultation led to a commitment from the Scottish Government to consolidate hate crime law in Scotland and, within that, extend the characteristics which fall within the purview of the criminal provisions.[159] In making such a pledge, there was a clear indicator that some action would finally be taken to address some of the notable gaps in Scottish hate crime that had persisted since 2009. For example, at the time of the One Scotland consultation, the gaps in the list of characteristics to which either hate crime offences or aggravations could apply included, for example, age and gender, but also stirring up of racial hatred.

With the culmination of the One Scotland consultation exercise, the Scottish Government tabled the Hate Crime and Public Order (Scotland) Bill on 23 April 2020, which became law on 10 May 2021. The Bill was something of a disappointment on a number of fronts. It did not include the protection of sex and/or gender as an extension to the list of characteristics, but did include age. Seemingly, despite three rounds of consultation, review and expert advisory input, the Scottish Government was still not prepared to commit to including characteristics of sex/gender within the hate crime framework. This is especially frustrating for a government that has poured so much time and resource into the development of a hate crime framework that is intended—as Yousaf and Campbell claimed in 2018—to be fit for the future.[160] It stands in stark contradiction to the *Equally Safe* commitments, and the recommendations of the NACWG (see Chap. 1, Sect. 1.3.1.), which is, at the very least, mixed messaging. It is also somewhat perplexing that the Scottish Government continue with

158 Scottish Government (2018b, p. 1).

159 Scottish Government (2019b, p. 33).

160 Scottish Government (2018b, p. 1).

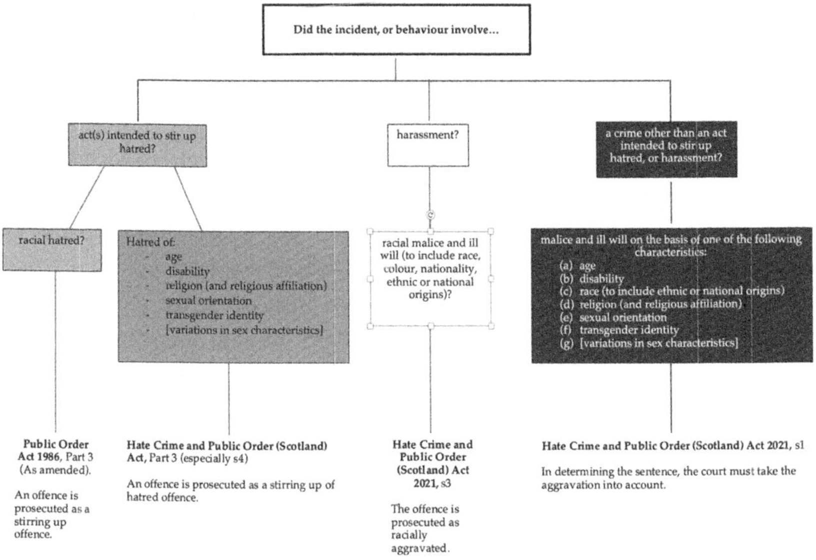

Fig. 3.2 Legislative remedies for hate crimes in Scotland after the enactment of the Hate Crime and Public Order (Scotland) Act 2021

"prevarication" over the more contentious elements of hate crime, especially in what was intended to be an "updating piece of legislation."[161]

The HCPOA 2021 also does not offer much—if anything—in the way of new offences, beyond filling gaps to ensure religious aggravation and the stirring up of religiously aggravated hatred are captured. Perhaps most significantly from the perspective of a holistic piece of law, it includes all of the characteristics in one place (see Fig. 3.2), and for the first time in the history of a devolved Scotland, there is one piece of legislation which captures all of the aggravations applicable to underlying criminal acts. Arguably the most significant thing the HCPOA 2021 has delivered on is consolidating scattered hate crime provisions. Through amending the Public Order Act 1986,[162] repealing section 50A of the Criminal Law (Consolidation) (Scotland) Act 1995,[163] Section 96 of the Crime and

[161] Barker and Jurasz (2020a).

[162] Hate Crime and Public Order (Scotland) Act 2021, sch. 2, para. 1 (asp 14).

[163] Ibid., para. 2.

Disorder Act 1998,[164] Section 74 of the Criminal Justice (Scotland) Act 2003[165] and the entirety of the Offences (Aggravation by Prejudice) (Scotland) Act 2009 (asp 8),[166] the HCPOA 2021 has—in some ways—simplified the statutory approach to hate crimes.

The early developments of both criminal justice legislation and hate crime laws in Scotland post-Devolution focused almost overwhelmingly on additions of characteristics to benefit from protection but also of increased punishments, and sentencing for those convicted of an offence. This approach was retained and embedded into the most recent reform agenda that culminated in the HCPOA 2021 (as Fig. 3.2 shows).

That is not to say that the HCPOA 2021 passed into law without controversy. There have been wide-ranging criticism expressed over the implications for freedom of expression as a result of the provisions contained within it. These concerns were noted both in the press[167] and in Parliament too, not least by Adam Tomkins MSP, who stated that, "We must guard against vagueness, and we must guard against overbreadth."[168] In outlining this need for caution, Tomkins was almost aligned in his conclusions with the court in *Miller*[169] in respect of the breadth of the things that could be captured by the draft bill. This correlation across two different legal systems in respect of different facets of the same legislative frameworks shows the gravity of the problem, but also the widespread investment in ensuring that there are limits between expression rights and hate crimes. This is not per se new territory for anything relating to hate crime, especially given the difficulties of policing hate versus protecting speech and expression, although the (then) Cabinet Secretary for Justice, Humza Yousaf MSP, stated that:

> Some have argued that there is a tension between hate crime law and freedom of expression, but I am not persuaded by that. I do not think that the

[164] Ibid., para. 3.

[165] Ibid., para. 4.

[166] Ibid., para. 5.

[167] Davidson (2020).

[168] Meeting of the Scottish Parliament, 10 March 2021, Official Report, col. 70.

[169] *R (Miller) v. The College of Policing* [2021] EWCA Civ. 1926.

two have to be mutually exclusive, and I think that there can be strong protections in law against hate crime and strong freedom of expression provisions.[170]

Nevertheless, the HCPOA 2021 is tainted from its enactment and has fallen short of the expectations that accompanied the consultative stages.

While the HCPOA 2021 reshaped legislative remedies for hate-related crimes in Scots Law, it also, to a degree, consolidated hate crime legislation—something the other nations in the UK have yet to do. That said, simply consolidating legislative provisions is not particularly forward-looking. In bringing together the majority of hate-related criminal provisions into one piece of legislation, there is a degree of clarity offered.[171] The addition of a longer list of characteristics, especially through the (now) inclusion of age, with the potential to add variations in sex characteristics, shows some limited (see Chap. 4) developmental thinking with respect to addressing the societal challenges of bias. Some of the amendments enacted through the HCPOA 2021 have shown forward-thinking. For example, the new legislation captures religiously aggravated prejudice through a new stirring-up offence, as well as ensuring that religious aggravations are considered at sentencing for underlying criminal offences, focusing on the introduction of aggravations rather than on lots of new offences. In addressing the lacuna surrounding religious aggravation and filling the gaps[172] left by the repeal of the Offensive Behaviour at Football and Threatening Communications (Scotland) Act 2012 (asp 1), and the jurisdictional limitation of the religious hatred provisions[173] in the POA 1986, for example, the HCPOA 2021 joins some of the dots left by previous scattered law reforms (though continues to raise questions over online forms of hatred and violence against women—see Chap. 6). While it has addressed, substantively, religious hatred, this is not particularly

[170] Meeting of the Scottish Parliament, 10 March 2021, Official Report, cols. 92–93.

[171] It should be noted though that not all hate crime provisions are found within the HCPOA 2021. The POA 1986 provisions relating to racial hatred remain in force, and now work in conjunction with the HCPOA 2021.

[172] Brown et al. (2016, pp. 211–212).

[173] Part 3A of the Public Order Act 1986 (as amended) applies only to England and Wales, therefore not extending the religious hatred offences to Scotland.

radical nor progressive, especially given the long-standing awareness that religion—and religious prejudice—is a polarising factor. Women increasingly participate in, for example, sport and religion, and yet the protections afforded to them have not developed in step with society. Times have changed, but it seems the law has yet to do so. The problem of legal blindless here cannot squarely be blamed on 'the law'—it is more an issue of legislator reluctance, and the consequence is that VAW is not taken as seriously as it could—and should—be.

Inevitably, though, gaps remain. The HCPOA 2021 falls somewhat short of being a true landmark piece of legislation—it does not, for example, address gender as a characteristic despite the previous debates in post-Devolution Scotland about such a topic (see Chap. 4). Nor does it do much to change the hate crime framework beyond what was in—admittedly piecemeal—legislation previously, even in including the power to add 'variations in sex characteristics' to the protected characteristics list at some point in the future is not novel—it is the same idea as that suggested by the HCWG 2004. As a stand-alone act, the HCPOA overlooks alternative approaches and models for tackling hate crimes, even legislatively. Given the concerning increases in the numbers of recorded hate crimes more generally, with records showing that the characteristics of race followed by sexual orientation were the most numerous hate crimes recorded across 2019–20,[174] the HCPOA is a disappointing effort. After race and sexual orientation, hatred aggravated by religion and disability follow close behind in terms of the volume of reports.[175]

In the most recent Police Scotland Quarterly Performance Reports, which track recorded instances of hate crimes, the statistics make for depressing reading given the numerous political and legal efforts at reforming hate crime in Scotland. While there are some distinct differences in the volume of reported hate crimes across 2020–21 and 2021–22, Police Scotland statistics show that there have been noticeable rises in the numbers of reports of hate crimes relating to aggravations based on transgender identity, disability or sexual orientation within a relatively short time period. For instance, there was a 6% increase in hate crime reports

[174] Scottish Government (2021a, p. 45).
[175] Ibid.

(totalling 103) recorded between April and June 2021–22 compared to the figures from the same period in previous year.[176] This reflects the year-on-year increases that have been recorded for disablist, transgender and sexual orientation aggravations.[177] Most shockingly, the latest statistics show a 76.7% increase in transgender aggravated hate crimes.[178] This is not an isolated issue, with a 29% increase in crimes recording multiple aggravators being reported too.[179] Police Scotland does not treat these statistics particularly pessimistically, noting that the reported figures for hate crimes relating to race and religion indicate "little variation."[180] In sum, while the total reported hate crimes show a slim increase from 3776 in 2020–21 to 3782 in 2021–22, and the overall percentage of transgender hate crimes represents only 2%, the percentage increase is still damaging for Scotland's ambitions of tolerance.[181] The bigger picture also shows that while the total number of recorded hate crimes may vary only slightly, the overall message is that there is a sustained trend towards a steady increase[182] in hate crimes in Scotland. This seems to stand at odds with the volume of resources dedicated to hate crime reform, at least from the perspectives of the criminal justice system. It is also a marker for the scale of the challenge, and the shifting sands of progress (and its measurement).

In seeking to reduce hate crimes and tackle societal prejudices, more legislation has been implemented, which, in turn, leads to more characteristics and more reporting, and therefore reported increases in hate crimes. It is not the role of legislation to tackle or prevent crimes, and, as Glover reiterates, statutory provisions cannot in any event "protect" groups,[183] but it is one of the strands of a wider strategy that is designed to address prejudice in society. If the legislation does not embody change, it is difficult to see it as part of a holistic scheme to address the problem.

---

[176] Police Scotland (2021a, p. 63).

[177] Police Scotland (2021b, p. 72).

[178] Ibid.

[179] Ibid.

[180] Ibid.

[181] Garton-Crosbie (2022).

[182] Police Scotland (2021a, p. 63).

[183] Glover (2017, p. 88).

Similarly, misunderstandings about the ability of legislation to protect[184] individuals, especially when coming from the office of the Justice Secretary, inspire little confidence that the system of hate crime is one which is understandable, let alone workable.

Similarly, statistics like legislative reform are only one element of the hate crime picture. They directly affect the responses to these crimes—for these statistics to show little other than a sustained level of offending suggests that other effective mechanisms beyond law are sorely needed. The HCPOA as a 'new' piece of legislation also presents some significant challenges for policing, with Police Scotland being caught somewhat off-guard and forced to request delays to their statutory reporting obligations to provide disaggregated data until the necessary systems are in place.[185] While the imposition of data duties on Police Scotland ought to be regarded as a positive step, delays to readiness—suggested to be until 2023[186]—do little to suggest that the HCPOA will have an immediate positive impact. Scotland has notionally taken steps to do things differently but has been dogged by delays[187]—both in Parliament and in policing. In some respects, the HCPOA 2021 is a safe measure—it consolidates rather than modernises and remains reliant upon other, underprepared stakeholders to give it teeth. In that, it is reflective of how Scotland and hate crime arrived at its current position.

3.6 Conclusion: Scotland's Post-HCPOA 2021 … Future?

Like equal opportunity and anti-discrimination laws before them, hate crime statutes usually only cover prejudice towards specified victim characteristics or categories of identity (eg: race, religion, sexual orientation or disability). Although the initial impetus for reform in this area came from

[184] See, for example, the confusion by Justice Secretary Kenny MacAskill in the Scottish Parliament debate on the Offences (Aggravation by Prejudice) (Scotland) Bill in Meeting of the Scottish Parliament, 18 March 2009, Official Report, cols. 15874–15875; Glover (2017, p. 88).

[185] Police Scotland (2021b, p. 72).

[186] Wade (2022).

[187] BBC News (2021).

> minority groups who successfully demonstrated to legislatures that their group identity or 'difference' from the majority made them vulnerable to prejudice-related violence and intimidation, the principle of equality before the law has meant that the vast majority of hate crime legislation has had to adopt a symmetrical approach to the protection of victim attributes or categories of identity (eg: race is the protected attribute not 'black-ness'). This generic construction of hate crime has also enabled the law to recognise crimes of prejudice that are committed by minority group members upon majority group members and minority-upon-minority offences. This has produced a tension between the original impetus for hate crime laws to protect marginalised and stigmatised minorities and their increasing application to disadvantaged groups and minority offenders. Gail Mason[188]

While Scotland claims to be distinctive in its approach and has shown a willingness to deliver on progressive legislative agendas, hate crime stands as something of an outlier. Scotland, it seems, has, at times and on occasion, adopted a proactive approach to legislative protections for some groups and characteristics, including that of transgender identity, which Hopkins described as being, at the time, "a first for hate crime in Europe."[189] While there is little evidence to cast doubt on the willingness of Scotland to engage with a more modern consideration of hate crimes, the traditional focus and English influences have been retained and, arguably, strengthened by the introduction of a specific hate crime act (HCPOA) and associated campaigns.

For instance, the One Scotland campaign of 2020 replicated some of Scotland's long-standing successes with poster campaigns which originates from the Zero Tolerance Campaign (see Chap. 2). The 2020 One Scotland Letters to Haters campaign replicated the use of a number of striking posters (see Fig. 3.3) displayed in public locations to raise awareness of hate crimes in Scotland, but also the need to report them.

The public awareness initiatives differ somewhat to Scotland's tendency to introduce legislation driven by punitive and retributivist demands. This legislative approach suggests that hate crime continues to be a challenging aspect of the criminal justice system. The legislative

[188] Mason (2014a, p. 63).

[189] Hopkins (2009, p. 24).

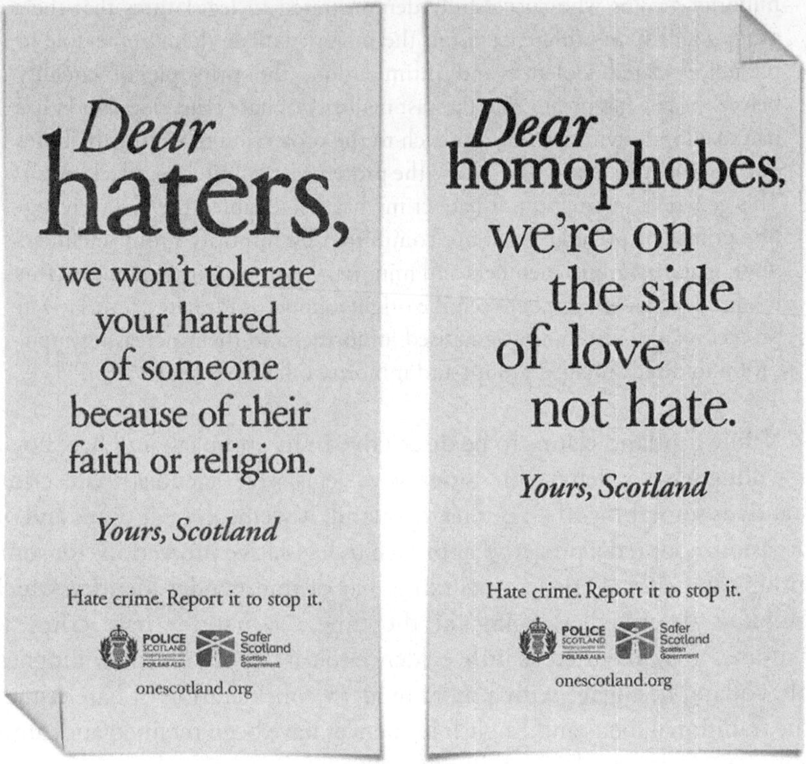

Fig. 3.3 Dear Haters and Dear Homophobes posters from the One Scotland Letters to Haters campaign to raise public awareness of hate crimes in Scotland

focus to fall on punishment and retribution remains problematic, not simply because hate crime is a social problem, but because social and political factors drive demands for legislation to enshrine responses to prejudice. The retributivist approach does not allow (nor encourage) the tackling of hate crime from perspectives beyond criminal punishment. Criminalisation will not and cannot change social attitudes—a point the Association of Scottish Police Superintendents make convincingly by suggesting that Scotland cannot simply arrest its way out of problems.[190] With hate crime provisions becoming increasingly numerous, it is

[190] Association of Scottish Police Superintendents (2020, p. 2).

difficult to see how adding more characteristics, more offences and greater scope to the hate crime provisions tackles the underlying societal challenges of prejudice, malice or ill will. In some respects, it is questionable whether the intent of the Scottish legislature to grapple with hate crime reform has contributed to tackling of social (in)cohesion or otherwise.

This is an ongoing concern which has been worthy of comment since Scotland first made its most significant departure from the approach adopted in England and Wales with the Offences (Aggravation by Prejudice) (Scotland) Act 2009 (asp 8), by introducing protections for sexual orientation, disability and transgender identity. Credit is due for taking steps to offer protection to minority groups, but the ways in which this protection was delayed and then finally added does not solve the problem of the origins of the underlying prejudice that is supposedly tackled through criminalisation. This is the case for criminal justice generally, but especially in the context of hate crime provisions specifically, not least because they overlook rehabilitative design principles[191] but because they do not accommodate nor encourage, for example, restorative justice even where it can be useful[192] and instead retain symbolic purposes.[193] Hate crime legislation in Scotland captures an ever-expanding list of characteristics—marking a departure from the original focus on minorities and the original rationale to protect these groups. In attempting to consolidate, the HCPOA is a bastion of conservative symbolism, but little else, because gender is *still* not a feature and is *still* not given even symbolic recognition within the hate crime framework.

By adding additional characteristics (and groups) benefitting from protection to the hate crime provisions (see Chap. 4), the problems of the visibility of prejudice and 'spikes' in hate crime are self-fulfilling. The more characteristics that are protected, the more numerous the reports of alleged hate incidents and resulting hate crimes are, alongside more spurious reports which have to be investigated but may not necessarily be much other than what Police Scotland describe as "vexatious."[194] In turn,

[191] Mason (2014a, p. 59).

[192] Gavrielides (2012, p. 3639).

[193] Mason (2014b, p. 78).

[194] Police Scotland (2020, p. 11).

these 'increases' are used to indicate that hate crimes are 'rising' and more must be done—but this is a misleading interpretation. Better or enhanced reporting or changes in reporting practices do not mean 'more' hate crimes are happening, nor that society is ready to accept them. Better reporting could mean that more reports are noted[195]—a point not always captured by media, nor through third-party recording mechanisms,[196] but nevertheless highlighted as a resourcing concern surrounding the feasibility of increasing the breadth of hate crimes under the HCPOA 2021.[197] Similarly, issues surrounding the reporting of incidents based on perception pose additional challenges—not only for the policing of hate crimes but also for gaining a more accurate picture of the prevalence of hatred and prejudice. Reporting based on perception was acted upon as a necessary change as a result of the Macpherson Report,[198] and yet was the subject of scrutiny—and comment—in *Miller*[199] where questions over the discretion to report (or not) non-crime hate incidents[200] arose. The breadth of the difficulties of perception-based reporting, especially for non-crime hate incidents, was highlighted by the court as being "extremely wide in scope"[201]—sufficiently so as to interfere with freedom of expression rights. The interference with speech rights is something that Maini-Thompson suggests will need to be carefully considered in redressing the balance between hate reporting and expression rights.[202] This presents additional problems when it comes to the reporting of incidents rather than crimes—issues that have arisen in Scotland too in respect of the HCPOA 2021.[203]

Changes in reporting practices and the hyperbole associated with the presumption that this causes increased hate crimes is something increasingly recognised—and commented on as caveats—in the evaluation of

[195] de Freytas-Tamura (2016).
[196] Wong et al. (2020, p. 81).
[197] Wade (2022).
[198] Home Office (1999, Recommendations 12 and 16).
[199] *Miller* (n 171).
[200] Ibid. [194].
[201] Ibid. [197].
[202] Maini-Thompson (2022).
[203] Nachiappan (2020).

hate crime statistical analyses in both Scotland[204] and England,[205] but also raised as an operational concern by Police Scotland as having a significant impact on the understanding its officers have of potential charging selections.[206] By implication, if the issues were not (previously) reported nor recorded, there is no way to demonstrate an increase or otherwise. Where reporting practices have changed—either to capture new characteristics or to reflect changes in policing practice—this also does not automatically mean increases in hate crime. As such, the justifications for 'stronger' or 'increased protections' are the design of increased legislative reform to begin with—and pay little consideration to other, non-legislative approaches to addressing the social prejudices underlying the justifications for hate crimes.

There has been little change in the approach towards the criminalisation of hate crime legislation post-Devolution. In 2021, similar drivers were evident in the HCPOA that have been present across the legislative history of hate crime. Similar approaches have been as dominant from the development of the O(ABP)A 2009 right through to the HCPOA 2021—more legislation, more offences, more aggravations and more sentencing have remained cornerstones of the legislative agenda on hate crime in Scots Law. In this, Scotland has done little differently to other jurisdictions.

That said, the approach of 'more' has so far not extended to gender in Scots Law. This is the reality even though "gender-bias crimes affect women collectively [and] [w]omen are constantly aware of their vulnerability and status as potential victims,"[207] and yet, still do not benefit from specific capture in the ever-growing list of protected groups and characteristics in the hate crime framework in Scotland. This is particularly perplexing given the growing awareness that hate crime frameworks have shifted in emphasis from protecting minorities, to capturing those subject to hostility and prejudice. Other areas of law—especially that of equalities—have recognised this. The hate crime framework in Scotland, less so.

---

[204] Scottish Government (2021a, p. 8).

[205] Allen and Zayed (2021, p. 4).

[206] Police Scotland (2020, p. 3).

[207] Hodge (2011, p. 8).

The legislative progressivism on display in (selected) areas of Scottish policy has not extended to women and the hate crime framework, nor has the willingness to engage with extending protection to additional groups not traditionally captured within hate crimes seen fit to encompass women. This omission—from policy and legislative perspectives—is a curious one given that gender has been an undercurrent of discussion in the almost constant hate crime reform discussions. Successive Scottish executives and governments have pledged to address hate crime and inequalities. In the early days of hate crime post-devolution, Scotland was forward-looking and prepared to engage in the difficult discussions. In some respects, Scotland was much more progressive in policy terms than any of the other jurisdictions within the UK; yet, when it mattered, Scotland, under Scottish Labour, shied away from the experimental approach to hate crime legislation that had been advocated for up until 2004. This situation changed somewhat, and a renewed vigour was evident when the political leadership shifted to the SNP. Unlike under Scottish Labour, the SNP were prepared to forge ahead with legislation, but like their predecessors, the hate crime reform agenda stagnated. The SNP remain committed to reform of hate crime, and pledge this regularly in political documents. Despite this, they have done little that is substantively different despite having been in power for over a decade. Luckily for the people of Scotland, MSPs have been willing to stand up and plug the gaps left by government inaction. At Holyrood, despite the flaws in the approach to moving forward on hate crime legislation, the process and interests of MSPs are transparent—a direct contrast to the situation at Westminster. The experimental approach and heavy reliance on the need for more and more research often referred to by the Scottish Government does at least offer some reassurance that measured decisions will be taken—even if they are frustratingly slow in addressing, meaningfully, the inclusion of previously excluded groups (and characteristics) within hate crime.

Statistical reporting can shed some (limited) light on some of the realities of hate crimes, but it also reinforces suggestions that while Scotland may have resolved its 'portmanteau' approach to hate crime legislation, there is still a significant amount of work to be done beyond legal initiatives to achieve societal equality. Scotland still has some way to go to improve upon the situation for minority groups and to meaningfully reduce hate crime, not just the reporting of it. On the multifarious journey of hate crime reform in Scotland though, there is seemingly, still—as we suggested in 2021—some "room for improvement."[208]

In the following chapter, the discussion focuses specifically on the issue of gender within the context of hate crime and explores why and how Scots Law has shied away from specific protections for gender within hate crime despite the overwhelming societal challenge posed by violence against women.

References

Allen, Grahame, and Yago Zayed. 2021. Hate Crime Statistics. House of Commons Library, Briefing Paper No 8357. https://researchbriefings.files.parliament.uk/documents/CBP-8537/CBP-8537.pdf. Accessed 10 February 2022.

Association of Scottish Police Superintendents. 2020. Justice Committee Hate Crime and Public Order (Scotland) Bill Submission. Scottish Parliament. REF NO. J/S5/20/HC/396. https://archive2021.parliament.scot/S5_JusticeCommittee/Inquiries/JS520HC396_The_Association_of_Scottish.pdf. Accessed 10 February 2022.

Asthana, Anushka, Ben Quinn, and Rowena Mason. 2016. UK Votes to Leave EU After Dramatic Night Divides Nation. *The Guardian*, June 24. https://www.theguardian.com/politics/2016/jun/24/britain-votes-for-brexit-eu-referendum-david-cameron. Accessed 10 February 2022.

Athwal, Harmit. 2002. Deaths with a (Known Or Suspected) Racial Element 1991–1999. Institute of Race Relations. https://irr.org.uk/article/deaths-with-a-known-or-suspected-racial-element-1991-1999/. Accessed 10 February 2022.

Barker, Kim, and Olga Jurasz. 2019. Submission of Evidence to One Scotland Consultation on Amending Scottish Hate Crime legislation. https://consult.gov.scot/hate-crime/consultation-on-scottish-hate-crime-legislation/consultation/view_respondent?show_all_questions=0&sort=submitted&order=ascending&_q__text=jurasz&uuId=167846602. Accessed 10 February 2022.

[208] Barker and Jurasz (2021, p. 14).

———. 2020a. Scots Hate Crime Bill: A Missed (Gender) Opportunity? University of Stirling Public Policy Blog. https://policyblog.stir.ac.uk/2020/05/01/scots-hate-crime-bill-a-missed-gender-opportunity/. Accessed 10 February 2022.

———. 2020b. Submission of Evidence to Justice Committee on Hate Crime and Public Order (Scotland) Bill 2020. Scottish Parliament. REF NO. J/S5/20/HC/34. https://archive2021.parliament.scot/S5_JusticeCommittee/Inquiries/JS520HC34_Barker_and_Jurasz(1).pdf. Accessed 10 February 2022.

———. 2021. Misogynistic Harassment: A Stumbling Block for Scots Hate Crime Reform? *Juridical Review* 1: 1–17.

BBC News. 2007a. Scottish Executive renames itself. *BBC News*, September 3. http://news.bbc.co.uk/1/hi/scotland/6974798.stm. Accessed 10 February 2022.

———. 2007b. Timeline: Scottish elections 2007. *BBC News*, May 4. http://news.bbc.co.uk/1/hi/scotland/north_east/6622335.stm. Accessed 10 February 2022.

———. 2013. Nigel Farage Blasts 'fascist' Protesters After Edinburgh Confrontation. *BBC News*, May 17. https://www.bbc.co.uk/news/uk-scotland-22566183. Accessed 10 February 2022.

———. 2021. Hate Crime Vote Delayed After Marathon Holyrood Debate. *BBC News*, March 10. https://www.bbc.co.uk/news/uk-scotland-scotland-politics-56349995. Accessed 10 February 2022.

Belfast Telegraph News Headlines. 2015. University of Ulster Director to Chair New Hate Crime Advisory Group. *Belfast Telegraph*, October 14. https://www.belfasttelegraph.co.uk/news/northern-ireland/university-of-ulster-director-to-chair-new-hate-crime-advisory-group-31610004.html. Accessed 10 February 2022.

Bell, Mark. 1999. The New Article 13 EC Treaty: A Sound Basis for European Anti-Discrimination Law? *Maastricht Journal of European and Comparative Law* 6 (1): 5–23.

Booth, Robert. 2019. Racism Rising Since Brexit Vote, Nationwide Study Reveals. *The Guardian*, May 20. https://www.theguardian.com/world/2019/may/20/racism-on-the-rise-since-brexit-vote-nationwide-study-reveals. Accessed 10 February 2022.

Brax, David. 2016. Motives, Reasons and Responsibility in Hate/Bias Crime Legislation. *Criminal Justice Ethics* 35 (3): 230–248.

Brooks, Libby. 2022. 'Darkest moment in our history': Raith Fans on David Goodwillie Row. *The Guardian*, February 4. https://www.theguardian.com/uk-news/2022/feb/04/darkest-moment-in-our-history-raith-rovers-fans-david-goodwillie-row. Accessed 10 February 2022.

Brown, Callum G., Thomas Green, and Jane Mair. 2016. Religion in Scots Law: The Report of an Audit at the University of Glasgow. Edinburgh: Humanist Society Scotland. https://www.humanism.scot/wp-content/uploads/2016/02/Religion-in-Scots-Law-Final-Report-22-Feb-16.pdf. Accessed 10 February 2022.

BT. n.d. Hope United. https://www.bt.com/hopeunited. Accessed 10 February 2022.

Burnett, Jon. 2017. Racial Violence and the Brexit State. *Institute of Race Relations* 58 (4): 85–97.

Chakraborti, Neil, and John Garland. 2015. *Hate Crime: Impact, Causes and Responses*. 2nd ed. London: SAGE Publications.

Chalmers, James, and Fiona Leverick. 2017. A Comparative Analysis of Hate Crime Legislation: A Report to the Hate Crime Legislation Review. https://consult.gov.scot/hate-crime/independent-review-of-hate-crime-legislation/supporting_documents/495517_APPENDIX%20%20ACADEMIC%20REPORT.pdf. Accessed 10 February 2022.

Corbett, Steve. 2016. The Social Consequences of Brexit for the UK and Europe: Euroscepticism, Populism, Nationalism and Societal Division. *International Journal of Social Quality* 6 (1): 11–31.

Curtice, John. 2016. Brexit: Behind the Referendum. *Political Insight* 7 (2): 4–7.

Dale, Iain, ed. 2000. *Labour Party General Election Manifestos 1900–1997*. With an Introduction by Dennis Kavanagh. London: Routledge.

Davidson, Gina. 2020. Insults Uttered During Scottish Independence Could Be Prosecuted as Hate Crime, MSPs Warned. *The Scotsman*, November 11. https://www.scotsman.com/news/politics/insults-uttered-during-scottish-independence-referendum-could-be-prosecuted-hate-crime-msps-warned-3031789. Accessed 10 February 2022.

Davidson, Lorraine. 2011. Law to Tackle Sectarianism in Football 'first act of government'. *The Times*, May 26. https://www.thetimes.co.uk/article/law-to-tackle-sectarianism-in-football-first-act-of-government-g9mpm7qhv6n. Accessed 10 February 2022.

de Freytas-Tamura, Kimiko. 2016. Britain's Increase in Hate Crimes Is Tied to Changes in How They Are Reported. *The New York Times*, November 5. https://www.nytimes.com/2016/11/06/world/europe/britain-hate-crimes.html. Accessed 10 February 2022.

Duffy, Judith. 2014. Eleven Arrests After Loyalist No Supporters' Descend on George Square. *The Herald*, September 21. https://www.heraldscotland.com/news/13181036.eleven-arrests-loyalist-no-supporters-descend-george-square/. Accessed 10 February 2022.

Electoral Commission, The. 2014. Scottish Independence Referendum: Report on the Referendum Held on 18 September 2014. ELC/2014/02. https://www.electoralcommission.org.uk/sites/default/files/pdf_file/Scottish-independence-referendum-report.pdf. Accessed 10 February 2022.

Engender. 2015. The 'S' Word: Women's Experiences of Intra-Christian Sectarianism in Scotland. https://www.engender.org.uk/content/publications/1432569345_The-S-Word%2D%2D-Womens-experience-of-intra-Christian-sectarianism.pdf. Accessed 10 February 2022.

Equality and Human Rights Commission. 2019. Background to the Equality Duty. https://www.equalityhumanrights.com/en/public-sector-equality-duty-scotland/background-equality-duty. Accessed 10 February 2022.

Eski, Yarin, Paul McGuiness, and Michele Burman. 2011. Changes to Scotland's Criminal Justice System Post-Devolution: Main Legislative Developments, Major Reviews of Policy and Procedure, and the Introduction of 'new' Bodies. Scottish Centre for Crime & Justice Research. https://www.sccjr.ac.uk/wp-content/uploads/2012/12/Changes-to-Criminal-Justice-in-Scotland-post-Devolution.pdf. Accessed 10 February 2022.

Furby, Liam. 2017. Our Plan for Scotland: Equality and Human Rights for All. SNP: News, September 19. https://www.snp.org/scotland-programme-for-government-equality-and-human-rights-for-all/. Accessed 10 February 2022.

Garton-Crosbie, Abbi. 2022. Scotland a "less welcoming place" for Trans People Amid Hate Crime Rise. *The National*, January 21. https://www.thenational.scot/news/19866850.scotland-less-welcoming-place-trans-people-amid-hate-crime-rise/ . Accessed 10 February 2022.

Gavrielides, Theo. 2012. Contextualizing Restorative Justice for Hate Crime. *Journal of Interpersonal Violence* 27 (18): 3624–3643.

Gawlewicz, Anna. 2020. 'Scotland's Different': Narratives of Scotland's Distinctiveness in the Post-Brexit Vote Era. *Scottish Affairs* 29 (3): 321–335.

Giles, Ellie. 2021. Do You Know the Offside Rule. #HerGameToo. https://www.hergametoo.co.uk/post/ellie-giles. Accessed 10 February 2022.

Glover, Philip. 2017. Statutory Aggravation by Religious Prejudice in Scotland: Correcting the "Lord Advocate's lacuna". *Juridical Review* 2: 85–105.

Guardian, The. 1999. And the Racist Killings Go On. *The Guardian*, February 24. https://www.theguardian.com/uk/1999/feb/24/lawrence.ukcrime5. Accessed 10 February 2022.

———. 2014. Scottish Independence Referendum: Final results in full. *The Guardian*, September 8. https://www.theguardian.com/politics/ng-interactive/2014/sep/18/-sp-scottish-independence-referendum-results-in-full. Accessed 10 February 2022.

Hall, Nathan. 2013. *Hate Crime*. 2nd ed. London: Routledge.

Harvie, Patrick. 2007. Proposed Sentencing of Offences Aggravated by Prejudice (Scotland) Bill: Statement of Reasons by Patrick Harvie MSP on Why No Further Consultation Is Required. https://archive2021.parliament.scot/S3_MembersBills/Draft%20proposals/prejudice_reasons.pdf. Accessed 10 February 2022.

Hayton, Richard. 2016. The UK Independence Party and the Politics of Englishness. *Political Studies Review* 14 (3): 400–410.

Hepburn, Eve. 2020. Uncharted Waters: The Social and Equality Impacts of Brexit. *Scottish Affairs* 29 (2): 141–178.

Herald, The. 2014a. Gay Councillor Targeted by Hardline Loyalists in Square. *The Herald*, September 21. https://www.heraldscotland.com/news/13181077.gay-councillor-targeted-hardline-loyalists-square/. Accessed 10 February 2022.

———. 2014b. Police Investigation into Fire Near Herald Office. *The Herald*, September 21. https://www.heraldscotland.com/news/13181064.police-investigation-fire-near-herald-office/. Accessed 10 February 2022.

Hills, Leslie. 2001. Why Engender? In *Women and Contemporary Scottish Politics: An Anthology*, ed. Esther Breitenbach and Fiona Mackay, 27–33. Edinburgh: Polygon.

Hodge, Jessica P. 2011. *Gendered Hate: Exploring Gender in Hate Crime Law*. Northeastern University Press.

Home Affairs Committee. 2009. The Macpherson Report – Ten Years On. HC 2008–09, 427. https://publications.parliament.uk/pa/cm200809/cmselect/cmhaff/427/427.pdf. Accessed 10 February 2022.

———. 2021. The Macpherson Report: Twenty-two years on. HC 2021–22, 139. https://committees.parliament.uk/publications/7012/documents/72927/default/. Accessed 10 February 2022.

Home Office. 1999. The Stephen Lawrence Inquiry: Report of an Inquiry by Sir William Macpherson of Cluny. Cm 4262-I. https://assets.publishing.service.gov.uk/government/uploads/system/uploads/attachment_data/file/277111/4262.pdf. Accessed 10 February 2022.

Hopkins, Tim. 2009. Scotland's Approach to Hate Crime Law. *Safer Communities* 8 (4): 19–26.

Hudson, Barbara. 2007. Diversity, Crime and Criminal Justice. In *Oxford Handbook of Criminology*, ed. Mike Maguire, Rod Morgan, and Rob Reiner, 158–175. Oxford: Oxford University Press.
Hunter, Eveline. 1979. *Scottish Woman's Place: A Practical Guide and Critical Comment on Women's Rights in Scotland*. Billings & Sons Ltd.
Husak, Douglas. 2004. The Criminal Law as a Last Resort. *Oxford Journal of Legal Studies* 24 (2): 207–235.
Iganski, Paul, and David Smith. 2011. Rehabilitation of Hate Crime Offenders: Research Report. Equality and Human Rights Commission. https://www.equalityhumanrights.com/en/our-work-scotland/our-work-scotland/research-scotland/rehabilitation-hate-crime-offenders. Accessed 10 February 2022.
Law, Alex. 2015. Sectarianism, Criminalisation and the Civilising Process in Scotland. In *Crime, Justice and Society in Scotland*, ed. Hazel Croall, Gerry Mooney, and Mary Munro, 99–114. London: Routledge.
Law Commission. 2021. Hate Crime Laws: Final Report. Law Com No 402. https://s3-eu-west-2.amazonaws.com/lawcom-prod-storage-11jsxou24uy7q/uploads/2021/12/Hate-crime-report-accessible.pdf. Accessed 10 February 2022.
Maini-Thompson, Sapan. 2022. Is "Perception-Based Recording" for Hate Crime Compatible with Freedom of Speech? *UK Human Rights Blog*, January 28. https://ukhumanrightsblog.com/2022/01/28/is-perception-based-recording-for-hate-crime-compatible-with-freedom-of-speech/. Accessed 10 February 2022.
Mason, Gail. 2014a. Legislating Against Hate. In *The Routledge International Handbook on Hate Crime*, ed. Nathan Hall, Abbee Corb, Paul Giannasi, John G.D. Grieve, and Neville Lawrence, 58–68. London: Routledge.
———. 2014b. The Symbolic Purpose of Hate Crime Law: Ideal Victims and Emotion. *Theoretical Criminology* 18 (1): 75–92.
McPhee, David. 2015. Racism in Scotland Since the Stephen Lawrence Report. *The Scotsman*, October 30. https://www.scotsman.com/news/racism-scotland-stephen-lawrence-report-1491145. Accessed 10 February 2022.
McSmith, Andy. 2014. Ukip's Women Problem: Nigel Farage Manages to Come Across as Sexist – Even While Admitting His Party 'looks a bit blokeish'. *The Independent*, October 9. https://www.independent.co.uk/news/uk/politics/ukip-s-women-problem-nigel-farage-manages-to-come-across-as-sexist-even-while-admitting-his-party-looks-a-bit-blokeish-9781885.html. Accessed 10 February 2022.

Mintchev, Nikolay. 2021. The Cultural Politics of Racism in the Brexit Conjuncture. *International Journal of Cultural Studies* 24 (1): 123–140.

Murray, Rainbow. 2015. UKIP Uses Women's Rights as a Trojan Horse to Attack Minorities. *The Conversation*, April 13. https://theconversation.com/ukip-uses-womens-rights-as-a-trojan-horse-to-attack-minorities-40096. Accessed 10 February 2022.

Nachiappan, Arthi. 2020. Scottish Hate Crime Bill Threatens Free Speech, Free to Disagree Campaign Group Warns. *The Times*, September 12. https://www.thetimes.co.uk/article/hate-crime-bill-threatens-free-speech-free-to-disagree-campaign-group-warns-hvd8pcsvd. Accessed 10 February 2022.

Nicoll, Ruaridh. 2007. From Executive to Government – What's Really in a Name? *The Guardian*, July 22. https://www.theguardian.com/commentisfree/2007/jul/22/scotland.devolution. Accessed 10 February 2022.

Perry, Barbara. 2001. *In the Name of Hate: Understanding Hate Crimes*. London: Routledge.

Piatkowska, Sylwia J., and Brendan Lantz. 2021. Temporal Clustering of Hate Crimes in the Aftermath of the Brexit Vote and Terrorist Attacks: A Comparison of Scotland and England and Wales. *The British Journal of Criminology* 61 (3): 648–669.

Police Scotland. 2020. Justice Committee Hate Crime and Public Order (Scotland) Bill Submission. Scottish Parliament. REF NO. J/S5/30/HC/366. https://archive2021.parliament.scot/S5_JusticeCommittee/Inquiries/JS520HC366_Police_Scotland.pdf. Accessed 10 February 2022.

———. 2021a. Quarter 1 Performance Report: Report April to June 2021/22. https://www.scotland.police.uk/spa-media/uutmvys2/q1-performance-report.pdf. Accessed 10 February 2022.

———. 2021b. Quarter 2 Performance Report: Report July to September 2021/22. https://www.scotland.police.uk/spa-media/oifbto5z/q2-performance-report-ppc.pdf. Accessed 10 February 2022.

Pratt, John, David Brown, Mark Brown, Simon Hallsworth, and Wayne Morrison, eds. 2005. *New Punitiveness: Trends, Theories, Perspectives*. London: Willan Publishing.

Press Association. 2016. Danny Simpson to Miss Out on Leicester Title Celebrations After Curfew Order. *The Guardian*, May 12. https://www.theguardian.com/football/2016/may/12/danny-simpson-leicester-city-curfew-title-celebrations. Accessed 10 February 2022.

Public Prosecution Service for Northern Ireland. 2010. *Hate Crime Policy.* https://www.ppsni.gov.uk/sites/ppsni/files/publications/PPS%20Hate%20Crime%20Policy.pdf. Accessed 10 February 2022.

Ross, Graham. 2009. Offences (Aggravation by Prejudice) (Scotland) Bill: Summary. SPICe. https://archive2021.parliament.scot/S3_Bills/Offences%20(Aggravation%20by%20Prejudice)%20(Scotland)%20Bill/Offencesprejudice.pdf. Accessed 10 February 2022.

Schweppe, Jennifer. 2021. 'What is a hate crime?' *Cogent. Social Sciences* 7 (1) https://doi.org/10.1080/23311886.2021.1902643.

Scotsman Newsroom, The. 2016. Hate Crimes in Scotland 'fell after Brexit vote'. *The Scotsman*, September 22. https://www.scotsman.com/news/politics/hate-crimes-scotland-fell-after-brexit-vote-1466617. Accessed 10 February 2022.

Scott, Kenneth B. 2011. Politics and the Police in Scotland: The Impact of Devolution. *Crime, Law and Social Change* 55: 121–132.

Scott, Kirsty. 2001. A Game of Two Halves. *The Guardian*, May 15. https://www.theguardian.com/world/2001/may/15/gender.uk. Accessed 10 February 2022.

Scottish Executive. 2002. Report of the Cross-Party Working Group on Religious Hatred. http://image.guardian.co.uk/sys-files/Politics/documents/2002/12/05/crosspartyreport.pdf. Accessed 10 February 2022.

———. 2006. Response to the Recommendations of the Working Group on Hate Crime.

Scottish Government. 2016a. A Plan for Scotland: The Government's Programme for Scotland 2016–2017. https://www.gov.scot/binaries/content/documents/govscot/publications/strategy-plan/2016/09/plan-scotland-scottish-governments-programme-scotland-2016-17/documents/00505210-pdf/00505210-pdf/govscot%3Adocument/00505210.pdf. Accessed 10 February 2022.

———. 2016b. Report of the Independent Advisory Group on Hate Crime, Prejudice and Community Cohesion. https://www.gov.scot/publications/report-independent-advisory-group-hate-crime-prejudice-community-cohesion/documents/. Accessed 10 February 2022.

———. 2018a. Independent Review of Hate Crime Legislation in Scotland: Final Report. https://www.gov.scot/binaries/content/documents/govscot/publications/progress-report/2018/05/independent-review-hate-crime-legislation-scotland-final-report/documents/00535892-pdf/00535892-pdf/govscot%3Adocument/00535892.pdf. Accessed 10 February 2022.

———. 2018b. One Scotland: Hate Has No Home Here: Consultation on Amending Scottish Hate Crime Legislation. https://www.gov.scot/publications/one-scotland-hate-home-here-consultation-hate-crime-amending-current-scottish-hate-crime-legislation/pages/1/. Accessed 10 February 2022.

———. 2019a. Developing Information on Hate Crime Recorded by the Police in Scotland. https://www.gov.scot/publications/developing-information-hate-crime-recorded-police-scotland/documents/. Accessed 10 February 2022.

———. 2019b. Protecting Scotland's Future: The Government's Programme for Work 2019–2020. https://www.gov.scot/publications/protecting-scotlands-future-governments-programme-scotland-2019-20/documents/. Accessed 10 February 2022.

———. 2021a. A Study into the Characteristics of Police Recorded Hate Crime in Scotland' February 2021. https://www.gov.scot/publications/study-characteristics-police-recorded-hate-crime-scotland/documents/. Accessed 10 February 2022.

———. 2021b. Hate Crime Bill Passed. https://www.gov.scot/news/hate-crime-bill-passed/. Accessed 10 February 2022.

———. 2021c. Understanding the Nature of Hate Crime. https://www.gov.scot/news/understanding-the-nature-of-hate-crime/. Accessed 10 February 2022.

Scottish National Party. 2007. Manifesto 2007: It's Time. http://news.bbc.co.uk/1/shared/bsp/hi/pdfs/12_04_07_snpmanifesto.pdf. Accessed 10 February 2022.

Scottish Parliament. 2007. Equal Opportunities Committee Report: Equalities in Scotland: A Review of Progress. SP Paper 781. https://archive.parliament.scot/business/committees/equal/reports-07/eor07-03.htm. Accessed 10 February 2022.

———. 2009. Hate Crime Bill Gets Committee Support. https://www.parliament.scot/newsandmediacentre/17086.aspx. Accessed 10 February 2022.

Scottish Parliament Justice Committee. 2009. Stage 1 Report on the Offences (Aggravation by Prejudice) (Scotland) Bill. SP Paper 225. https://archive2021.parliament.scot/S3_JusticeCommittee/Reports/jur09-06.pdf. Accessed 10 February 2022.

Stewart, Catriona. 2021. Sense Over Sectarianism Is Tackling Issue in Glasgow's Schools and Beyond. *Glasgow Evening Times*, May 22. https://www.glasgowtimes.co.uk/news/19321654.sense-sectarianism-tackling-issue-glasgows-schools-beyond/. Accessed 10 February 2022.

Thorp, Arabella, Jane Fiddick, and Edward Wood. 1998. The *Crime and Disorder Bill [HL]*, Bill 167 of 1997–1998: Anti-social Neighbours, Sex Offenders, Racially Motivated Offences and Sentencing Drug-Dependent Offenders. House of Commons Library, Research Paper 98/44. https://researchbriefings.files.parliament.uk/documents/RP98-44/RP98-44.pdf. Accessed 10 February 2022.

UK Independence Party. 2010. *Restoring Britishness: A Cultural Policy for an Independent Britain*. UKIP.

Wade, Mike. 2022. Police Struggle to Cope as New Hate Crime Law Leads to Surge in Reports. *The Times*, January 21. https://www.thetimes.co.uk/article/police-struggle-to-cope-as-new-hate-crime-law-leads-to-surge-in-reports-rhnv7jp6k?shareToken=8646e8073d4db6f5d076fd7439337d26. Accessed 10 February 2022.

Walters, Mark A., Rupert Brown, and Susann Wiedlitzka. 2016. Research Report 102: Causes and Motivations of Hate Crime. Equality and Human Rights Commission. https://www.equalityhumanrights.com/sites/default/files/research-report-102-causes-and-motivations-of-hate-crime.pdf. Accessed 10 February 2022.

Weaver, Matthew. 2016. 'Horrible spike' in Hate Crime Linked to Brexit Vote, Met Police Say. *The Guardian*, September 28. https://www.theguardian.com/society/2016/sep/28/hate-crime-horrible-spike-brexit-vote-metropolitan-police. Accessed 10 February 2022.

Wong, Kevin, Kris Christmann, Michelle Rogerson, and Neil Monk. 2020. Reality Versus Rhetoric: Assessing the Efficacy of Third-Party Hate Crime Reporting Centres. *International Review of Victimology* 26 (1): 79–95.

Working Group on Hate Crime. 2004. Working Group on Hate Crime Report. Scottish Executive. https://www.hatecrimescotland.org/wp/wp-content/uploads/2014/08/Scottish-Working-Group-on-Hate-Crime-Report-2004.pdf. Accessed 10 February 2022.

4

Gender and Hate: A Scottish Perspective

4.1 Introduction

We have the opportunity to do something different, substantial and meaningful in relation to the abuse that women suffer day and daily. I have to ask myself the question: what is the point of pursuing the same legislative approach that we have seen decade after decade? That approach has not produced any better results for women; it has not delivered for women.[1] (Annabelle Ewing MSP (SNP))

Silence is no longer an option. We can no longer afford to pick and choose what forms of prejudice and hate we will stand up against. Most crucially of all, we must find allies. We must not think that the solution is talking only to people with whom we identify. We must build alliances with people who are subject to all forms of prejudice and hate. We must come together to root it out of our society, politics, public discourse and communities around the country.[2] (Anas Sarwar MSP (Scottish Labour))

---

[1] Scottish Parliament (2021b, Annabelle Ewing).

[2] Meeting of the Scottish Parliament, 28 March 2019, Official Report, col. 37.

K. Barker, O. Jurasz, *Violence Against Women, Hate and Law*, Palgrave Hate Studies,
https://doi.org/10.1007/978-3-030-99375-7_4

As demonstrated in Chap. 3, proposals to include gender within hate crime frameworks are far from new—yet, such discussions reoccur regularly, not only in Scotland but also in England and Wales, always attracting a significant level of controversy. In Scotland alone, the issue of whether to include sex and/or gender within the legal framework of hate crime has been on the agenda for nearly two decades. The debate(s) over the inclusion or exclusion of gender within hate crime contexts seems to reappear with alarming regularity, but—to date—to no avail.

Scotland is currently emerging from its most recent attempt to modernise its hate crime framework and to reflect—thus far unsuccessfully—women's experiences within in. This chapter traces recent developments in bringing the 'women's perspective' to hate crime reform in Scotland. Building on the history of hate crime outlined in Chap. 3, we explore five years of attempted policy and law reform, starting from Lord Bracadale's Review, through the One Scotland Consultation to the passing of the Hate Crime and Public Order (Scotland) Act 2021 (asp 14) (HCPOA 2021) and, latterly, the Working Group on Misogyny and Criminal Justice in Scotland.

4.2 Hate (Re)defined and Gender Perspectives

> I always thought I don't care how someone becomes a woman or a man; it does not matter to me. It is just part of their specificity, their uniqueness, like everyone else's. Anybody who identifies as a woman, wants to be a woman, is going around being a woman, as far as I'm concerned, is a woman.[3] (Catharine A. MacKinnon)

It is astounding to witness the levels of controversy surrounding the proposed expansion of the hate crime framework to include gender. This is even more so given that transphobic hate (or, to be more accurate, the protected characteristic of 'transgender identity') has already been

[3] Williams (n.d.: https://www.transadvocate.com/sex-gender-and-sexuality-the-transadvocate-interviews-catharine-a-mackinnon_n_15037.htm).

successfully incorporated within the legal frameworks in Scotland as well as in England and Wales. The notion of 'gender' then, albeit in a specific category (i.e. 'transgender'), has already been successfully reflected within the law. Nonetheless, proposals to include sex and/or gender in hate crime frameworks in Scotland were met with a significant degree of polarisation amongst society, but particularly so, within some women's groups. The key issues dividing the groups were the impact of gender self-identification and Gender Recognition Act reform in Scotland on the use—or alleged abuse—of the hate crime protections. These deeply divisive and heated debates have been a permanent feature of the last five years of attempts to reform the hate crime framework in Scotland and—as we argue later in this chapter—are likely to continue against a background of proposals to create a stand-alone offence of misogynistic harassment.

4.2.1 Why Gender, Not Sex

Hate crime is heavily rooted in societal prejudice as well as perceptions—those held by the victim, other persons—including bystanders—and the perpetrator. However, an important caveat to the position presented here is that, as we argue in Chap. 1, hate crime discourse does not offer an explanation for all forms of VAW. Not all VAW is hateful and/or misogynistic by default. Whilst some acts of VAW are motivated by the hatred of women because they are women (or perceived as women), the motives of the perpetrators of VAW vary.[4] We argue that adopting the socially constructed meaning of being a 'woman' ('gender') rather than one based on biology ('sex') within the hate crime framework provides for a more adequate capturing of factors leading up to the commission of a hate crime perpetrated 'against a woman because she is a woman.'

Prejudice towards women, and its rampant survival throughout centuries, is socially conditioned: its pernicious livelihood is maintained by gender stereotypes, structural inequality and systematic discrimination of women, as well as unequal power relations. The intersecting complexity

---

[4] Hamberger et al. (1997); Roberts (2021).

of these phenomena is strengthened by other factors, such as race, religion, class, economic status or geopolitical locations (to name a few) which—when combined—are reflected in targeted violence and abuse towards women because they are *perceived* to be socially positioned as 'women.' For instance, as noted by Mason-Bish and Zempi, street harassment of Muslim women wearing a veil is an example of using harassment as means of punishment of "women who participate in the street for not performing gender appropriately."[5] In this example, women are targeted not merely because they are perceived by the perpetrator to be 'women' but because of the broader connotations associated with the expected manner in which women's gender roles are performed (or not). In this context, it is not inconceivable that gender-based hate can be perpetrated against women (especially those who break social mores) by other women—for example, to enforce certain culturally conditioned perceptions of 'womanhood'—therefore subverting somewhat the preconditioned assumption that gender-based hate requires a male perpetrator and a female victim. Zempi and Chakraborti demonstrate that women who do not wear a veil are equally subject to street harassment,[6] even from other women, albeit, as argued by Davis, "[w]omen's comments directed toward other women are not situated in the same place of power as are men's comments."[7] The aforementioned example is an illustration of a combination of gender-based and Islamophobic hate which plays out in this particular scenario of street harassment. Nonetheless, it illustrates a broader point about gender (and the associated perceptions of what is expected/involved in performing one's gender role) rather than sex being a driver behind some instances of violence perpetrated against women. It also emphasises the issue of perceptions as contributory to the commission of a hate crime. Similarly, acts of violence perpetrated against women by incels are not simply about men's frustration with their 'involuntarily celibate' status. To the contrary, incels' expressions of hate towards women are driven by an extreme belief in women's inferiority to men, as well as their subservient status with sex and extreme violence against them used

[5] Mason-Bish and Zempi (2019, p. 556).

[6] Zempi and Chakraborti (2014).

[7] Davis (1994, p. 139).

as a method of punishment. The power aspect is mirrored in the words of Elliot Rodger, an "incel hero"[8] responsible for the 2014 Isla Vista attacks in California:

> I will slaughter every single spoiled stuck-up blonde slut.... You will finally see I'm the superior one. The true alpha male.[9]

As such, it is the gender/power relations rather than either biologically determined sex or a physical appearance as 'female' that lies at the heart of extreme misogyny, as encapsulated in the aforementioned example. Similarly, the perpetrator's *perception* that a victim is a woman also rests entirely in the extreme misogynistic beliefs (and values) that breed the hatred captured in such behaviours. Despite increased recognition that this is the case, the law in Scotland (and in other jurisdictions) largely fails to follow suit. Whilst the addition of gender to the hate crime framework would not work as a panacea for this deeply entrenched societal prejudice, it may nonetheless signal the societal recognition of the role of gender in perpetration of hate crime.

Furthermore, applying the lens of 'gender' to hate crime also allows it to reflect that power relations and the positioning of women within society are far from stagnant—they vary, change and fluctuate depending on a number of factors and contexts, including those that are geopolitical in nature. Albeit not regarding hate crime, Hunter remarked that

> The reforms that changed women's legal rights, the vote, equal pay, legal abortions, may have been hard fought for, but they were often conceded more to satisfy other fancied needs of the country than women's emancipation. Thus nurseries are provided during war to allow women into the factories, contraception becomes available when governments worry about overpopulation, and equal pay is sought by male trade unionists anxious about women undercutting their wages. It is not that the reforms we have won are not worthwhile in themselves. Yet they do not necessarily reflect a real change in attitude towards women's "role". [...] History has a tendency not only to give things away when it is easy to do so, but it also takes them

[8] BBC News (2018).

[9] The Fifth Estate (2019).

> back again when they are no longer convenient to those in control, the employers, the government and men.[10]

This give-take away dichotomy finds reflections in contemporary history too—for instance, illustrated by the regression in women's rights and a rise in VAW following the Arab Spring despite women's active and equal participation during the revolutions in the Middle East.[11] As such, the societal perceptions—including men's perceptions—of what is or is not associated with 'being a woman' or a woman's role in society are also subject to change (in either direction). These changing perceptions are likely to be reflected in prejudices which inform/motivate hate crime—something that a fixed category of 'sex' is unlikely to satisfactorily capture. Interestingly, the 2020 Report by Galop showed that even within the category of transphobic hate, the majority of transphobic incidents have been committed against respondents who identified as female/women/femme[12]—once again pointing towards one's perceived gender rather than biological sex as influencing the experiences of hate.

Importantly, prejudice related to the perception of the victim by the perpetrator is crucial to considerations of gender and hate crime. The actual identity of the victim—or whether or not the victim actually belongs to the protected group/has a protected characteristic—is irrelevant to the determination of hate crime. Rather, the emphasis lies on the motivation of the perpetrator which is likely informed by long-held prejudices. Consequently, "the person does not have to be a member of the social group being targeted by the perpetrator to be the victim of a hate crime"[13]—a matter also clarified in *R (Miller) v. The College of Policing*:

> A victim of a hate crime or incident does not have to be a member of a minority group or someone who is generally considered to be vulnerable. For example, a heterosexual man who is abused leaving a gay bar may well perceive that the abuse is motivated by hostility based on sexual orientation

[10] Hunter (1979, p. 1).

[11] Jurasz (2013).

[12] Bradley (2020, p. 7).

[13] Scottish Government (2021, p. 6).

although he himself is not gay. Anyone can be a victim of a hate incident or crime.[14]

Therefore, it is ultimately the perpetrator's perception of a victim as a 'woman' that is the determinative factor in gender-based hate.[15]

Proponents of the inclusion of 'sex' rather than 'gender' in hate crime legislation frequently rely on the Equality Act 2010[16] to support their approach which is now also reflected in the Scottish Government's position on this issue.[17] It is nonetheless curious for the Scottish Government to adopt this position given its parallel commitment and efforts to incorporate CEDAW into Scots Law. The CEDAW Committee has repeatedly interpreted VAW to be gender-based (rather than sex-based), including recognition that "the *opinio juris* and State practice suggest that the prohibition of gender-based violence against women has evolved into a principle of customary international law."[18] Given Scotland's expressed ambitions for the incorporation of CEDAW as well as the prominence of CEDAW's norms across a number of Scottish Government's policies concerning VAW (not least, *Equally Safe*), it is surprising that the terminology of gender was abandoned without even as much as a debate of that aspect during the passage of the HCPOA 2021 in the Scottish Parliament.

4.2.2 Gender and Hate Crime: Challenges and Opportunities

As we argue elsewhere, the addition of 'gender' to the hate crime framework in Scotland, but also in England and Wales, is long overdue,

---

[14] *R (Miller) v. The College of Policing* [2021] EWCA Civ. 1926 [16] at (vi) (quoting the Revised Guidance).

[15] The issue of the perception of a victim applies equally to other characteristics. For example, attacking a heterosexual person leaving a gay bar or directing Islamophobic abuse at a non-Muslim person.

[16] Equality Act 2010, s. 11 mentions 'sex' as a protected characteristic. In contrast, 'gender' appears under protected characteristics only in relation to 'gender reassignment'; see ibid., s. 7.

[17] Scottish Government (2020).

[18] Committee on the Elimination of Discrimination against Women (2017, para. 2).

resulting "in the production of an incomplete picture and knowledge concerning hate crime and its gender dimension."[19] This is not only for symbolic reasons[20] or to achieve party with other protected characteristics[21] but, more importantly, to ensure visibility of gender-based hate within the law, especially in the relevant cases involving VAW. For Maher et al., extending protected characteristics to include gender has the symbolic value of illuminating "systematic and underpinning social attitudes in relation to everyday violence against women" and "for gendered hate to become more visible, more readily contested and, ultimately, less acceptable."[22] The latter is important, although, as emphasised in Chap. 1, the view taken here is that not all VAW is motivated by hate and the law should not assume this position as default. However, in instances where an act of VAW is motivated by gender-based hate—or where it is perceived as such—there ought to be appropriate legal avenues to enable this recognition, also at sentencing. That said, this approach should not overshadow the pressing need to address the problem of VAW in law and policy, nor should it in any way lead to decreases in the governmental budgetary commitments to tackle VAW.

More crucially, however, the inclusion of gender within hate crime would acknowledge the gendered nature of a range of harms arising from gender-based hate crimes. In general, there is a conceptual deficit in how harms arising from gender-based abuse and VAW—hateful or not—are judicially and legally recognised.[23] Whilst there is an overwhelming acceptance of physical harms associated with VAW, the recognition of non-physical aspects of harms is still lacking. This includes participatory harms in the form of limited participation of women in the public sphere (for example, resulting from the impact of street harassment[24] or online violence against women (OVAW), including online misogynistic abuse[25]) as well as the wider societal harms of the normalisation of VAW. The former is captured in what Iganski and Lagou refer to as

[19] Barker and Jurasz (2019b, p. 101).
[20] Mason (2014).
[21] Choundas (1995, p. 1072).
[22] Maher et al. (2015, pp. 192–193).
[23] Barker and Jurasz (2021d, pp. 256–259).
[24] Mason-Bish and Zempi (2019).
[25] Barker and Jurasz (2021a, pp. 540–541); Barker and Jurasz (2021c, p. 57).

"behavioural injury"[26] resulting in the change of behaviour of the hate crime victim to avoid future victimisation. This notion is closely related to concerns expressed by Vera Grey and Kelly in their work on women and street harassment, which demonstrated that women continuously alter their behaviours and trade their freedoms for safety[27] when in public spaces—especially in the streets and on public transport. Furthermore, extending the scope of the protected characteristics to include gender would enable—albeit to a small extent—recognition of the intersectional nature of hate crime, where it involves gender and one or multiple other characteristics. This feature is currently obscured in that the legal framework on hate crime "turns a blind eye to the variety of characteristics (outside those already deemed as 'protected') which contribute to the complex nature of the identity of many of the hate crime victims."[28] This point was aptly highlighted by Diane Abbott MP (Labour) who publicly emphasised that the alarming volumes of abuse she has been receiving as a black *and* female politician are both racist *and* sexist.[29] However, the criminal justice system still lags behind the social reality of hate crime and its often intersectional nature in that it allows the victims to officially 'tick' only one protected characteristic—even if that is not the case in their lived experience of hate crime. As such, by such favouring legalistic (over) simplicity and 'neatness,' the criminal justice system ignores the fact that "identity is messy [and] it is time for hate crime policy to better acknowledge this."[30]

4.3 Gender and Hate: Regulatory Lacuna

Following the recommendation of Independent Advisory Group on Hate Crime, Prejudice and Community Cohesion to the Scottish Government to reassess "whether the existing criminal law provides sufficient protections for those who may be at risk of hate crime, for example based on

[26] Iganski and Lagou (2014, p. 43).
[27] Vera-Grey (2018).
[28] Barker and Jurasz (2019b, p. 102).
[29] Sylvester and Thomson (2018).
[30] Mason-Bish (2014, p. 31).

gender,"[31] the key step in reviving the long-standing question over the inclusion of gender-based hate in the Scottish hate crime framework was Lord Bracadale's Review of Hate Crime Legislation in Scotland. The Bracadale Review was announced on 26 January 2017[32] with the remit to review whether the law in Scotland should be clarified and harmonised, and whether additional protected groups should be included. In his Review, Lord Bracadale specifically sought views on whether new categories of hate crime should be created that would be inclusive of gender[33] as well as considering the term 'misogyny' in the context of hate crime.[34] In doing so, Lord Bracadale reflected the findings of the research report associated with the Review, which stipulated that gender (alongside age) is one of the two characteristics most commonly appearing in other jurisdictions but which, thus far, have been absent in Scots Law.[35]

Following a period of wide public consultation,[36] Lord Bracadale reported the results of his review on 31 May 2018. The Bracadale Review recommended that a statutory aggravation related to gender (gender hostility) be introduced. In Lord Bracadale's view,

> where an offence is committed, and it is proved that the offence was motivated by hostility based on gender, or the offender demonstrates hostility towards the victim based on gender during, or immediately before or after, the commission of the offence, it would be recorded as aggravated by gender hostility. The court would be required to state that fact on conviction and take it into account when sentencing.[37]

The recommendation reflected the overall view from the consultation responses. These opinions "did not demonstrate any clear consensus on the general principle of extending hate crime legislation, [showed] strong

[31] Scottish Government (2016, p. 18).

[32] Meeting of the Scottish Parliament, 26 January 2017, Official Report, col. 49.

[33] Scottish Government (2017, pp. 2 and 62).

[34] Scottish Government (2018a, para. 4.12).

[35] Chalmers and Leverick (2017).

[36] A total of 356 responses to the Consultation were received, with consent to be made public. The actual number of responses is likely higher: seehttps://consult.gov.scot/hate-crime/independent-review-of-hate-crime-legislation/consultation/published_select_respondent.

[37] Scottish Government (2018a, p. vii: Recommendation 9).

support among both individual and organisational respondents for some kind of provision relating to gender or misogyny."[38] The Report also touched upon, though very slightly, the contested issue of terminology of 'sex' vs 'gender' used in the context of hate crime reform. Lord Bracadale's rationale was very simple: "I have used the term 'gender' rather than 'sex' throughout this part, because that is the term used by most (though not all) organisations and consultation respondents."[39] However, the argument went further, invoking a human-rights-based approach:

> I have carefully considered the arguments whether an aggravation should apply to all forms of gender hostility, or whether it should be 'one-way' and only cover hostility or malice and ill-will towards women. Although I agree that the essence of the conduct which we are seeking to cover is usually against women, it is not inconceivable that there could be hostility against a man (or non-binary person) based on their gender. I have some concern that an approach which focused only on hostility towards women would risk stereotyping (all) men as perpetrators and (all) women as victims, which I do not consider to be an accurate or helpful message. A human rights-based approach suggests that having a consistent approach which is capable of applying in equivalent cases, regardless of the sex of the victim, is better.[40]

Whilst this approach can be appreciated, it appears to have been a missed opportunity to take a more informed, elaborate and firm position on this highly debated issue and its remit within hate crime legislation. The outcomes of such analysis would most certainly cause huge controversy (irrespective of the position taken), but it would have nonetheless allowed for a more detailed legal analysis of the issue, potentially also moving away from a singular focus on the Equality Act 2010 characteristics (and, therefore, the category of 'sex').

The conclusion of the Bracadale Review irrespective of this (intended) oversight caused controversy enough, especially given that it went against the views and suggestions expressed by key women's and equality

[38] Ibid., paras. 4.13–4.14 and 4.17.

[39] Ibid., para.4.11.

[40] Ibid., para.4.43.

organisations in Scotland. In a joint statement, Rape Crisis Scotland, Scottish Women's Aid and Engender said:

> We think the recommendations put forward in this report do not pay enough attention to international experience and evidence. Other nations and states have found that simply adding gender to a laundry-list of groups protected by hate crime legislation leads to underreporting, under-investigation, and under-prosecution.[41]

The organisations expressed further disappointment and concern over the absence of recommendations that would meaningfully tackle misogyny and misogynistic hate and harassment in Scotland. In part, this disappointment was palpable because of the lived experience of a long-standing misogynistic society (see Chap. 2) but more especially in light of recommendations from Engender to create a "standalone misogynistic hate offence as a way of disrupting epidemic levels of misogynistic hate in schools, in the workplace, on city streets, and online."[42]

This sentiment was supported by Scottish Labour who also expressed disappointment over "the lack of a recommendation for a specific law against misogyny."[43] Interestingly, at that point, the then Communities Minister Annabelle Ewing indicated that whilst Lord Bracadale's Report would be used as a basis for the Scottish Government's future work to consolidate hate crime legislation in Scotland,[44] there was less support for creation of a stand-alone offence.[45]

Ultimately, the Scottish Government departed from the earlier position of relying on Lord Bracadale's recommendations amidst concerns from a number of women's groups as to whether "the hate crime framework provides an appropriate model for dealing with gender-based violence."[46] It is an interesting development, especially given the lack of clarity on what 'model' entails here. At a basic level, the model could

[41] Engender (2018).
[42] Ibid.
[43] Davidson (2018).
[44] Brooks (2018).
[45] Barker and Jurasz (2020a); Barker and Jurasz (2021b).
[46] Scottish Government (2020).

comprise of existing and/or future criminal law provisions capturing VAW to which a statutory aggravation based on gender (as a proposed protected characteristic) could be added. However, as noted by Lord Bracadale, this approach would not apply to all offences concerning VAW, especially where offences are quite focused/specific and have a clear 'gender element,' such as, for example, FGM, forced marriage and the sexual offences under the Sexual Offences (Scotland) Act 2009 (asp 9).[47] In Lord Bracadale's opinion, in such cases:

> [t]he nature of the conduct is clear from the offence itself and so an aggravation is not necessary to provide clarity in the offender's record or inform any subsequent criminal justice intervention. The offences implicitly involve the concept of gender, are already treated very seriously by society so the penalties imposed reflect this. It might therefore be concluded that there is no need to send an additional 'message' through hate crime legislation that the conduct is unacceptable.[48]

It is therefore difficult to see how this would undermine the existing approach of the legal system to deal with VAW. The offences dealing with VAW sit outside the hate crime framework—hence, if there are concerns over their appropriateness in capturing the essence, motives, root causes of VAW or justice to the victims, they are to do with Scots criminal law/ criminal justice system but separate from hate crime. In such cases—to put it somewhat bluntly—the 'only' practical element that is different is the fact that upon prosecution of the offence involving VAW as a hate crime, higher sentencing is possible and so is symbolic recognition—through official case records—that a crime was motivated by gender. What would, however, be inappropriate is the suggestion that all cases involving VAW *should* be viewed as hate crime, as this approach would likely detract focus from the complex nature of VAW, which is not always motivated by gender-based hate.

Despite a clear recommendation in the Bracadale Report, the Scottish Government proceeded to introduce a further consultation on the matter

[47] Scottish Government (2018a, para. 4.31).

[48] Ibid., para. 4.33.

of hate crime reform in Scotland. The *One Scotland: Hate Has No Home Here* consultation was launched in November 2018.[49] Following a number of issues raised by Bracadale Report, the government sought further views on the aspects of gender and the hate crime framework, including questions concerning a statutory aggravation for gender[50] as well as a proposal for a stand-alone offence of misogynistic harassment.[51]

Unsurprisingly, the consultation respondents were divided on this matter, with no clear consensus reached. However, the analysis of responses to questions concerning gender revealed a certain pattern. Responses from organisations were generally in favour of the statutory aggravation model for gender, whereas third-sector organisations in Scotland "with specialist expertise in women's issues"[52] favoured the option to create a stand-alone offence of misogynistic harassment over that of a statutory aggravation. Despite the fact that only eight third-sector organisations expressed a definitive 'no' answer to the proposal for a statutory aggravation for gender hostility, the Scottish Government ultimately decided not to include such provision in the Hate Crime and Public Order (Scotland) Bill 2020,[53] reflecting the majority view (see Fig. 4.1) expressed amongst individual respondents (64%).

In contrast, the Scottish Government did not follow the same approach where the question of misogynistic harassment was concerned. With the exception of the public sector, the vast majority of respondents (76%) were either unsure or negative about the proposal to create a stand-alone offence of misogynistic harassment (see Fig. 4.2 below). Only 29% of third-sector organisations expressed clear support for the creation of the offence, although more generally, "respondents in favour of a standalone offence of misogynistic harassment generally made the point that this option was favoured by organisations with specialist expertise in this area."[54] The opponents of this approach drew attention to the problematic use

[49] Scottish Government (2018b).

[50] Ibid., p. 13.

[51] Ibid., p. 17.

[52] Scottish Government (2019, p. 34).

[53] This position was maintained when the Hate Crime and Public Order (Scotland) Act 2021 (asp 14) (HCPOA 2021) was enacted in April 2021.

[54] Ibid., p. 40.

Table 6.1: Q7 – Do you agree with Option A to develop a statutory aggravation for gender hostility?

	Yes		No		Unsure		Total	
Respondent type	n	%	n	%	n	%	n	%
Third sector organisations	13	43%	8	27%	9	30%	30	100%
Public sector / partnerships	18	82%	3	14%	1	5%	22	100%
Faith groups	3	38%	5	63%	–	0%	8	100%
Other organisations	7	78%	1	11%	1	20%	9	100%
Total organisations	**41**	**59%**	**17**	**25%**	**11**	**16%**	**69**	**100%**
Total individuals	108	23%	300	64%	64	14%	472	100%
Total (organisations and individuals)	**149**	**28%**	**317**	**59%**	**75**	**14%**	**541**	**100%**

Percentages may not total 100% due to rounding.

Fig. 4.1 Responses to *One Scotland* Consultation Paper on whether to develop a statutory aggravation based on gender hostility (Scottish Government (2019, p. 36).)

Table 6.2: Q8 – Do you agree with Option B to develop a standalone offence for misogynistic harassment?

	Yes		No		Unsure		Total	
Respondent type	n	%	n	%	n	%	n	%
Third sector organisations	9	29%	7	23%	15	48%	31	100%
Public sector / partnerships	6	26%	9	39%	8	35%	23	100%
Faith groups	–	0%	7	100%	–	0%	7	100%
Other organisations	3	38%	3	38%	2	25%	8	100%
Total organisations	**18**	**26%**	**26**	**38%**	**25**	**36%**	**69**	**100%**
Total individuals	108	23%	281	61%	73	16%	462	100%
Total (organisations and individuals)	**126**	**24%**	**307**	**58%**	**98**	**18%**	**531**	**100%**

Percentages may not total 100% due to rounding.

Fig. 4.2 Responses to *One Scotland* Consultation Paper on whether to develop a stand-alone offence for misogynistic harassment (Scottish Government (2019, p. 40).)

of terms 'misogyny'/'misogynistic,' which "was too broad to be of practical use for the purposes of establishing a criminal offence, since it included both criminal and non-criminal behaviour"[55] as well as conceptual discomfort (Figs. 4.3 & 4.4) in using the concept of misogyny as the underpinning cause of all crimes of violence against women.[56]

---

[55] Ibid., p. 42.

[56] Ibid. See also Barker and Jurasz (2019a).

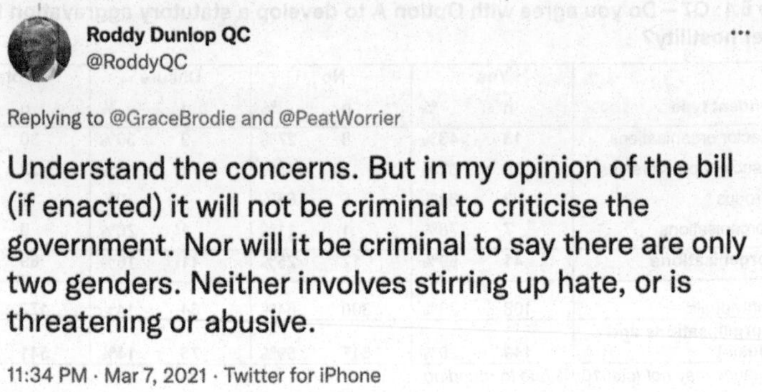

Fig. 4.3 A tweet from Roddy Dunlop QC (Twitter (2021b: @RoddyQC, 7 March 2021, 11:34 pm).)

Fig. 4.4 Tweets by Kate Joester and Patrick Harvie (Twitter (2021a: @patrickharvie, 4 March 2021, 5:26 pm).)

Interestingly, however, the Scottish Government's approach towards the use of terminology of sex/gender in *One Scotland* aligned with that of Lord Bracadale, stating that "for ease of consistency of references with Lord Bracadale's report, this consultation paper takes the same approach to the use of the term 'gender as opposed to 'sex' as is taken in the report."[57]

[57] Scottish Government (2018b, p. 14).

Nonetheless, this approach would be departed from in the next (albeit not yet final) crucial step in the saga of amending hate crime legislation in Scotland: the drafting and passage of the Hate Crime and Public Order (Scotland) Bill 2020.

4.4 The Legacy of Failure: Hate Crime Act 2021

> Of course, legislation will not change attitudes on its own but it can do two things. First, clearly-defined hate crime legislation and well-developed procedures in the criminal justice system to deal with it will increase awareness of hate crime and give victims more confidence that it will be taken seriously by the police, prosecutors and the courts. Secondly, it can contribute to attitudinal change." Lord Bracadale[58]

On 23 April 2020, the Scottish Government introduced the Hate Crime and Public Order (Scotland) Bill. It was a long-awaited piece of legislation, culminating from the Bracadale Review and One Scotland consultation. However, despite the high hopes that were held for the Bill to take a pioneering approach to gender and hate crime, the result was crushing for supporters of the introduction of gender into the hate crime framework in Scotland. The Bill became law—the Hate Crime and Public Order (Scotland) Act 2021 (asp 14)—on 23 April 2021, passed by a vote of 82 for 32 against, with 4 abstentions.

Since its early days—when introduced as a Bill—the (now) HCPOA has proved contentious and even been described as the "most controversial in the Scottish Parliament's history."[59] This is not only because of the gender/sex tensions and polarisation of the debate on that aspect of the proposed law, but also due to concerns about it having a chilling effect on the freedom of expression.[60] In particular, criticism has been raised concerning stirring up offences, especially in relation to what is considered as

[58] Scottish Government (2018a, p. ii).

[59] Merson (2021).

[60] Joyce (2021).

"abusive or threatening" by a "reasonable" person and how these thresholds will be interpreted, for example, alongside the (then) proposed gender amendments.

For Hunter Blackburn, the two issues—gender and freedom of expression—combined prompted a concern "in relation to issues around sex and gender identity, and the risk of furthering chilling effects in an area of debate that people are already afraid to enter."[61] This view was reinforced during the stage 3 debate on the Bill, with Elaine Smith MSP (Labour) noting that "the Government's amendments will not be enough to prevent the chilling effect on women's ability to discuss and debate their rights."[62]

The resulting passage of the Bill was far from smooth, with an outstanding number of proposed amendments, lengthy debates and delays to the vote.[63] It is fair to say that it is relatively rare to see a piece of legislation attracting such wide and long-lasting critique—from politicians, law makers, third-sector organisations, religious organisations, the general public, but also famous public figures such as Val McDermid and Peter Tatchell.[64] The early draft of the Bill was criticised by the Law Society of Scotland for having a perceived low threshold for prosecution of stirring up offences,[65] whilst the Scottish Police Federation expressed concerns over the "policing of speech" should the Bill be passed.[66]

The most heated aspect of the debate, however, was the one surrounding issues of sex/gender. Johann Lamont MSP (Labour) tabled a series of amendments to the Bill which prompted the debate on various aspects of the sex/gender incorporation into the hate crime framework as well as sex/gender more generally. In particular, Lamont sought incorporation of 'sex' as a protected characteristic, therefore enabling recognition of a statutory aggravation based on sex, alongside clarification within the Bill that

[61] Blackburn (2021).

[62] Scottish Parliament (2021b, Elaine Smith).

[63] Davidson (2021).

[64] Sutherland (2020).

[65] Law Society of Scotland (2020, p. 14).

[66] Stevenson (2020).

there are only two sexes.[67] Lamont saw it as paramount to ensure that the Bill offered clarity on the meaning of 'woman' as a 'female of any age' and 'man' as a 'male of any age,'[68] reflecting the meaning of sex under the Equality Act 2010.[69] Lamont's amendments were not without controversy—whilst they attracted support from some MSPs (e.g., Joan McAlpine MSP (SNP) who decided to vote against the government's whip to support Lamont's amendment), others objected to the proposed amendments in a strong fashion, including Patrick Harvie MSP (Scottish Greens) who accused Lamont of "vicious transphobia."[70] Given Harvie's pivotal role in securing hate crime reform between 2007 and 2009, particularly in relation to transgender identity characteristics, this criticism was notable. The tension evident in Harvie-Lamont exchange is an illustration of how deeply divisive the sex/gender debate in the context of hate crime is, with Joan McAlpine referring to it as "polarised, but [...] dynamic and changing"[71] and the then co-leader of the Scottish Green's, Andy Wightman, resigning from the party amidst

> the intolerance shown by some party members to an open and mature dialogue about the tensions and conflicts around questions of sex and gender in the context of transgender rights and women's rights.[72]

McAlpine continued to critique the Bill, especially the notion of a 'reasonable person' in light of this challenge:

> The bill's "reasonable person" safeguard is welcome and will work well in most instances, but it will not work where views are polarised. In particular, the debate around women's rights and trans identity means that views that might be considered inoffensive and factual by some people will be perceived as hateful and abusive by others.[73]

---

[67] Scottish Parliament (2021a: Group 1: Characteristic of sex (Johann Lamont); amendment 11B (Johann Lamont)).

[68] Ibid., amendment 17 (Johann Lamont).

[69] Scottish Parliament (2021b, Johann Lamont).

[70] Ibid.

[71] Ibid., Joan McAlpine.

[72] Wightman (2020).

[73] Scottish Parliament (2021b, Joan McAlpine).

Disappointingly, despite the Bill debate palaver, there are no apparent 'winners' as no substantive amendments regarding sex/gender were legislated for explicitly. The HCPOA 2021 went in the opposite direction to the Bracadale Report in that a gender aggravation was not introduced. However, the HCPOA 2021 also failed to incorporate an aggravation based on sex making it clear that—no matter the views on sex/gender—the issue of capturing hate directed against women because they are women has been parked, once again. Instead, the term 'variations in sex characteristics'[74] was incorporated into the Act, with an aim of departing from the use of 'intersex.'[75] Given the indecisiveness of the Scottish Parliament in taking a position on the sex/gender amendments to—what appeared to be—a major piece of legislation modernising and consolidating the hate crime framework in Scotland, a rather curious feature of the Act is the "power to add the characteristic of sex" in Section 12. As explained in the Policy Memorandum:

> The enabling power provides flexibility to allow sex to be included as an additional characteristic to the hate crime legislative framework at a later date and to define that characteristic. This power could therefore be used, at a later date, to extend the scope of the statutory aggravation in Part 1 of the Bill so that it also applies in relation to characteristic of sex and/or to extend the scope of the offences of stirring up hatred in section 3(2) and 5(2) of the Bill so that one or both also apply in relation to this characteristic.[76]

In reaching this decision, significant reliance was placed on the then newly convened Working Group on Criminal Justice and Misogyny in Scotland, chaired by Baroness Helena Kennedy QC:

> Recognising that there is a clear need to tackle misogyny and gender based prejudice in Scotland, the Scottish Government is committed, in principle, to developing a standalone offence on misogynistic harassment and is establishing a Working Group to take this work forward. Provision is also

[74] HCPOA 2021, s. 1(2)(g).

[75] Scottish Parliament (2020, para. 204).

[76] Ibid., para. 241.

included in this Bill for an enabling power to allow the characteristic of sex to be added to the hate crime legislative framework at a later date, after the Bill has passed if this is, for example, recommended by the Working Group.[77]

Whilst at the time of writing this book, the Working Group has not reported its final conclusions, the Policy Memorandum on the Bill has assumed that it is likely to be sex rather than gender that may be added in the future. This in itself is presumptuous of the direction that the Working Group could (or would) take and somewhat puts in question the extent to which the Working Group has taken a truly independent and evidence-informed approach to their work/recommendations. It remains curious as to why, given neither sex nor gender was explicitly included in Section 1(2) or elsewhere in the Act, Section 12 provides powers of adding only the characteristic of sex instead of retaining the flexibility to introduce sex and/or gender.

What has become apparent throughout the process of passing HCPOA 2021 is that the creation of the Working Group provided a 'way out' for the Scottish Parliament to avoid taking a position on one of the most controversial issues debated today. The pertinent question is: for how long, and to what end?

As we note elsewhere, "It seems that not only has the legislative and parliamentary appetite to address gender-based prejudice fallen away, but misconceptions around hate crime will continue to persist."[78] Whilst the Working Group is expected to provide a long-awaited clarification of the definitional scope of 'misogyny' and the proposal to create a stand-alone offence of misogynistic harassment, it is naive to assume that this would end the polarising debate that has been dominating hate crime reform conversations in Scotland but also south of the border. The proposal to create an offence of misogynistic harassment sooner or later will bring back the sex/gender debate, especially in relation to the adopted *legal* meaning of misogyny and its implications. For example, it is likely that a question of transmisogyny would need to be presumably addressed. As such, the lack of clear legislative positioning of sex/gender within the

[77] Ibid., para. 240.

[78] Barker and Jurasz (2020b).

HCPOA 2021 has only postponed the inevitable and complex conversations about a controversial societal challenge that Scottish politicians and broader society are yet to resolve.

Ultimately, the Scottish Government has failed to put to bed the question of gender within the hate crime framework. It has also failed to meaningfully address the issue of hate crime reform in Scotland beyond consolidation. The Hate Crime and Public Order (Scotland) Bill 2020 may have been enacted as the HCPOA 2021, but it remains like the hate crime framework in Scots Law—as a result of political hesitancy and legislative dithering—incomplete.

4.5 Conclusion

Scotland has certainly embarked upon the uneasy journey to modernise its hate crime framework. From the legal perspective, the HCPOA 2021 has certainly marked a step forward in terms of consolidating hate crime legislation in Scotland—but it remains an achievement not without a cost, especially for women. The passing of the HCPOA 2021 can hardly be described as a sign of legislative progressivism, despite the opportunity, the promise and the potential that the Scottish Parliament had to bring to an end years (if not decades) of overlooking gender within hate crime. It is not only a missed opportunity but a disappointment to women who have been or may be victims of crimes motivated by gender-based hate. Furthermore, the Scottish Parliament gave a green light to prolonging the inevitable need to address the issue of sex/gender within hate crime, especially given increased public debate about misogyny as well as concerns about a pandemic of misogynistic harassment and abuse. It is hard not to agree with Johann Lamont's criticism of the Scottish Parliament in that "there's too much of 'well we pass a bit of legislation to show how much we care, to send a message', and then do nothing else."[79]

With all eyes and hope now resting on the forthcoming report of the Working Group, it appears that the next opportunity for the Scottish Parliament to rescind the failures of the current legislative approach

[79] Learmonth (2021).

would be to show a different approach towards legislating on the proposed stand-alone offence of misogynistic harassment. It is to that which we turn next.

References

Barker, Kim, and Olga Jurasz. 2019a. *Expert Response to One Scotland Consultation on Amending Scottish Hate Crime Legislation. Scottish Parliament.* https://consult.gov.scot/hate-crime/consultation-on-scottish-hate-crime-legislation/consultation/view_respondent?show_all_questions=0&sort=submitted&order=ascending&_q__text=barker&uuId=167846602. Accessed 10 February 2022.

———. 2019b. *Online Misogyny as a Hate Crime: A Challenge for Legal Regulation?* London: Routledge.

———. 2020a. Misogynistic Harassment: Advancing Scots Criminal Law? University of Stirling Public Policy Blog. https://policyblog.stir.ac.uk/2020/01/27/misogynistic-harassment-advancing-scots-criminal-law/. Accessed 10 February 2022.

———. 2020b. Scots Hate Crime Bill: A Missed (Gender) Opportunity? University of Stirling Public Policy Blog. https://policyblog.stir.ac.uk/2020/05/01/scots-hate-crime-bill-a-missed-gender-opportunity/. Accessed 10 February 2022.

———. 2021a. Gender-Based Abuse Online: An Assessment of Law, Policy and Reform in England and Wales. In *The Palgrave Handbook of Gendered Violence and Technology*, ed. Anastasia Powell, Asher Flynn, and Lisa Sugiura, 529–544. London: Palgrave Macmillan.

———. 2021b. Misogynistic Harassment: A Stumbling Block for Scots Hate Crime Reform? *Juridical Review* 1: 1–17.

———. 2021c. Online Misogyny as a Hate Crime: An Obstacle to Equality? *GenIUS: Rivista di studigiuridicisull'orientamentosessuale e l'identità di genere* 1: 51–66.

———. 2021d. Text-Based (Sexual) Abuse and Online Violence Against Women: Toward Law Reform? In *The Emerald Handbook of Technology-Facilitated Violence and Abuse*, ed. Jane Bailey, Asher Flynn, and Nicola Henry, 247–264. Bingley: Emerald Publishing.

BBC News. 2018. Elliot Rodger: How Misogynist Killer Became 'incel hero'. *BBC News*, April 26. https://www.bbc.co.uk/news/world-us-canada-43892189. Accessed 10 February 2022.

Blackburn, Lucy Hunter. 2021. Chilling Effect: How the Hate Crime Bill Threatens Free Speech. *Holyrood*, March 10. https://www.holyrood.com/comment/view,chilling-effect-how-the-hate-crime-bill-threatens-free-speech. Accessed 10 February 2022.

Bradley, Cerys. 2020. Transphobic Hate Crime Report 2020: The Scale and Impact of Transphobic Violence, Abuse and Prejudice. Galop. https://galop.org.uk/wp-content/uploads/2021/06/Trans-Hate-Crime-Report-2020.pdf. Accessed 10 February 2022.

Brooks, Libby. 2018. Scotland Declines to Introduce Misogynistic Harassment Law. *The Guardian*, May 31. https://www.theguardian.com/society/2018/may/31/scotland-declines-to-introduce-law-for-misogynistic-harassment. Accessed 10 February 2022.

Chalmers, James, and Fiona Leverick. 2017. A Comparative Analysis of Hate Crime Legislation: A Report to the Hate Crime Legislation Review. https://consult.gov.scot/hate-crime/independent-review-of-hate-crime-legislation/supporting_documents/495517_APPENDIX%20%20ACADEMIC%20REPORT.pdf. Accessed 10 February 2022.

Choundas, George P. 1995. Neither Equal nor Protected: The Invisible Law of Equal Protection, the Legal Invisibility of its Gender-Based Victims. *Emory Law Journal* 44: 1069–1185.

Committee on the Elimination of Discrimination Against Women. 2017. General Recommendation No. 35 on Gender-Based Violence Against Women, Updating General Recommendation No. 19. UN Doc. CEDAW/C/CG/35. https://digitallibrary.un.org/record/1305057. Accessed 10 February 2022.

Davidson, Gina. 2021. Controversial Hate Crime Bill vote delayed after fiery Holyrood debate. *The Scotsman*, March 11. https://www.scotsman.com/news/politics/controversial-hate-crime-bill-vote-delayed-after-fiery-holyrood-debate-3161789. Accessed 10 February 2022.

Davidson, Jenni. 2018. Gender and Age Should Be Added to Hate Crime Laws, Lord Bracadale Report Recommends. *Holyrood*, June 1. https://www.holyrood.com/news/view,gender-and-age-should-be-added-to-hate-crime-laws-lord-bracadale-report-recommends_8802.htm. Accessed 10 February 2022.

Davis, Deirdre. 1994. The Harm That Has No Name: Street Harassment, Embodiment, and African American Women. *UCLA Women's Law Review* 4 (2): 133–178.

Engender. 2018. Women's Organisations Disappointed by Lord Bracadale's Recommendations, Seek Further Dialogue with Scottish Government.

https://www.engender.org.uk/news/blog/womens-organisations-disappointed-by-lord-bracadales-recommendations-seek-further-dialogue/. Accessed 10 February 2022.

Fifth Estate, The. 2019. Why Incels Are a 'real and present threat' for Canadians. *CBC News*, January 27. https://www.cbc.ca/news/canada/incel-threat-canadians-fifth-estate-1.4992184. Accessed 10 February 2022.

Hamberger, L.K., J.M. Lohr, D. Bonge, and D.F. Tolin. 1997. An Empirical Classification of Motivations for Domestic Violence. *PubMEd: Violence Against Women* 3 (4): 401–423.

Hunter, Eveline. 1979. *Scottish Woman's Place: A Practical Guide and Critical Comment on Women's Rights in Scotland*. Billings & Sons Ltd.

Iganski, Paul, and Spiridoula Lagou. 2014. The Personal Injuries of 'hate crime'. In *The Routledge International Handbook on Hate Crime*, ed. Nathan Hall, Paul Giannasi AbbeeCorb, John G.D. Grieve, and Neville Lawrence, 34–46. London: Routledge.

Joyce, Helen. 2021. Scotland's New Hate Crime Act Will Have a Chilling Effect on Free Speech. *The Economist*, November 8. https://www.economist.com/the-world-ahead/2021/11/08/scotlands-new-hate-crime-act-will-have-a-chilling-effect-on-free-speech. Accessed 10 February 2022.

Jurasz, Olga. 2013. Women of the Revolution: The Future of Women's Rights in Post-Gaddafi Libya. In *The 'Arab Spring': New Patterns for Democracy and International Law*, ed. Carloa Panara and Gary Wilson, 123–144. Leiden: MartinusNijhoff.

Law Society of Scotland. 2020. Response to the Call for Evidence: Hate Crime and Public Order (Scotland) Bill. https://www.lawscot.org.uk/media/369185/2020-07-24-call-for-evidence-hate-crime-and-public-order-scotland-bill-2020.pdf. Accessed 10 February 2022.

Learmonth, Andrew. 2021. Johann Lamont: The Scottish Parliament Has Not Improved the Lives of Scotland's Women. *Holyrood*, April 15. https://www.holyrood.com/news/view,johann-lamont-scottish-parliament-has-not-been-good-for-women. Accessed 10 February 2022.

Maher, Jane Maree, Jude McCulloch, and Gail Mason. 2015. Punishing Gendered Violence as Hate Crime: Aggravated Sentences as a Means of Recognising Hate as Motivation for Violent Crimes Against Women. *Australian Feminist Law Journal* 41 (1): 177–193.

Mason, Gail. 2014. The Symbolic Purpose of Hate Crime Law: Ideal Victims and Emotion. *Theoretical Criminology* 18 (1): 75–92.

Mason-Bish, Hannah. 2014. Beyond the Silo: Rethinking Hate Crime and Intersectionality. In *The Routledge International Handbook on Hate Crime*, ed. Nathan Hall, Paul Giannasi AbbeeCorb, John G.D. Grieve, and Neville Lawrence, 24–33. London: Routledge.

Mason-Bish, Hannah, and Irene Zempi. 2019. Misogyny, Racism and Islamophobia: Street Harassment at the Intersections. *Feminist Criminology* 14 (5): 540–559.

Merson, Adele. 2021. Hate Crime Bill Passes Holyrood Vote Despite Free Speech Concerns. *The Press and Journal*, March 11. https://www.pressandjournal.co.uk/fp/politics/scottish-politics/2966239/hate-crime-vote/. Accessed 10 February 2022.

Roberts, Yvonne. 2021. The Perpetrators: Inside the Minds of Men Who Abuse Women. *The Guardian*, November 7. https://www.theguardian.com/society/2021/nov/07/the-perpetrators-inside-the-minds-of-men-who-abuse-women. Accessed 10 February 2022.

Scottish Government. 2016. Report of the Independent Advisory Group on Hate Crime, Prejudice and Community Cohesion. https://www.gov.scot/publications/report-independent-advisory-group-hate-crime-prejudice-community-cohesion/documents/. Accessed 10 February 2022.

———. 2017. Independent Review of Hate Crime Legislation in Scotland: Consultation Paper. https://consult.gov.scot/hate-crime/independent-review-of-hate-crime-legislation/user_uploads/final-paper-1.pdf. Accessed 10 February 2022.

———. 2018a. Independent Review of Hate Crime Legislation in Scotland: Final Report. https://www.gov.scot/binaries/content/documents/govscot/publications/progress-report/2018/05/independent-review-hate-crime-legislation-scotland-final-report/documents/00535892-pdf/00535892-pdf/govscot%3Adocument/00535892.pdf. Accessed 10 February 2022.

———. 2018b. One Scotland: Hate Has No Home Here: Consultation on Amending Scottish Hate Crime Legislation. https://www.gov.scot/binaries/content/documents/govscot/publications/consultation-paper/2018/11/one-scotland-hate-home-here-consultation-hate-crime-amending-current-scottish-hate-crime-legislation/documents/one-scotland-hate-home-here-consultation-amendin. Accessed 10 February 2022.

———. 2019. One Scotland: Hate Has No Home Here: Consultation on Amending Scottish Hate Crime Legislation: Analysis of Responses. https://www.gov.scot/binaries/content/documents/govscot/publications/consultation-analysis/2019/06/consultation-amending-scottish-hate-crime-

legislation-analysis-responses/documents/one-scotland-hate-no-home-here-consultation-amending-scottish-hate-crime-. Accessed 10 February 2022.
———. 2020. Hate Crime and Public Order (Scotland) Bill: Information Note: Sex/Gender. https://www.gov.scot/binaries/content/documents/govscot/publications/factsheet/2020/04/hate-crime-bill-what-it-will-do/documents/hate-crime-bill-sex-and-gender/hate-crime-bill-sex-and-gender/govscot%3Adocument/Hate%2BCrime%2BBill%2B-%2BInformation%2BNote%2BPdf%2B-%2BSex-Gender%2B-%2BRevised%2BAugust%2B2020.pdf. Accessed 10 February 2022.
———. 2021. A Study into the Characteristics of Police Recorded Hate Crime in Scotland. https://www.gov.scot/binaries/content/documents/govscot/publications/research-and-analysis/2021/02/study-characteristics-police-recorded-hate-crime-scotland/documents/study-characteristics-police-recorded-hate-crime-scotland/study-characteristics-police-r. Accessed 10 February 2022.
Scottish Parliament. 2020. Hate Crime and Public Order (Scotland) Bill: Policy Memorandum. https://www.parliament.scot/-/media/files/legislation/bills/current-bills/hate-crime-and-public-order-scotland-bill/introduced/policy-memorandum-hate-crime-and-public-order-scotland-bill.pdf. Accessed 10 February 2022.
———. 2021a. Hate Crime and Public Order (Scotland) Bill: Groupings of Amendments for Stage 3. https://www.parliament.scot/-/media/files/legislation/bills/current-bills/hate-crime-and-public-order-scotland-bill/stage-3/timed-groupings-at-stage-3.pdf. Accessed 10 February 2022.
———. 2021b. Hate Crime and Public Order (Scotland) Bill: Stage 3 Amendments: Debate on the Proposed Changes (10 March 2021). https://www.parliament.scot/bills-and-laws/bills/hate-crime-and-public-order-scotland-bill#target4. Accessed 10 February 2022.
Stevenson, Lesley. 2020. New Hate Crime Bill Could Devastate Police Relationship with the Scottish Public. Scottish Police Federation. https://spf.org.uk/new-hate-crime-bill-could-devastate-police-relationship-with-the-scottish-public/. Accessed 10 February 2022.
Sutherland, Fraser. 2020. Coalition of Artists, Authors, Journalists and Campaigners Call for Changes to Hate Crime Bill. Humanist Society Scotland. https://www.humanism.scot/what-we-do/news/coalition-of-artists-authors-journalists-and-campaigners-call-for-changes-to-hate-crime-bill/ . Accessed 10 February 2022.

Sylvester, Rachel, and Alice Thomson. 2018. Diane Abbott Interview: 'Why am I abused so much? I'm both black and a woman'. *The Times*, April 28. https://www.thetimes.co.uk/article/diane-abbott-saturday-interview-why-am-i-abused-so-much-i-m-both-black-and-a-woman-fd2vhdrc5. Accessed 10 February 2022.

Twitter. 2021a. @patrickharvie, 4 March 2021, 5:26pm. https://twitter.com/patrickharvie/status/1367526902848757764. Accessed 10 February 2022.

———. 2021b. @RoddyQC, 7 March 2021, 11:34pm. https://twitter.com/RoddyQC/status/1368706626639826945. Accessed 10 February 2022.

Vera-Grey, Fiona. 2018. *The Right Amount of Panic: How Women Trade Freedom for Safety*. Bristol: Policy Press.

Wightman, Andy. 2020. Resignation from the Scottish Green Party. *Land Matters*, December 18. https://andywightman.scot/archives/710. Accessed 10 February 2022.

Williams, Cristan. n.d. Sex, Gender, And Sexuality: The TransAdvocate Interviews Catharine A. MacKinnon. *The TransAdvocate*, Undated. https://www.transadvocate.com/sex-gender-and-sexuality-the-transadvocate-interviews-catharine-a-mackinnon_n_15037.htm. Accessed 10 February 2022.

Zempi, Irene, and Neil Chakraborti. 2014. *Islamophobia, Victimisation and the Veil*. London: Palgrave Macmillan.

5

Misogynistic Harassment

5.1 Introduction

[…]
These words, they're like Tuesdays,
there's one every week.
I've held them between pressed palms
and Yale locks.
Consulted them like a guidebook
to my own hometown.
Clenched them tight in fists that now mark the imprint of
nameless men trying to name me.
I stare hard at hands and fists and feet
don't walk don't look don't think don't be—
that key in my hand turning a lock in my throat—don't
feel another man's teeth as I walk these streets
of you and me, yet
I exist, somewhere between
'are you Asian?'
and
'Nice tits!'

K. Barker, O. Jurasz, *Violence Against Women, Hate and Law*, Palgrave Hate Studies,
https://doi.org/10.1007/978-3-030-99375-7_5

And let's just name the problem here:
these streets I've walked I've walked in fear,
and never once have these words begun
in a woman's mouth.
Still,
I'm leaving them here. Nadine Aisha Jassat[1]

Despite decades of campaigning, advocacy and legal protections being introduced across various jurisdictions, harassment—both offline and now also online—remains a persistent problem for women. According to the UN Women UK YouGov survey carried out in January 2021, 71% of women (n = 1098) of all ages experienced sexual harassment in public spaces, with the figure rising to 86% amongst women aged 18–24.[2] In all, 17% of women in the UK were subjected to online comments or jokes which made them feel uncomfortable.[3] However, there are signs of a gradual social change in attitudes.

According to the Scottish Social Attitudes Survey 2019, attitudes towards sexual harassment in Scotland are changing, with an increasing number of respondents finding various forms of harassment "very seriously wrong." For example, 45% of respondents found workplace sexual harassment "very seriously wrong" and an astounding majority (94%) considered the behaviour of a man putting up his ex-girlfriend's naked pictures on the Internet as such too (as compared with 88% of respondents in 2014).[4] Wolf-whistling was considered to be "very seriously wrong" by 39% of respondents, marking an increase of 14% since the 2014 survey (Fig. 5.1).[5]

Although social attitudes in Scotland have migrated towards increasingly larger parts of Scottish society condemning various forms of harassment faced by women, it remains a serious problem and concern for women and girls in Scotland. The 2018 Girls in Scotland survey found that 33% of girls and young women aged 13–25 experienced sexual

[1] See 'Hopscotch' in Jassat (2019, pp. 80–81).
[2] UN Women and APPG for UN Women (2021, p. 6).
[3] Ibid., p. 15.
[4] Scottish Government (2020, p. 7).
[5] Ibid.

Table 1.1: Experiences of gender-based violence (%)

	2014	2019
Been in a relationship where you felt your partner/husband/wife was regularly trying to stop you doing what you wanted to do	14	15
Been regularly verbally abused, put down or criticised by a partner, husband or wife	12	14
Been physically attacked or abused by a partner, husband or wife	11	11
Had unwanted sexual contact (e.g. sexual assault, rape)	7	11
Been touched inappropriately by a boss or colleague	5	8
Been a victim of stalking (either in person or online)	5	6
No, none of these	69	68
Don't know/Refused	2	2
Unweighted base	1,428	952

Base: All respondents who completed the self-completion

Fig. 5.1 A comparison of experiences of gender-based violence in Scotland in 2014 and in 2019 (Scottish Government (2020, p. 16))

harassment in their local community. In all, 21% said they experienced this while at school, college or university,[6] prompting calls from MSP Pauline McNeill to increase prevention of harassment in schools.[7] The prevalence of sexual harassment in higher education was highlighted in a 2014 report by Edinburgh University Students' Association—the report, based on a research survey of 781 students on Student's Experiences of Sexual Harassment in Edinburgh, found that nearly one in three Edinburgh University students experienced sexual harassment during their time at the University.[8] In 2021, Glasgow University was criticised over the manner in which it (mis)handled complaints of sexual harassment[9] as well as a failure to recognise sexual harassment misconduct by a

[6] Girlguiding Scotland (n.d.: https://www.girlguidingscotland.org.uk/girls-taking-action/our-campaign-work/ending-sexual-harassment-in-schools/).

[7] Paterson (2021).

[8] Shaw (2014); McCullough et al. (2017).

[9] Martin (2021).

former lecturer.[10] Online harassment and street harassment remain a significant challenge too. In 2021, 23% of girls aged 11–16 and 33% of young women aged 17–21 reported having been harassed online in the preceding year alone,[11] while a ScotPulse survey carried out in March 2021 revealed that 1 in 4 women has been harassed 'on the street,' with a staggering 97% of women taking measures to try to reduce any risk of harassment.[12]

Harassment of women—be it sexual or non-sexual, on the streets, in the workplace or in schools/universities—is a significant problem in Scotland, but also globally. Yet, harassment is not a statutory offence in Scotland despite other advancements in the law concerning, for example, stalking[13] as well as abusive and threatening behaviours.[14] The statistics suggest that despite gradually changing social attitudes towards sexual harassment and despite laws that address behaviours tantamount to harassment (in its various forms), harassment of women and girls—because they are women and girls—is pervasive and, arguably, not adequately captured within Scots Law. One proposed mechanism to address this came from Engender, suggesting the creation of a stand-alone offence of 'misogynistic harassment.'[15] Although garnering praise and support initially, including from the Scottish Government, it too has stalled given the numerous legal questions and uncertainties[16] surrounding it.

This chapter explores the history and development of the legal positioning of 'harassment' of women, including street and sexual harassment, leading to consideration of the Scottish proposals to create a stand-alone offence of misogynistic harassment. In doing so, the discussion questions the adequacy of describing harassment faced by women as 'misogynistic' before proposing an alternative approach to capturing such behaviours within Scots Law.

---

[10] Daviesand Al Jazeera Investigative Unit (2021).

[11] Girlguiding Scotland (2021, p. 21).

[12] Mitchell (2021).

[13] Criminal Justice and Licensing (Scotland) Act 2010 (CJL(S)A 2010), s. 39 (asp 13).

[14] Ibid., s. 38.

[15] Engender (2019).

[16] Barker and Olga (2020a); Barker and Jurasz (2021a).

5.2 Harassment

Nowadays, the term 'harassment' is commonly used and understood (albeit the latter is not always the case in relation to the *legal* meaning of harassment). The term has been significantly popularised in the aftermath of #MeToo, which amplified women's voices about their experiences of sexual harassment. However, the term harassment was coined in the 1970s in the USA, and only subsequently following a significant amount of campaigning, awareness-raising and litigation, was it reflected in law and policy in the USA and also in other jurisdictions.

Harassment now takes on a myriad of forms, types, and captures—as a term—a broad range of behaviours. In principle, legal avenues for seeking redress for victims of harassment exist, but these are still relatively rarely pursued. Even when they are, the seriousness of alleged behaviours directed at women is questioned as "high jinks"[17]—attitudes reflective of the dismissiveness with which sexual harassment, and the harassment of women more generally, are treated.

Recognition of behaviours amounting to sexual harassment and the influence on legal innovation that has followed such a conceptualisation cannot be understated—if not for legal importance, then at least for societal importance. Before assessing the suggested reforms to legal conceptions of harassment in Scots Law, this chapter turns to understanding the origins of harassment, and sexual harassment in particular.

5.2.1 Harassment, Sex and the Workplace

Although the rise of the term 'harassment' was closely contextually tied to workplace sexual harassment of women, harassment of women (sexual or otherwise) takes place in a number of spaces and contexts. It appears

[17] *Fitzpatrick v. Scottish Ministers*, Judgment of the Employment Tribunal (Case No: 4103399/2020, 13 January 2022) [217]; Mitib (2022).

in the streets,[18] on public transport,[19] in schools[20] and universities,[21] in the military,[22] by[23] and in[24] the police force, but to name a few.

The origins of the term 'harassment' are attributed to Lin Farley. Farley, then instructor at Cornell University and director of the women's section of the Human Affairs Program, first used the term 'sexual harassment' in public in April 1975 whilst testifying in a hearing on women in the workplace by the New York City Human Rights Commission.[25] The term was subsequently popularised, also in the media, following the publication of a *New York Times* article titled 'Women Begin to Speak Out Against Sexual Harassment at Work' in August 1975.[26] Naming behaviour(s) that many women experienced on an everyday basis was a monumental step towards tackling the phenomenon of harassment. Farley recalls the momentum around the birth of the concept of sexual harassment:

> [...]it felt as if the term had the potential to change everything. Working women immediately took up the phrase, which finally captured the sexual coercion they were experiencing daily. No longer did they have to explain to their friends and family that 'he hit on me and wouldn't take no for an answer, so I had to quit.' What he did had a name.[27]

Naming and calling out 'sexual harassment' paved the way for subsequent successful litigation (albeit following rather difficult beginnings)[28] but also established the basis for rooting the act of 'harassment' in law. Within feminist legal literature, the work of Catherine MacKinnon pioneered the conceptualisation of 'sexual harassment' as a form of sex

[18] Mitchell (2021).
[19] Brown (2021).
[20] Davidson (2021).
[21] McCullough et al. (2017); Davies and Al Jazeera Investigative Unit (2021).
[22] Gregory (2021).
[23] Dodd (2022); Fern (2021).
[24] Brown et al. (2018).
[25] Farley (2017).
[26] Nemy (1975).
[27] Farley (2017).
[28] For an overview and assessment of early cases involving workplace sexual harassment, see MacKinnon (1979, ch. 4).

discrimination, especially in the workplace context. For MacKinnon, "sexual harassment, most broadly defined, refers to the unwanted imposition of sexual requirements in the context of a relationship of unequal power."[29] As such, the occurrence of sexual harassment at work is seen as a result of sexual and material inequalities faced by women intersecting and mutually reinforcing, thereby enabling the harassment to take place.[30]

This is illustrated in contemporary Scotland by the case of DeeAnn Fitzpatrick, a civil servant who sued the Scottish Government (unsuccessfully) with regard to the alleged incident at Marine Scotland's Scrabster office. In particular, Fitzpatrick alleged being harassed and bullied—sent anonymous cards from colleagues as well as tied to a chair with her mouth taped over—when she spoke out about behaviours of two male colleagues.

Whilst the employment tribunal criticised Marine Scotland's "general office culture of puerile pranks [which] was at the furthest extreme of such misbehaviour"[31] and indicated that "some behaviours at the office were entirely wrong,"[32] including the photograph of the claimant that was "not acceptable in the modern workplace,"[33] it ultimately dismissed the claim over findings of the claimant's "dishonesty" and delays in reporting the alleged harassment.[34] The Tribunal remarked that it was

> likely that at the time she was privately upset by it, but that she did not actively and openly protest about it at the time either with her line mangers or HR as a means of fitting in to the office, and dealing with the general practice of misbehaviour which had taken place directed towards her and others. […] She did not, we infer, consider it sufficiently important at the time either to record it in writing or to raise it clearly.[35]

---

[29] Ibid., p. 1.

[30] Ibid.

[31] *Fitzpatrick* (n. 18) [219].

[32] Ibid., [228].

[33] Ibid., [225].

[34] Ibid., [220]–[221].

[35] Ibid., [220].

In *Majrowski v. Guy's and St Thomas' NHS Trust*, Lady Hale observed that

> [a] great deal is left to the wisdom of the courts to draw sensible lines between the ordinary banter and badinage of life and genuinely offensive and unacceptable behaviour.[36]

Irrespective of the ultimate outcome of the case, the remarks of the Employment Tribunal in *Fitzpatrick* are concerning in the post-#MeToo era—especially regarding the 'delayed' reporting of harassment and nature of behaviours to which Fitzpatrick was subjected. Rhoda Grant MSP (Scottish Labour) described this as a case of "institutional racism, sexism, harassment and abuse"[37]—an indicator of the severity of the behaviours it failed to offer redress for. As Fitzpatrick's case demonstrates, there is still a long way to go in addressing harassment—especially harassment of women—including its conceptualisation and operationalisation within the law, strengthening processes supporting victims of harassment and, last but not least, capturing the nature and typology of harassment adequately within the law itself. It also evidences the continuing need to address the underlying power dynamics that, left unchecked, encourage tolerance of harassing behaviours.

5.2.2 Harassment: Power and Sex

Power dynamics and inequalities are at the core of the conceptual underpinnings of sexual harassment. Importantly, sexual harassment is not only centred around unequal power relations between a victim and the perpetrator but is additionally reinforced by other iterations of inequality including, but not limited to, race and class.[38] Whilst sexual harassment is a product of intersectional power relations, its emanations, typology and the spaces in which it occurs most certainly vary. But to follow MacKinnon, it

> does not mean that the same things must happen (or feel the same) to each and every woman, or happen to each victim in the same way. It does mean

---

[36] *Majrowski v. Guy's and St Thomas' NHS Trust* [2006] UKHL 34 [66].

[37] Meeting of the Scottish Parliament, 28 March 2019, Official Report, col. 26.

[38] MacKinnon (1979, pp. 29–30).

> that the factors that explain and comprise the experience of sexual harassment characterize all women's situation in one way or another, not only that of direct victims of the practice. It is this level of commonality that makes sexual harassment a women's experience, not merely an experience of a series of individuals who happen to be of female sex. Ultimately, to me, this is also what makes sexual harassment sex discrimination.[39]

However, the concept of sexual harassment has also been criticised for its predominantly heteronormative narrative, with Butler noting that "the sexual harassment of gay people may well take place not in the service of shoring up a gender hierarchy, but in promoting gender normativity."[40] Furthermore, inequalities which speak directly to power relations underpinning sexual harassment play out not only in the commission of it, but influence who can speak out as well as "shape whether sexual harassment can be challenged and, indeed, the degree of success such challenges may have."[41] This in turn is further reinforced by the social and geopolitical locations of victims and perpetrators alike. For instance, whilst the Global North hailed the relative success of the #MeToo movement and women speaking out about sexual harassment, for many women in the Global South, sexual harassment remains an everyday reality for which women pay the highest price and #MeToo—despite its praise—offered little transformational opportunity.[42] The murder of a young Dalit woman, Jeyasre Kathiravel, in the garment factory in India illustrates a deadly dynamic between gender, class, socio-economic inequalities and sexual harassment: the woman was murdered by her supervisor following long-term sexual harassment, verbal abuse and sexual assaults which became 'normalised' in the factory.[43] Similarly, Zarkov and Davis recall clashing social locations of Dominique Strauss-Khan and New York hotel maid Nafissatou Diallo who accused him of sexual assault in 2011 as an example of this unequal dynamic:

---

[39] Ibid., p. xiii.

[40] Butler (1990, p. xiii).

[41] Lazard (2020, p. 34).

[42] Ranganathan (2019).

[43] Kelly (2021).

> [...]who speaks and who is heard remains crucial![...]She stood no chance, precisely because their social locations were so hugely, un-comparably different: she was a black immigrant hotel maid, he was a white national of a powerful European state and the director of one of the most powerful financial agencies in the world.[44]

The concept of power—or rather, unequal power relations—is particularly significant to legal considerations of (sexual) harassment. It speaks not only to the ultimate question of the power of the law in combatting (sexual) harassment of women—and, by extension, violence against women (VAW) generally—but also the question of justice for women who experience harassment. Arguably, it also more adequately captures the nature of harassment received by women, especially in public spaces, as opposed to, for example, the concept of misogyny which has been favoured in the Scottish proposals for the creation of an offence of 'misogynistic harassment' (see below at Sect. 5.5). However, in order to assess these proposals comprehensively, also in light of Scotland's legislative ambitions to incorporate CEDAW and end the discrimination of women in private and public spaces, it is necessary to take stock of the current state of the law in Scotland concerning harassment.

5.2.3 360 Degrees of Harassment

The problem of the harassment of women that came to prominence in the 1970s is, sadly, not just history. Harassment continues to be pervasive in the twenty-first century and is very much a lived, everyday experience in contemporary society across the globe and across various contexts. Although the vast majority of countries criminalise harassment, this has not translated into its elimination or, to be more realistic, significant reduction, showing how deeply rooted the practice of harassment is in unequal power relations as well as social and structural inequalities. Movements such as #MeToo and #TimesUp, despite their flaws, have contributed to the public debate about the sexual harassment of women

[44] Zarkov and Kelly (2018, p. 5).

and stripped much of the 'taboo cloak' surrounding harassment. Importantly, it enabled women to publicly speak out about their experience of sexual harassment on an unprecedented scale. In doing so, to follow MacKinnon, "#MeToo has done what the law could not—[…] eroding the two biggest barriers to ending sexual harassment in law and in life: the disbelief and trivializing dehumanization of its victims."[45]

Even where law reform is concerned, there are signs of the growing discontent surrounding harassment of women and a willingness to challenge it through new and more contemporary forms of legal regulation—be it the proposed offence of misogynistic harassment in Scotland[46] or the offence of public sexual harassment as recommended by the Law Commission in England and Wales.[47] The growing public support for treating harassment of women as hate crime[48]—however problematic from other angles—is indicative of the increasing social appreciation of the harmful effects of such behaviours. It mirrors calls from international organisations, such as the Council of Europe, to end the harassment of women in public space,[49] including online spaces.[50]

However, women's everyday experiences of harassment and its reports in the media have a rather chilling effect on any—however small—hope for progress. The accounts of harassment in the 1970s are replicated and rewritten 50 years on, now also expanding to the online sphere and perpetrated using new technologies. Although there exist laws to challenge it, workplace (sexual) harassment is still pervasive at all levels of employment—as aptly demonstrated by #MeToo and #TimesUp. What is more, in the words of Lin Farley, sexual harassment has become a word that "the corporate world would feel comfortable tossing around"[51] and has arguably lost its teeth in institutional and human resource policies,

[45] MacKinnon (2018).

[46] Engender (2019).

[47] Law Commission (2021, p. 127 at para. 5.6 and p. 208 at para. 5.397).

[48] Brooks (2018).

[49] Council of Europe (2017).

[50] Council of Europe (2021).

[51] Farley (2017).

"corporate-friendly legalese,"[52] and increasingly common uses of NDAs (non-disclosure agreements) which conveniently 'cleanse' (or rather, mask) the real extent and realities of contemporary workplace sexual abuse.

It is not just the 'corporatisation' of the term sexual harassment which highlights the pervasiveness of the challenge in addressing the underlying behaviours and attitudes. The acceptance of the term, as giving a 'name' to the behaviours, is an indicator of the lack of substantive progress in reality for women since the 1970s. The Reclaim the Night marches of 1970s and early 1980s are far from being a mere historical note, with women's public/street harassment peaking and women taking to the streets, once again, in protest over the lack of public safety. Reclaim These Streets (as well as #ReclaimTheseStreets) protests continue amidst relentless, everyday, yet invisible,[53] "safety work"[54] of many women in Scotland, the UK and worldwide to maximise their own safety, even at the cost of adapting their own behaviours or giving up their freedoms.[55] Yet, whilst women are constantly forced to exercise 'caution' and adapt their behaviours to maximise their own safety, the old, fixed stereotypes and institutional prejudice thrive in unchanged forms, calling on women to be "streetwise"[56] or trivialising the reality of their experiences of harassment. The latter is truly an everyday challenge, as shown most recently by fears for women's safety following the rise in drink spiking in Scotland—an alarming near 100% rise in the last five years[57]—as well as the reaction of the hospitality sector to help tackle this problem by supporting the 'Ask for Angela' campaign (Fig. 5.2).[58]

This sign of solidarity with women over tackling harassment in public spaces is certainly welcome—nonetheless, it does not diminish the fact that the burden of ensuring one's safety still heavily lies on women. This is the case in relation to not only individual safety in public but also

---

[52] Ibid.

[53] Vera-Grey (2018, ch. 4).

[54] Kelly (2012).

[55] Vera-Grey (2018).

[56] BBC News (2021).

[57] Clark (2021).

[58] Meehan and Blackstock (2021); Gall (2017).

Fig. 5.2 A campaign poster: 'Ask for Angela'

safety of other women. For instance, the Strut Safe initiative was started by Alice Jackson and Rachel Chung in Edinburgh in the aftermath of Sarah Everard's and Sabina Nessa's murders, and offers free walks home in Edinburgh and a phone service for the entire UK to support women who may feel unsafe when alone in public spaces.[59] The popularity of the service—gathering over 77,000 followers on Instagram—is a testament to the wide demand for such a service and, sadly, the scale of the problem. Although in the words of the Strut Safe founders, "It's like the Hinge of social services. Designed to be deleted!,"[60] the current reality firmly points towards such services being far from obsolete, especially given the growing distrust amongst women towards the police force. What is more, the wide-ranging impacts of the problem of street/public safety—beyond threats of physical violence—remain conspicuous, yet unaddressed. For

[59] Strut Safe (n.d.: https://www.strutsafe.org/).

[60] Loffhaggen (2022).

example, research by Mason-Bish and Zempi[61] demonstrated the negative impact of street harassment of veiled Muslim women on their participation in the public sphere, with men effectively acting as "public gatekeepers," using harassment as a means of punishing "women who participate in the street for not performing gender appropriately."[62] We argue elsewhere that similar effects can be observed in relation to the impact of online social media abuse on women's participation in online public spaces.[63] Consequently, the limited focus on threats to women's public safety (offline and online) gives rise to participatory harms which, whilst harmful, remain outside the scope of legal or judicial recognition.[64]

As the public conscience is shaken time and again and the names of women who paid the highest price for their presence in the streets are trending on social media, the pressing question arises: can the law better tackle the harassment of women?

5.3 Harassment and the Law

> The aim of this Bill is to protect the victims of harassment. It will protect all such victims whatever the source of the harassment—so-called stalking behaviour, racial harassment, or anti-social behaviour by neighbours. I am sure that all Members of this House have been moved, as I have, by the details of the cases which have come to public attention in the past year or two. Those cases have highlighted the devastating effect that those who cause harassment to others can have on the lives of their victims. The remedies contained in this Bill will, I believe, provide effective relief for those victims. The Lord Chancellor, Lord Mackay of Clashfern.[65]

---

[61] Mason-Bish and Zempi (2019).

[62] Ibid., p. 556.

[63] Barker and Jurasz (2019).

[64] Barker and Jurasz (2021b, pp. 256–259).

[65] HL Deb 24 January 1997, vol. 577, col. 917 (available at https://hansard.parliament.uk/Lords/1997-01-24/debates/32a77a2f-06bf-4f6a-a609-82ed93ce6dae/ProtectionFromHarassmentBill).

These opening remarks of the Lord Chancellor introducing the (then) Protection from Harassment Bill in the House of Lords in 1997 bore great promise and aspiration: to provide an effective remedy to the victims of harassment. Twenty-five years on, this statement is crudely subverted by the commonplace occurrence, volume and invasiveness of harassment in its various forms and spaces. As noted by Farley in 2017, "[t]oday the term "sexual harassment" may be ubiquitous; the behavior [sic], unfortunately, remains ubiquitous, too."[66]

Since the enactment of the Protection from Harassment Act (PHA) 1997, the law—both in Scotland and in England and Wales—has evolved to be more specific and to capture discrete behaviours which (previously) were likely to be subsumed under 'harassment.' Harassment has moved away from being used as a catch-all phrase, and we have witnessed the emergence of offences reflecting specific behaviours akin to harassment within the law: stalking,[67] voyeurism[68] (including upskirting) and, now (potentially)—in Scotland—misogynistic harassment.[69] Despite these advances in law, the proposal for creation of misogynistic harassment—albeit not entirely unproblematic, from legal and labelling perspectives—remains contested.

There is also a clear commitment by the Scottish Government to tackle the harassment of women, especially its sexual forms. The Scottish Government's position on sexual harassment states:

> Sexual harassment or abuse of any form whether in the workplace, in the home or in society, is completely reprehensible and must stop. It is a form of gender based violence and we are committed to tackling it. Everyone has the right to work and live their life free of abuse, harassment and intimidation—the Scottish Government encourages anyone who has experienced this to report it. We know that Sexual Harassment is not a problem specific to any one institution. We must tackle the underlying attitudes and

66 Farley (2017).

67 CJL(S)A 2010, s. 39.

68 Ibid., s. 43.

69 Engender (2019).

inequalities and the culture that perpetuates this behaviour. It is the responsibility of all society and for us as individuals to take action.[70]

This policy commitment corresponds with the Scottish Government's approach of allocating budgets to tackling VAW (see Chap. 1), for example, by funding[71] the Sexual Harassment Legal Service run by the Scottish Women's Rights Centre which "provides information, advice, and representation to women who have encountered sexual harassment in the workplace, in university or college, online, and in the street."[72] Furthermore, the government's pledge to tackle sexual harassment extends also to filling gaps in existing laws including, as confirmed by the response of the Scottish Government to the 2020 Report and Recommendations of the First Minister's National Advisory Council on Women and Girls (NACWG),[73] consideration of creating a stand-alone offence of misogynistic harassment.

5.3.1 Harassment in Scots Law

Although the PHA 1997 was a landmark piece of legislation establishing the offence of harassment in England and Wales, its applicability to Scotland has always been limited. Unlike in England and Wales, the criminal law provisions of the PHA 1997 did not create statutory offences in Scots Law. At the time, it was assumed that the existing common law in Scotland already captured and criminalised conduct which the PHA 1997 sought to address.[74] This approach was further confirmed in *Marinello v. City of Edinburgh Council*[75] where the First Division commented on the scope and interpretation of Section 8 of the PHA 1997: "[t]his section is intended to provide similar protection against harassment

[70] First Minister's National Advisory Council on Women and Girls (2018).

[71] Scottish Government (2021b, p. 28).

[72] Scottish Women's Rights Centre (n.d. https://www.scottishwomensrightscentre.org.uk/sexual-harassment/).

[73] Scottish Government (2021b, p. 4).

[74] HL Deb 24 January 1997, vol.577, col.920 (available at https://api.parliament.uk/historic-hansard/lords/1997/jan/24/protection-from-harassment-bill#column_920).

[75] *Marinello v. City of Edinburgh Council* [2011] CSIH 33.

in Scotland as that provided by section 1 for England and Wales. Although the language in section 8 is not identical to the language in section 1, the effect of the provisions is the same."[76]

As such, the focus of the PHA 1997in Scotland remains on civil remedies as a key avenue for protecting victims of harassment. Section 8(1) of the PHA 1997 establishes the right to be free from harassment:

> (1) Every individual has a right to be free from harassment and, accordingly, a person must not pursue a course of conduct which amounts to harassment of another and—
>
> (a) is intended to amount to harassment of that person; or
> (b) occurs in circumstances where it would appear to a reasonable person that it would amount to harassment of that person.

For purposes of Section 8, the act of harassment is understood as causing an individual alarm and distress by conduct which may include speech,[77] on at least two occasions. The exception to the latter applies only in cases of domestic abuse, where a single occurrence of such conduct is sufficient.[78]

Under Section 8(2) of the PHA 1997, the victims/pursuers may bring a civil action for harassment against an alleged harasser, including the harasser's employer, as confirmed by the House of Lords in *Majrowski v. Guy's and St Thomas' NHS Trust*.[79] The latter aspect opens up avenues for

[76] Ibid., [8].

[77] Protection from Harassment Act 1997 (PHA 1997), s. 8(3).

[78] Ibid., s. 8A(3)(a), as amended by the Domestic Abuse (Scotland) Act 2011 (asp 13).

[79] [2006] UKHL 34 [40] (Lord Nicholls):

> A final point should be noted on the interpretation of the 1997 Act. Sections 1 to 7 of the 1997 Act apply to England and Wales. Sections 8 to 11 make corresponding provision for Scotland. During the oral hearing of this appeal my noble and learned friend Lord Hope of Craighead drew attention to section 10. Section 10 inserts a new section, section 18B, into the Prescription and Limitation(Scotland) Act 1973. As explained by Lord Hope in his speech, the new section 18B envisages that the employer of a person responsible for harassment may be the defender in an action of harassment. In other words, section 18B appears to assume that in Scotland an employer may be vicariously liable. This is confirmatory of the conclusion expressed above regarding England and Wales. Parliament cannot have intended that in this respect the position would be different north and south of the border.

pursuing a legal claim against this specific type of harassment—a significant development given the volume of workplace harassment experienced by women. That said, given the costs associated with a civil action, questions remain about the accessibility and affordability of such a remedy by women who experienced it. Furthermore, as noted by Middlemiss, an action for harassment in employment under the PHA 1997 may be more favourable than a more traditional route for pursuing an action under discrimination legislation—a point demonstrated by the case of DeeAnn Fitzpatrick discussed earlier in this chapter. An action under the PHA 1997 means that "employers may be liable without having subjected the victim to discriminatory behaviour as such (and that) employees may proceed with a claim up to six years after the event"[80] as opposed to three months under discrimination claims.

The possible outcomes of an action for harassment in Scotland include award of damages,[81] grant of interdict/interim interdict[82] or grant of a non-harassment order (Section 8(5) of the PHA 1997). Non-harassment orders are designed to protect the victim from further harassment "if [the court] is satisfied that it is appropriate for it to do so."[83] That said, following the passage of the landmark Domestic Abuse (Scotland) Act 2018 (asp 5), non-harassment orders become a default option in cases involving domestic abuse unless the court can explain why victims of domestic abuse (including children) would be safe in the absence of a non-harassment order.[84] Under the PHA 1997, a breach of a non-harassment order is a criminal offence punishable by up to five years' imprisonment or a fine or both,[85] with powers of arrest (without warrant) attached.[86]

Protection from harassment—or acts akin to it—is also enshrined in other discrete parts of legislation. Section 149 of the Equality Act 2010

[80] Middlemiss (2006, p. 308).

[81] PHA 1997, s. 8(5)(a).

[82] Ibid., s. 8(5)(b)(i).

[83] Ibid., s. 8(5)(b)(ii).

[84] Criminal Procedure (Scotland) Act 1995, s. 234AZA, as amended by the Domestic Abuse (Scotland) Act 2018, sch., pt. 1, ch. 4 (asp 5). See also *Finlay v. Procurator Fiscal, Perth* [2020] SAC (Crim) 1 [8].

[85] PHA 1997, s. 9(1).

[86] Ibid., s. 9(3).

creates a public sector equality duty (PSED) which places a positive obligation on public authorities to eliminate harassment:

> A public authority must, in the exercise of its functions, have due regard to the need to—
>
> (a) eliminate discrimination, harassment, victimisation and any other conduct that is prohibited by or under this Act.

This provision applies equally across Scotland, England and Wales, despite jurisdictional differences between the three. It offers an additional layer of legal protection from harassment, albeit not directly creating a specific offence nor an avenue for redress, but rather influencing public sector governance practices to be free from harassment.

Scots Law has gone further, and specifically developed precise statutory offences which criminalise abusive or threatening behaviours (Section 38 of the Criminal Justice and Licensing (Scotland) Act 2010 (asp 13) (CJL(S)A 2010)) as well as stalking (Section 39 of the CJL(S)A 2010). Although these acts are not named as harassment (in the understanding of harassment under the PHA 1997), they contain elements of the offence which share some conceptual resemblance to the articulation of harassment offered under the PHA 1997.

Section 39 of the CJL(S)A 2010 creates an offence of stalking, which, unlike the Section 38 offence, requires the course of conduct to cause "fear or alarm"[87] on at least two occasions.[88] In contrast, the three distinct elements of the Section 38 offence are:

(1) behaviour of the accused in a manner which is threatening or abusive;[89]
(2) this behaviour would likely cause a reasonable person to suffer fear or alarm;[90]

[87] CJL(S)A 2010, s 39(3).

[88] Ibid., s. 39(6)(j), confirmed in *McBride v. HM Advocate* [2016] HCJAC 66.

[89] Ibid., s. 38(1)(a).

[90] Ibid., s. 38(1)(b).

(3) the intention of the accused for their conduct to cause fear or alarm or recklessness of the accused as to whether their behaviour would cause fear or alarm.[91]

The Section 38 offence moves away from the notion of conduct causing "alarm and distress" (as per PHA 1997) towards "suffering fear or alarm." As such, it covers a potentially broad range of behaviours, including, for example, using abusive language towards a former partner whilst the partner was having a consultation with their lawyer[92] and injuring a police officer with a sword whilst shouting and swearing at other officers.[93] Whether behaviour is abusive or threatening is determined through a test of reasonableness, that is, would the conduct in question cause a reasonable person (interpreted to mean "someone who is not of abnormal sensitivity")[94] fear or alarm. This test is an objective test, and no real person has to actually suffer fear or alarm.

Commenting on Section 38 and Section 39 offences, Ferguson and McDiarmid note that they not only "avoid the public/private difficulties" but also have

> the potential significantly to reduce the Crown's reliance on common law breach of peace and indeed it seems that they have already done so: there was a 34 per cent decrease in the number of breach of the peace offences being recorded by the police in the year following the coming into force of the 2010 Act.[95]

Furthermore, Section 38 and Section 39 offences, whilst not labelled as misogynistic nor sex or gender specific (i.e., unlike the proposed 'misogynistic harassment' offence), capture a range of behaviours which are commonly experienced by women in public and in private, as well as online. As such, they advance Scots Law with regard to providing a statutory basis for the criminalisation of such behaviours and to which,

---

[91] Ibid., s. 38(1)(c).

[92] *Reilly v. Robertson* [2012] HCJAC 76.

[93] *Urquhart v. HM Advocate*[2015] HCJAC 101.

[94] *Paterson v. Harvie* [2014] HCJAC 87[19] (Lord Justice-General Gill).

[95] Ferguson and McDiarmid (2014, p. 428).

in principle, the protected characteristics of hate crime legislation could apply. Therefore, we propose that a preferable approach of capturing the 'misogynistic' nature of some instances of harassment would be to create a statutory offence of 'harassment' to which a protected characteristic of 'gender' (if one is included in the future) could be applied. We provide a detailed proposal and explanatory rationale for such a solution in Chap. 7.

5.4 Harassment in International Law

At an international level, sexual harassment has long been recognised as a form of VAW,[96] and is viewed as a form of discrimination[97] as well as an obstacle to women's enjoyment of other human rights and fundamental freedoms.[98] Despite this recognition at the UN level, harassment is not explicitly prohibited in any of the UN human rights treaties. This contrasts with the European approach where the Istanbul Convention defines sexual harassment and places an obligation on state parties to

> take the necessary legislative or other measures to ensure that any form of unwanted verbal, non-verbal or physical conduct of a sexual nature with the purpose or effect of violating the dignity of a person, in particular when creating an intimidating, hostile, degrading, humiliating or offensive environment, is subject to criminal or other legal sanction.[99]

However, the CEDAW Committee addressed harassment in numerous General Recommendations,[100] drawing on the various con-

[96] Declaration on the Elimination of Violence against Women, UNGA Res 48/104 (20 December 1993)art. 2(b); Beijing Declaration: United Nations (1995, para.113).

[97] Beijing Declaration: United Nations (1995, para.71).

[98] Ibid., para.224.

[99] Council of Europe Convention on preventing and combating violence against women and domestic violence (opened for signature 11 May 2011, entered into force 1 August 2014) CETS 210 (Istanbul Convention) art. 40.

[100] Committee on the Elimination of Discrimination against Women (1989); Committee on the Elimination of Discrimination against Women (1992); Committee on the Elimination of Discrimination against Women (2017).

texts in which it takes place, including workplaces and access to justice.[101] Furthermore, the Beijing Declaration and Platform for Action recognised that "the fear of [...] harassment, is a permanent constraint on the mobility of women and limits their access to resources and basic activities"[102] and that "the experience of sexual harassment is an affront to a worker's dignity and prevents women from making a contribution commensurate with their abilities."[103]

Recent years have seen renewed attention paid to the problem of the harassment of women, and sexual harassment specifically, across UN bodies and agencies. There is an increased recognition of intersecting factors—such as disability[104] or race[105]—which shape women's experiences of sexual harassment and amplify the harms arising from it. Equally, the UN acknowledged a long-standing problem of sexual harassment within the organisation itself, committing to a zero-tolerance approach to tackling it.

For instance, the creation of the UN Secretary General's Chief Executives Board Task Force on Sexual Harassment[106] and the establishment of the Group of Friends to Eliminate Sexual Harassment[107] by the Member States of the United Nations in New York in 2018 are amongst some of the developments in response to the highlighted problem of sexual harassment within the organisations of the UN system (Fig. 5.3).

From the legal perspective, the most significant development aimed at combatting sexual harassment originated from the work of the International Labour Organisation (ILO). In June 2019, the ILO adopted a landmark instrument, the Violence and Harassment Convention (No. 190), which is the first international treaty to recognise the right to work

[101] Committee on the Elimination of Discrimination against Women (1989, para. 1); Committee on the Elimination of Discrimination against Women (2015, paras. 15(i) and 18(g)).

[102] Beijing Declaration: United Nations (1995, para.117).

[103] Ibid., para.161.

[104] Committee on the Rights of Persons with Disabilities (2016, para. 58).

[105] Beijing Declaration: United Nations (1995, para.178(b)).

[106] UN System Chief Executives Board for Coordination (n.d.: https://unsceb.org/topics/addressing-sexual-harassment).

[107] Twitter (2018: @NLatUN, 13 September 2018, 9:34pm).

Fig. 5.3 A tweet from the Permanent Mission of the Kingdom of the Netherlands to the United Nations in New York announcing the launch of the Group of Friends to Eliminate Sexual Harassment in 2018

in environments free from harassment and violence—including, importantly, gender-based violence and gender-based harassment. The Convention defines violence and harassment as

> a range of unacceptable behaviours and practices, or threats thereof, whether a single occurrence or repeated, that aim at, result in, or are likely to result in physical, psychological, sexual or economic harm, and includes gender-based violence and harassment.[108]

[108] Convention (No. 190) concerning the elimination of violence and harassment in the world of work (adopted 21 June 2019, entered into force 25 June 2021) UNTS I-56938 (ILO

and 'gender-based violence and harassment' specifically as "violence and harassment directed at persons because of their sex or gender, or affecting persons of a particular sex or gender disproportionately, and includes sexual harassment."[109]

The significant aspect of the Convention is that it creates a legal obligation on state parties to the Convention to "adopt laws and regulations requiring employers to take appropriate steps […] to prevent violence and harassment in the world of work, including gender-based violence and harassment"[110] and to provide enforcement mechanisms and remedies for the victims,[111] therefore increasing the accountability of states in relation to such practices. The Convention opens an avenue for pursuing remedies for workplace violence and harassment at an international level too, with Bequiraj optimistically noting the in-principle possibility of 'last resort' to the International Court of Justice (ICJ) in cases of non-compliance.[112] This perspective remains unlikely given the track record to date of the types of cases which have been adjudicated by the ICJ and their fairly limited focus on issues of violence against women or gender discrimination.

However, the promise of the Convention is somewhat undermined by the fact that (as of January 2022) only 10 States have ratified it. The UK is not a party to the Convention either, despite the Scottish National Party MP, Martyn Day, questioning the Secretary of State for Work and Pensions, Mims Davies, about the government's progress towards its ratification in February 2020.[113] That said, a systematic comparison of national legislation in 193 UN Member States carried out by Raub et al.[114] revealed that in fact two-thirds of the States have adopted national legislation prohibiting sexual harassment in the workplace. Nonetheless, one-third of these countries use narrow definitions, and only 15% include in their definitions harassment by third parties (e.g., contractors,

Convention), Art. 1.

[109] Ibid., art. 1(b).

[110] Ibid., art. 9.

[111] Ibid., art. 10.

[112] Beqiraj (2019, pp. 1168–1169).

[113] UK Parliament (2020).

[114] Raub et al. (2021, p. 391).

customers).[115] The ILO Convention No. 190 has potential for closing these gaps and offers a glimmer of hope in tackling workplace sexual harassment—however, its success ultimately depends on the degree of ratification to ensure its "universal application in the world of work."[116]

5.5 Misogynistic Harassment

> For over four decades, Scotland has been grappling with questions about how it responds to the types of crimes that victimise women because they are women. Engender[117]

In November 2019, Engender published a report *Making women safer in Scotland: the case for a standalone misogyny offence.*[118] The report presents a case for the creation of a stand-alone offence of 'misogynistic harassment' and outlines some broad principles for its development. The proposal emerged generally as a response to the challenge of capturing crimes which victimise women because they are women but also partly as an alternative to incorporating sex and/or gender as a protected characteristic under hate crime legislation. The timing of the proposal was undoubtedly driven by the latter, especially given Engender's discontent with the suggestions put forward in the Bracadale Review (see Chap. 4).

At the time when the offence of misogynistic harassment was first mooted, it appeared—at least in principle—as an attractive legislative option and one which, potentially, would calm the heated debates over inclusions of sex and/or gender within the hate crime framework in Scotland. More importantly, if created, the offence would allow the capture of some abusive behaviours motivated by misogyny which, neither at the time nor at the time of writing this book,[119] is legally possible due to the lack of appropriate legal avenues to do so. This solution was favoured by other key women's organisations in Scotland (Scottish Women's Aid

[115] Ibid.

[116] Sahan (2020, p. 294).

[117] Engender (2019, p. 3).

[118] Ibid.

[119] Correct as of February 2022.

and Rape Crisis Scotland), but also appeared to align with expressed commitments of Humza Yousaf, the then Cabinet Secretary for Justice, to "be part of the solution" in the "fight against misogyny" and to consult on "whether to make hate motivated by misogynistic harassment an offence."[120]

However, the offence of misogynistic harassment attracts many legal questions, especially in the Scottish context—not least, as noted by Engender, "there is insufficient data at present to say precisely how the offence should operate."[121] The law in Scotland (and in other jurisdictions of the UK) does not define misogyny, which is one of the concepts within the proposed offence. As such, the legal meaning of 'misogynistic' remains unspecified, including the pertinent question of proving such conduct in Scots Law. The second key issue centres around the course of conduct, which here is harassment. Given that harassment is currently not a statutory offence in Scotland[122] (see above), the creation of an offence of misogynistic harassment would likely require the establishment of a statutory offence of 'harassment' first. Thus far, there has been no attempt to resolve or clarify this issue, including what definition of harassment ought to be adopted for this purpose under Scots Law. A somewhat obvious possibility would be to mirror the definition of harassment under the PHA 1997, or, alternatively, rely on the Scottish articulation of the offence of abusive or threatening behaviour under Section 38 of the CJL(S)A 2010. It is also worth noting that the proposed offence is likely to deal only with incidents that are individual harassing behaviours rather than including group behaviours which could amount to harassment.[123]

The issue of terminology, definitions and thresholds is not to be underestimated. Naming the offence accurately and transparently is crucial, not only to convey the social problem that it attempts to tackle, but also to clearly characterise the elements of behaviour for which criminalisation is sought. In doing so, legislators ought to reflect on whether the

[120] Yousaf (2018).

[121] Scottish Government (2018, para. 4.45).

[122] Barker and Jurasz (2021a, p. 15).

[123] Barker and Jurasz (2020a).

proposed offence is indeed 'fit for purpose' and be mindful of its operation within the existing legal system in Scotland. For example, would misogynistic harassment substantively differ from the Section 38 offence, and, if so, to what extent?

Clarity around the use of the term 'misogynistic' in this context is absolutely paramount. As we argue elsewhere, "in light of the lack of an accepted legal definition of 'misogyny,' the word has been often used relatively loosely, frequently pointing towards different meanings and describing different behaviours."[124] Not infrequently, terminology of 'misogyny' or 'misogynistic' is invoked whenever a crime has been committed against a woman. This raises a significant set of questions—is all harassment committed against women to be viewed as misogynistic? Or would characterisation of harassment as sexual give rise to a claim that it is misogynistic too? To answer these questions in the affirmative would presuppose that it is the victim's identity as a woman that makes the offence of harassment misogynistic rather than the offender's prejudice towards the victim because she is a woman. The view taken here is that not all harassment committed against women (just as not all VAW, as argued in Chap. 1) is misogynistic per se and to categorise it as such does not account for the multiplicity of motives behind harassment, not least the aspect of unequal power relations between the victim and the offender. Unlike the concept of hate that is ingrained into misogyny, the concept of power provides a more conceptually rooted explanation of the occurrence of the harassment of women, in a number of contexts. That said, harassment can be hateful, and misogynistic—however, as we argue elsewhere, a more adequate route for capturing these incidents (i.e., where motivation is gender-based hate) is through the hate crime framework and the addition of a protected characteristic of 'gender.'[125]

Given the definitional conundrum surrounding the offence of 'misogynistic harassment,' not an insignificant amount of hope and expectation lies on the Working Group on Misogyny and Criminal Justice in Scotland, chaired by Baroness Helena Kennedy QC, which is yet to report on its work. The Working Group, although independent, was established by

---

[124] Barker and Jurasz (2021a, p. 15).

[125] Ibid., p. 16.

the Scottish Government in response to the recommendation of the NACWG in 2020 to "criminalise serious misogynistic harassment, filling gaps in existing laws."[126] As such, the group was set up to "independently consider how the Scottish criminal justice system deals with misogyny"[127] and tasked with considering "gaps in the law that could be addressed by a specific criminal offence."[128] The remit of the group includes building "a picture of the experiences of women and girls in Scotland" and setting out "the principles which will support a shared understanding of how these experiences are influenced and/or driven by misogynistic behaviour and/or attitudes and where this behaviour is, or should be, a criminal offence."[129] Importantly, the remit also extends to the development of "an agreed working definition of misogyny."[130]

The fate of the offence of misogynistic harassment, which is still *in nascendi*, largely relies on the recommendations of the Working Group. Although the Scottish Government appears committed to legislating in favour of misogynistic harassment, the ultimate outcome remains to be seen, especially given the government's U-turn on the inclusion of gender in the recent process of reforming Scotland's hate crime framework,[131] but also its longer-term habit of avoiding legislating on aspects of gender-based prejudice (see Chaps. 3 and 4).

The term(s) 'misogyny'/'misogynistic' remains a political hot potato, and, as evidenced by experiences south of the border,[132] particularly prone to being misunderstood, misapplied and co-opted to other agendas rather than providing a meaningful avenue to tackle the epidemic of VAW in society. Somewhat worryingly, an early indicator of the common misunderstanding of the legal implications of misogynistic harassment (and its intended purpose) amongst the general public arose in the 2021 study by

[126] Scottish Government (2021b, p. 4).

[127] Scottish Government (n.d.: https://www.gov.scot/groups/misogyny-and-criminal-justice-in-scotland-working-group/).

[128] Ibid.

[129] Scottish Government (2021a).

[130] Ibid.

[131] Barker and Jurasz (2020b).

[132] Barker and Jurasz (2020c).

the HM Inspectorate of Constabulary in Scotland.[133] The report from the study stated that:

> One of the key issues raised across the survey by many people was the belief that the characteristic of sex/gender should be added to the list of protected characteristics for hate crime, in order that misogynistic harassment be included as a hate crime/incident (in line with the Hate Crime Bill going through parliament at the time of the survey). [...] Being unable to report such incidents as hate crime meant that many did not have confidence in the criminal justice system to address their concerns.[134]

This statement suggests that, to respondents, misogynistic harassment is a stand-alone offence to which, additionally, protected characteristics of sex/gender should be applied. Although not impossible, questions arise over whether the proposed offence is in fact fit for purpose and adequately reflects the behaviour that it seeks to criminalise. First, the intention behind proposing misogynistic harassment was to remove such behaviours from the legal landscape of hate crime on the premise that there is insufficient "evidence to suggest a gender hostility, gender, or sex aggravation will expand access to justice for women and girls."[135] Second, the application of the hate crime lens (be it through gender hostility or sex/gender aggravation) to a crime that is already explicitly labelled as 'misogynistic' appears to be linguistically redundant and questionable from a legal perspective too, unlike, for instance, where aggravation is based on race or religion and therefore enables the capturing of potentially intersectional aspects of the harassment (e.g., gender *and* race).

Assuming that the statutory offence of misogynistic harassment is introduced, challenges surrounding the enforcement of it, especially with regard to police attitudes, remain a concern. The 2021 study by the HM Inspectorate of Constabulary in Scotland[136] demonstrated significant dis-

---

[133] HM Inspectorate of Constabulary in Scotland (2021).

[134] Ibid., pp. 101–102.

[135] Engender (2019, p. 26).

[136] HM Inspectorate of Constabulary in Scotland (2021).

trust in the police force handling hate crimes, which also translates into hesitation by women in reporting these incidents. This is particularly true for crimes which are perceived by the complainer to be motivated by their sex/gender or misogyny. Some of the respondents noted:

> I think bi-women would be more likely to report if attacks on them as women were taken seriously too. I never get harassed as a bi-woman in a way that isn't also about me being female. (Respondent 297)[137]
>
> As a female who is aware of the low prosecution and conviction rates of men who commit crimes against women, why would I [report]? Further, it's my understanding that women aren't protected under anti "hate" legislation. (Respondent 321)[138]
>
> I don't think the law or the police consider crime against women and girls to be taken seriously. (Respondent 368)[139]
>
> One of the biggest barriers for women (in general) reporting any crime is fear of being judged, disbelieved and blamed for the crime they are reporting to…Basically attitude needs to be addressed if any changes to structure, policy and practice are to be effective. (Respondent 535)[140]

However, the work of Sheridan, Scott and Nixon analysing perceptions of stalking amongst police officers in England and Scotland demonstrated that despite the existence of relational biases amongst police officers in both forces, Scottish police officers were less susceptible to these biases than English police officers.[141] Scottish police officers were also more likely to label behaviour as harassment.[142] Although these findings are not a conclusive indicator that Scottish police attitudes towards misogynistic harassment will follow suit, it suggests the need for further research into Scottish police attitudes towards misogyny/misogynistic harassment as well as perceptions of the offence.

---

[137] Ibid., p. 92.

[138] Ibid., p. 102.

[139] Ibid.

[140] Ibid.

[141] Sheridan et al. (2016).

[142] Ibid., p. 11.

5.6 Conclusions: "See It, See It, Not Sort It?"[143]

Harassment of women continues to be a contemporary challenge—not only to women's safety, but also their participatory rights. Although the past 50 years or so have brought about significant legislative developments at domestic and international levels to address harassment, these have not translated into a decrease in frequency nor change in typology of such behaviours. Quite to the contrary, we keep witnessing a rise in concerns over women's safety in public spaces, with new spaces and tools used to harass women, even in the post-#MeToo era.

In light of these ongoing challenges, the proposal to create a standalone offence of misogynistic harassment in Scotland is certainly bold. Although, not unlike any other innovation, it suffers from some conceptual shortcomings, it nonetheless sends a loud and clear message that Scotland is taking the matters of women's harassment seriously and is prepared to tackle it through law. That in itself is praiseworthy given the lethargic response to this pressing issue across other jurisdictions of the UK.

That said, it is equally important not to bury this momentum and initial enthusiasm to tackle VAW, and women's harassment specifically, through creating a legally uncertain (and possibly unsatisfactory) but politically attractive addition to the legislative landscape in Scotland. As we argued earlier in this chapter, naming the offence accurately is crucial—misnaming it for the sake of symbolism or under the pretence of progressivism, however well intended, is likely to be catastrophic.

Irrespective of the fate of the proposed new offence, women should demand more from law (and those who make it) than a magic noun ('misogyny') or adjective ('misogynistic'). Calling harassment 'misogynistic' appears to contribute little to increasing women's safety in public or, from what's been mooted thus far, suggest a tangible and accessible

[143] "See it, see it, not sort it" is a word play on the public campaign slogan of the British Transport Police: see British Transport Police (n.d.: https://www.btp.police.uk/police-forces/british-transport-police/areas/campaigns/see-it-say-it-sorted/#:~:text=If%20you%20see%20something%20that,or%20text%20us%20on%2061016).

avenue for redress or offer higher degree of punishment for acts of 'misogynistic' harassment. The symbolism of creating an offence of 'misogynistic harassment' should not overshadow the overarching aim behind criminalising such behaviours, that is, to provide meaningful redress to the victims and to end long-standing impunity for such harassing behaviours which give rise to wide-ranging personal and societal harms.

However perfect or progressive the legislation, ultimate change will not come from law alone. Structural changes accompanied by a change in public and police attitudes towards harassment of women, including its more novel forms (see Chap. 6), are required. The slower progress in relation to the latter should not be a barrier to creating a progressive legal framework which truly works for women rather than merely name-dropping them.

References

Barker, Kim, and Olga Jurasz. 2019. Online Misogyny: A Challenge for Digital Feminism? *Journal of International Affairs* 72 (2): 95–114.

———. 2020a. Misogynistic Harassment: Advancing Scots Criminal Law? University of Stirling Public Policy Blog. https://policyblog.stir.ac.uk/2020/01/27/misogynistic-harassment-advancing-scots-criminal-law/. Accessed 10 February 2022.

———. 2020b. Scots Hate Crime Bill: A Missed (Gender) Opportunity? University of Stirling Public Policy Blog. https://policyblog.stir.ac.uk/2020/05/01/scots-hate-crime-bill-a-missed-gender-opportunity/. Accessed 10 February 2022.

———. 2020c. Why Misogyny and Hate Crime Reforms Need More Than Slick Campaigns. *The Conversation*, March 26. https://theconversation.com/why-misogyny-and-hate-crime-reforms-need-more-than-slick-campaigns-134265. Accessed 10 February 2022.

———. 2021a. Misogynistic Harassment: A Stumbling Block for Scots Hate Crime Reform? *Juridical Review* 1: 1–17.

———. 2021b. Text-Based (Sexual) Abuse and Online Violence Against Women: Toward Law Reform? In *The Emerald Handbook of Technology-Facilitated Violence and Abuse*, ed. Jane Bailey, Asher Flynn, and Nicola Henry, 247–264. Bingley: Emerald Publishing.

BBC News. 2021. Sarah Everard murder: Police Boss Philip Allott Urged to Quit Over Comments. *BBC News*, October 1. https://www.bbc.co.uk/news/uk-england-york-north-yorkshire-58762029. Accessed 10 February 2022.

Beqiraj, Julinda. 2019. Convention Concerning the Elimination of Violence and Harassment in the World of Work (Int'L Lab. Org.). *International Legal Materials* 58 (6): 1167–1176.

British Transport Police. n.d. See It. Say It. Sorted. https://www.btp.police.uk/police-forces/british-transport-police/areas/campaigns/see-it-say-it-sorted/#:~:text=If%20you%20see%20something%20that,or%20text%20us%20on%2061016. Accessed 10 February 2022.

Brooks, Libby. 2018. UK Police Chiefs Urged to Adopt Harassment of Women as Hate Crime. *The Guardian*, July 9. https://www.theguardian.com/world/2018/jul/09/uk-police-chiefs-urged-to-adopt-harassment-of-women-as-hate. Accessed 10 February 2022.

Brown, Hannah. 2021. Women's Safety Scotland: Anti-sexual Harassment British Transport Police Patrols Launched on Trains During Festive Period. *The Scotsman*, December 6. https://www.scotsman.com/news/crime/womens-safety-scotland-anti-sexual-harassment-british-transport-police-patrols-launched-on-trains-during-festive-period-3482456. Accessed 10 February 2022.

Brown, Jennifer, Ioanna Gouseti, and Chris Fife-Schaw. 2018. Sexual Harassment Experienced by Police Staff Serving in England, Wales and Scotland: A Descriptive Exploration of Incidence, Antecedents and Harm. *Police Journal (Chichester)* 91 (4): 356–374.

Butler, Judith. 1990. *Gender Trouble: Feminism and the Subversion of Identity.* London: Routledge.

Clark, John Paul. 2021. Edinburgh Drink Spiking Figures for Last Year Released by Police Scotland. *Edinburgh Live*, December 27. https://www.edinburghlive.co.uk/news/edinburgh-drink-spiking-figures-last-22579387. Accessed 10 February 2022.

Committee on the Elimination of Discrimination Against Women. 1989. General Recommendation No. 12: Violence Against Women. https://tbinternet.ohchr.org/Treaties/CEDAW/Shared%20Documents/1_Global/INT_CEDAW_GEC_5831_E.pdf. Accessed 10 February 2022.

———. 1992. General Recommendation No. 19: Violence Against Women. UN Doc. A/47/38. https://tbinternet.ohchr.org/Treaties/CEDAW/Shared%20Documents/1_Global/INT_CEDAW_GEC_3731_E.pdf. Accessed 10 February 2022.

———. 2015. General recommendation No. 33 on women's access to justice. UN Doc. CEDAW/C/GC/33. https://digitallibrary.un.org/record/807253. Accessed 10 February 2022.

———. 2017. General Recommendation No. 35 on Gender-Based Violence Against Women, Updating General Recommendation No. 19. UN Doc. CEDAW/C/CG/35. https://digitallibrary.un.org/record/1305057. Accessed 10 February 2022.

Committee on the Rights of Persons with Disabilities. 2016. General Comment No. 3 (2016) on Women and Girls with Disabilities. UN Doc. CRPD/C/GC/3.

Council of Europe. 2017. Putting an End to Sexual Violence and Harassment of Women in Public Space. Parliamentary Assembly Res 2177, Adopted 29 June 2017. https://assembly.coe.int/nw/xml/XRef/Xref-XML2HTML-EN.asp?fileid=23977. Accessed 10 February 2022.

———. 2021. GREVIO General Recommendation No. 1 on the Digital Dimension of Violence Against Women. https://rm.coe.int/grevio-rec-no-on-digital-violence-against-women/1680a49147. Accessed 10 February 2022.

Davidson, Gina. 2021. Rise in Sexual Harassment at Scottish Schools Needs Urgent Action on Access to Porn, Say Campaigners. *The Scotsman*, June 30. https://www.scotsman.com/news/politics/rise-in-sexual-harassment-at-scottish-schools-needs-urgent-action-on-access-to-porn-say-campaigners-3290684. Accessed 10 February 2022.

Davies, Deborah, and Al Jazeera Investigative Unit. 2021. Glasgow University Accused of Failing to Recognise Misconduct. *Aljazeera*, October 26. https://www.aljazeera.com/news/2021/10/26/glasgow-university-accused-of-failing-to-protect-against-misconduct. Accessed 10 February 2022.

Dodd, Vikram. 2022. Met Officers Joked About Raping Women, Police Watchdog Reveals. *The Guardian*, February 1. https://www.theguardian.com/uk-news/2022/feb/01/met-officers-joked-raping-women-police-watchdog-racist. Accessed 10 February 2022.

Engender. 2019. Making Women Safer in Scotland: The Case for a Standalone Misogyny Offence. https://www.engender.org.uk/content/publications/Making-Women-Safer-in-Scotland%2D%2D-the-case-for-astandalone-misogyny-offence.pdf. Accessed 10 February 2022.

Farley, Lin. 2017. I Coined the Term 'Sexual Harassment.' Corporations Stole It. *New York Times*, October 18. https://www.nytimes.com/2017/10/18/opinion/sexual-harassment-corporations-steal.html?_r=0. Accessed 10 February 2022.

Ferguson, Pamela R., and Claire McDiarmid. 2014. *Scots Criminal Law: A Critical Analysis*. 2nd ed. Reprinted 2019. Edinburgh: Edinburgh University Press.

Fern, Hannah. 2021. Police Me Too Is the Movement Working to Expose Domestic Abuse of Women by Officers. *The Independent*, October 31. https://www.independent.co.uk/life-style/women/police-me-too-women-sexual-assault-b1946111.html. Accessed 10 February 2022.

First Minister's National Advisory Council on Women and Girls. 2018. Sexual Harassment – What We Already Know. https://onescotland.org/wp-content/uploads/2018/05/Sexual-Harassment-Scottish-Government.pdf. Accessed 10 February 2022.

Gall, Charlie. 2017. Bars and Pubs in Scotland Launch Code Word System for People Who Feel Unsafe on Dates. *Daily Record*, March 9. https://www.dailyrecord.co.uk/news/scottish-news/bars-pubs-scotland-launch-code-9991363. Accessed 10 February 2022.

Girlguiding Scotland. 2021. Girls' Attitudes Survey 2021: A Snapshot of Girls' and Young Women's Lives. https://www.girlguiding.org.uk/globalassets/docs-and-resources/research-and-campaigns/girls-attitudes-survey-2021-report.pdf. Accessed 10 February 2022.

———. n.d. Ending Sexual Harassment in Schools. https://www.girlguiding-scotland.org.uk/girls-taking-action/our-campaign-work/ending-sexual-harassment-in-schools/. Accessed 10 February 2022.

Gregory, Andrew. 2021. Revealed: Scale of Abuse and Sexual Harassment of Women in UK Military. *The Guardian*, October 25. https://www.theguardian.com/uk-news/2021/oct/25/revealed-scale-of-abuse-and-sexual-harassment-of-women-in-uk-military. Accessed 10 February 2022.

HM Inspectorate of Constabulary in Scotland. 2021. Thematic Inspection of Hate Crime. https://www.hmics.scot/sites/default/files/publications/HMICS%20Thematic%20Inspection%20of%20Hate%20Crime%202021.pdf. Accessed 10 February 2022.

Jassat, Nadine Aisha. 2019. *Let Me Tell You This*. 404 Ink.

Kelly, Liz. 2012. Standing the Test of Time? Reflections on the Concept of the Continuum of Sexual Violence. In *Handbook on Sexual Violence*, eds. Jennifer Brown and Sandra Walklate, xvii–xxvi. London: Routledge.

Kelly, Annie. 2021. Worker at H&M Supply Factory Was Killed After Months of Harassment, Claims Family. *The Guardian*, February 1. https://www.theguardian.com/global-development/2021/feb/01/worker-at-hm-supply-factory-was-killed-after-months-of-harassment-claims-family. Accessed 10 February 2022.

Law Commission. 2021. Hate Crime Laws: Final Report. Law Com No 402. https://s3-eu-west-2.amazonaws.com/lawcom-prod-storage-11jsxou24uy7q/uploads/2021/12/Hate-crime-report-accessible.pdf. Accessed 10 February 2022.

Lazard, Lisa. 2020. *Sexual Harassment, Psychology and Feminism: #MeToo, Victim Politics and Predators in Neoliberal Times*. London: Palgrave Macmillan.

Loffhaggen, Emma. 2022. Strut Safe: The Service Helping Women Feel Safe Walking Home at Night. *Evening Standard*, February 2. https://www.standard.co.uk/insider/strut-safe-service-helping-women-feel-safe-night-sarah-everard-b979310.html. Accessed 10 February 2022.

MacKinnon, Catharine A. 1979. *Sexual Harassment of Working Women: A Case of Sex Discrimination*. New Haven: Yale University Press.

———. 2018. #MeToo Has Done What the Law Could Not. *New York Times*, February 4. https://www.nytimes.com/2018/02/04/opinion/metoo-law-legal-system.html. Accessed 10 February 2022.

Martin, Hazel. 2021. Glasgow University students 'let down' over sexual harassment reports. *BBC News*, July 12. https://www.bbc.co.uk/news/uk-scotland-57804932. Accessed 10 February 2022.

Mason-Bish, Hannah, and Irene Zempi. 2019. Misogyny, Racism and Islamophobia: Street Harassment at the Intersections. *Feminist Criminology* 14 (5): 540–559.

McCullough, Aimee, Melanie McCarry, and Anni Donaldson. 2017. Rapid Review of Scottish Higher Education Responses to Gender Based Violence. Equally Safe in Higher Education project report. Glasgow: University of Strathclyde. https://www.strath.ac.uk/media/1newwebsite/departmentsubject/socialwork/documents/Rapid_Review_of_SHEI_Responses_to_GBV_(April_2017)Final.pdf. Accessed 10 February 2022.

Meehan, Abbie, and Gordon Blackstock. 2021. Scottish Bars Band Together in Safe Word Scheme for People Who Fear Being Spiked. *Edinburgh Live*, October 26. https://www.edinburghlive.co.uk/news/edinburgh-news/scottish-bars-band-together-safe-21970114.amp. Accessed 10 February 2022.

Middlemiss, Sam. 2006. Liability of Employers Under the Protection from Harassment Act 1997. *Edinburgh Law Review* 10 (2): 307–309.

Mitchell, Jenness. 2021. Majority of Scottish Women Sexually Harassed Or Assaulted. *STV News*, March 17. https://news.stv.tv/feature/majority-of-scottish-women-sexually-harassed-or-assaulted. Accessed 10 February 2022.

Mitib, Ali. 2022. Marine Scotland Official Tied to Chair Loses £500k Claim as Tribunal Deems It 'high jinks'. *The Times*, January 19. https://www.thetimes.

co.uk/article/marine-scotland-official-tied-to-chair-loses-500k-claim-as-tribunal-rules-it-high-jinks-rkxtgx3cv. Accessed 10 February 2022.

Nemy, Enid. 1975. Women Begin to Speak Out Against Sexual Harassment at Work. *New York Times*, August 19. https://www.nytimes.com/1975/08/19/archives/women-begin-to-speak-out-against-sexual-harassment-at-work.html. Accessed 10 February 2022.

Paterson, Stewart. 2021. Glasgow MSP Calls for More Work to Prevent Sexual Harassment in Schools. *Glasgow Times*, December 3. https://www.glasgowtimes.co.uk/news/19758979.glasgow-msp-calls-work-prevent-sexual-harassment-schools/. Accessed 10 February 2022.

Ranganathan, Deepa. 2019. Myths and Realities of #MeToo: Young Feminists in the Global South Speak Out. https://www.openglobalrights.org/myths-and-realities-of-metoo-young-feminists-in-the-global-south-speak-out/. Accessed 10 February 2022.

Raub, Amy, Elizabeth Wong VaheKhachadourian, Aleta Sprague, Milad Pournik, and Jody Heymann. 2021. Ending Sexual Harassment at Work: Creating a Baseline on Laws in 193 Countries. *Human Rights Quarterly* 43 (2): 378–393.

Sahan, Makbule. 2020. The First International Standard on Violence and Harassment in the World of Work. *Business and Human Rights Journal* 5 (2): 289–295.

Scottish Government. 2018. Independent Review of Hate Crime Legislation in Scotland: Final Report. https://www.gov.scot/binaries/content/documents/govscot/publications/progress-report/2018/05/independent-review-hate-crime-legislation-scotland-final-report/documents/00535892-pdf/00535892-pdf/govscot%3Adocument/00535892.pdf. Accessed 10 February 2022.

———. 2020. Scottish Social Attitudes Survey 2019: Attitudes to Violence Against Women in Scotland. https://www.gov.scot/binaries/content/documents/govscot/publications/statistics/2020/12/scottish-social-attitudes-survey-2019-attitudes-violence-against-women-scotland/documents/scottish-social-attitudes-survey-2019-attitudes-violence-against-women-scotla. Accessed 10 February 2022.

———. 2021a. Misogyny and Criminal Justice in Scotland Working Group: Remit. https://www.gov.scot/publications/misogyny-and-criminal-justice-in-scotland-working-group-remit/. Accessed 10 February 2022.

———. 2021b. Scottish Government Response to the First Minister's National Advisory Council on Women and Girls: 2020 Report and Recommendations.

https://www.gov.scot/binaries/content/documents/govscot/publications/progress-report/2021/12/scottish-government-response-first-ministers-national-advisory-council-women-girls/documents/scottish-government-response-first-ministers-national-advisory-counci. Accessed 10 February 2022.

———. n.d. Misogyny and Criminal Justice in Scotland Working Group. https://www.gov.scot/groups/misogyny-and-criminal-justice-in-scotland-working-group/. Accessed 10 February 2022.

Scottish Women's Rights Centre. n.d. Sexual Harassment Legal Service. https://www.scottishwomensrightscentre.org.uk/sexual-harassment/. Accessed 10 February 2022.

Shaw, Alex. 2014. Nearly a Third of Edinburgh University Students Have Experienced Sexual Harassment, Survey Finds. *The Independent*, May 1. https://www.independent.co.uk/student/news/nearly-a-third-of-edinburghuniversity-students-have-experienced-sexual-harassment-survey-finds-9305482.html. Accessed 10 February 2022.

Sheridan, Lorraine, Adrian J. Scott, and Keri Nixon. 2016. Police Officer Perceptions of Harassment in England and Scotland. *Legal and Criminological Psychology* 21 (1): 1–14.

Strut Safe. n.d.. https://www.strutsafe.org/. Accessed 10 February 2022.

Twitter. 2018. @NLatUN, 13 September 2018, 9:34pm. https://twitter.com/nlatun/status/1040337876691681282. Accessed 10 February 2022.

UK Parliament. 2020. Violence and Harassment Convention: Question for Department for Work and Pensions. UIN 12984, Tabled on 5 February 2020 and Answered on 14 February 2020. https://questions-statements.parliament.uk/written-questions/detail/2020-02-05/12984. Accessed 10 February 2022.

UN System Chief Executives Board for Coordination. n.d. Addressing Sexual Harassment. CEB. https://unsceb.org/topics/addressing-sexual-harassment. Accessed 10 February 2022.

UN Women and APPG for UN Women. 2021. Prevalence and Reporting of Sexual Harassment in UK Public Spaces. https://www.unwomenuk.org/site/wp-content/uploads/2021/03/APPG-UN-Women-Sexual-Harassment-Report_Updated.pdf. Accessed 10 February 2022.

United Nations. 1995. Beijing Declaration and Platform for Action. https://www.unwomen.org/sites/default/files/Headquarters/Attachments/Sections/CSW/PFA_E_Final_WEB.pdf. Accessed 10 February 2022.

Vera-Grey, Fiona. 2018. *The Right Amount of Panic: How Women Trade Freedom for Safety*. Bristol: Policy Press.

Yousaf, Humza. 2018. Justice Secretary Humza Yousaf's Speech to SNP Conference. *SNP News*, October 7. https://www.snp.org/justice-secretary-humza-yousafs-speech-to-snp-conference/. Accessed 10 February 2022.

Zarkov, Dubravka, and Kathy Kelly. 2018. Ambiguities and Dilemmas Around #MeToo: #ForHowLong and #WhereTo? *European Journal of Women's Studies* 25 (1): 3–9.

6

Online Violence: A Blanket of Digital Sexism?

6.1 Introduction

> Forty years ago women took to the streets to challenge attitudes and demand action against harassment on the streets. ... Today the internet is our streets and public spaces.
>
> Yet for some people online harassment, bullying, misogyny, racism or homophobia can end up poisoning the internet and stopping them from speaking out. We have responsibilities as online citizens to make sure the internet is a safe space.[1] (Yvette Cooper MP (Labour))

> What makes me angry when I read that kind of abuse about me is, I worry about that it's putting the next generation of young women off politics. So, I feel a responsibility to challenge it, not so much on my own behalf, but on behalf of young women out there who are looking at what people say about me and thinking 'I don't ever want to be in that position'.[2] (Nicola Sturgeon MSP (SNP))

[1] Laville (2016).

[2] Amnesty International (2018).

K. Barker, O. Jurasz, *Violence Against Women, Hate and Law*, Palgrave Hate Studies,
https://doi.org/10.1007/978-3-030-99375-7_6

Amongst discussions across Scotland relating to legislative reform in the areas of hate crime and/or misogynistic harassment, scant attention has been paid to their 'online dimension.' Just as women have a history of taking to protest in physical spaces, so too women have turned to online spaces in the pursuit of 'reclaiming' these as well. The Reclaim the Night marches of the 1970s and Reclaim These Streets protests have contemporary online and digital mirrors in the Reclaim the Internet campaign that unfolded in 2016 demonstrating—nearly 50 years on—that women still need to fight for their (safe) presence in public spaces.[3] While the parallel is striking—and shows a constant need for women to 'claim' spaces in which they can be safe—it also demonstrates that the safety of women is not guaranteed *anywhere.*

Online spaces have shown themselves in recent years to be as unsafe, unwelcoming and openly hostile to women, and women's voices, as physical spaces continue to be. The epidemic of abuse, intimidation, hostility, harassment and violence that is dominating the Internet today, and women's engagement with it, is quite different to the World Wide Web as invented by Tim Berners Lee—who (in)famously declared that it "is for everyone."[4] The Internet today is far from being a space where all are welcome and able to participate freely, and without repercussions.

Rampant online abuse, harassment, hatred and violence undermine the value of the Internet. With reports of hate crime fluctuating in Scotland (records show 6300–7000 crimes between 2014–15 and 2019–20),[5] and reports of threats of violence also rising—with 51% of hate crimes being recorded under the offence of 'threatening or abusive behaviour' under Section 38 of the Criminal Justice and Licensing (Scotland) 2010 (asp 13)[6]—there is almost a concurrent likelihood that these issues will also occur, increasingly, online. Unlike the situation with hate crime, and offline harassment, however, the regulation of online violence—or lack thereof—cannot squarely be placed on the Scottish Government or on the justice system. The addition of the 'digital' and

[3] Fawcett Society (2020).

[4] Verdegem (2021).

[5] Scottish Government (2021, p. 9).

[6] Ibid., p. 10.

'online' element to considerations of VAW presents a different challenge for policy-makers, law enforcement bodies and the organs of the justice system. In part, this is because siloed approaches, or approaches based purely on the physical borders of Scotland, are insufficient to address the behaviours, attitudes and harms posed by acts amounting to online violence against women (OVAW). It is also partially due to the fact that Scotland (by virtue of Devolution) has only limited powers to legislate for matters relating to communications (see 6.3.2.).[7]

This chapter outlines the breadth of online misogynistic behaviours that are prevalent, though it must be noted that not all OVAW is misogynistic, and not all misogyny online will amount to acts of OVAW. In so doing, it explores the phenomenon of OVAW, and its myriad forms, highlighting the challenge posed by digital and online[8] forms of violence directed at and targeted towards women. It then outlines the current piecemeal provisions in Scots Law that could be used to address some of these acts, before considering how the reforms proposed for both hate crime and harassment in Scotland could tackle these behaviours. The discussion here questions whether enough attention has been paid to the online context in law reform discussions across Scotland, suggesting that Scotland has not (yet) focused on the digital elements of VAW. In understanding why that might be a failure for women in Scotland, the discussion turns first to an understanding of what is meant by OVAW.

6.2 Online Violence Against Women: A Harmful Digital Epidemic

While the phenomenon of VAW is now recognised, the same cannot be as readily said for its online forms, despite the overwhelming indicators that it is a phenomenon on its own. OVAW shares many of the features

---

[7] Scotland Act 1998, s. 29(4). The UK Government has reserved powers in this area: see Barker and Jurasz (2019a, p. 41).

[8] We draw a distinction between digital forms of violence—taken here to mean those forms committed through the use of technology, for example, the sending of abuse text messages—and online forms of violence, for example, the sending or posting of messages via social media and Internet-based platforms. While digital forms of violence can be included in OVAW, OVAW specifically refers to the Internet dimension of forms of VAW. Digital violence may already be captured through coercive control offences, whereas OVAW may not.

of VAW, but is facilitated through technological means, making digital and online spaces as unsafe for women as physical, offline spaces.[9] It is difficult to fathom why such scant attention has been paid to an unfolding epidemic of VAW perpetrated in digital forms, and across online spaces, especially when its prevalence is considered.

Growing concern about the breadth and spread of OVAW has been noted at international levels, with the United Nations Special Rapporteur on Violence Against Women, its causes and consequences remarking in 2018 that:

> Despite the benefits and empowering potential of the internet and [information and communications technology], women and girls across the world have increasingly voiced their concern at harmful, sexist, misogynistic and violent content and behaviour online.[10]

It is not just something that the UN Special Rapporteur has noted though. The overall prevalence of OVAW reaches—at least—85% of women across the globe,[11] though this figure may be a conservative statistic given the underreporting of OVAW[12] more generally. This is not a one-off report, with corroboration coming from other sources which indicate similar findings. For instance, the UN Women Sexual Harassment UK Report 2021 indicates that 17% of UK women reported feeling unsafe and/or uncomfortable as a result of comments or jokes made online.[13] This, again, is not an isolated finding, with Amnesty International reporting in 2017[14] that 21% of women experienced online abuse, and within that, 27% received threats—directly or indirectly—of violence (either physical or sexual). In all, 36% of women experiencing online abuse or harassment were concerned about their physical safety[15] as a result. Similarly, 37.8% of those surveyed in the UK by the Cybersmile

[9] Barker and Jurasz (2021e, p. 253).

[10] United Nations Human Rights Council (2018, para. 14).

[11] The Economist Intelligence Unit (2021).

[12] Ibid.; Barker and Jurasz (2022, forthcoming).

[13] UN Women and APPG for UN Women (2021, p. 15).

[14] Amnesty International (2017, p. 3).

[15] Ibid.

Foundation in 2017 reported seeing harassment online.[16] In 2020, over 50% of girls around the world reported being harassed or abused online, with 25% fearing for physical safety as a consequence.[17] In 2021, 71% of young women (aged 7–21) reported experiencing some form of online harm,[18] including online hate speech and harassment. In all, 50% of young women in Scotland report experiencing sexist comments,[19] with 28% recalling harassment online,[20] while perhaps the most staggering is that 82% of those surveyed report encountering online harm of some kind.[21] In 2018, girls in Scotland reported experiencing sexual harassment in a number of contexts, with 27% of 13–25-year-olds having experienced it online via social media.[22] Worryingly, 34% of girls reported feeling uncomfortable talking about sexual harassment, while 84% reported learning very little about sexual harassment and abuse.[23] To compound this, the "worst thing" about being a girl is the harassment that is received from men, because "they think they can talk to you in any way they want, and can talk about 'tapping' or 'shagging' you any time they want."[24] This reflects the staggering 2022 finding that only 15% (of the 1002 women and girls polled) believe social media to be a safe place for them.[25] These statistics—while not exhaustive—offer an indication of the scale of OVAW, at all levels—locally, nationally, regionally and internationally. They also demonstrate that OVAW (in its myriad forms) is not isolated, one-off nor localised—it is very much a pervasive global phenomenon.[26]

Part of the challenge of the epidemic of OVAW relates to the categorisation of it, and the behaviours it is perceived to include. With the

[16] The Cybersmile Foundation (2017, p. 5).
[17] Plan International (2020).
[18] Girlguiding (2021, p. 5).
[19] Ibid., p. 19.
[20] Ibid.
[21] Ibid.
[22] Girlguiding Scotland (2018, p. 8).
[23] Ibid., p. 13.
[24] Ibid.
[25] Girlguiding UK (2022, p. 2); Booth (2022).
[26] Barker and Jurasz (2019a, p. 24).

unfolding recognition and awareness of offline forms of VAW has come a greater awareness of the types of behaviours which can—and do—amount to forms of violence. This has included a growing awareness that it extends beyond physical and sexual abuse and includes other behaviours including—in Scotland—controlling behaviours that are designed to either isolate;[27] control, monitor or regulate;[28] or deprive or restrict a person's freedom.[29] While recognition of a greater range of offline behaviours amounting to VAW is in progress, the same cannot be said for OVAW, and the acts that fall within it. This is due, in part, to the enduring "trivialisation"[30] that seems to accompany complaints of online abuse, online harassment and online violence. Suggestions that abusive messages or online threats are 'only online' and can be ignored if an individual is to 'log out' are unhelpful and do not reflect the reality of online abuse, which can (but does not have to) transgress online and offline spaces. However, these suggestions reiterate the messaging that such forms of abuse are to be expected for women who engage online, while replicating historical and structural attitudes that issues of gender-based violence (GBV) and VAW matter little.[31] This attitude also reinforces perceptions that such behaviours have no real impact on the women receiving them—which is sadly not the case.

There is growing recognition of some of the behaviours that contribute to OVAW—and their similarities to VAW—as well as the inherent manifestation of what Southern and Harmer refer to as "ambient sexism."[32] This is a clear signal that women's voices are not welcome online. This message has been a constant since the earliest days of interactive, social spaces online—many of which were traditionally dominated by men,[33] with the emergence of OVAW being, at least in part, the result of a backlash to the idea of online spaces becoming shared spaces with women. Despite this long-standing attitude, there is an emerging awareness—if

---

[27] Domestic Abuse (Scotland) Act 2018, s. 2(3)(b) (asp 5).

[28] Ibid., s. 2(3)(c).

[29] Ibid., s. 2(3)(d).

[30] Barker and Jurasz (2021e, p. 254).

[31] Barker and Jurasz (2021d, p. 795).

[32] Southern and Harmer (2019, p. 192).

[33] Barker and Jurasz (2021d, p. 787).

not yet recognition—that the lasting impacts of OVAW are incredibly damaging—both to the women's movement generally, but also to gender equality. For instance, while aspects of the women's movement such as #MeToo have shed light on experiences of abuse and harassment, they have also triggered further challenges for women generally, not least through the backlash it generates.[34] Fox, Cruz and Lee highlight, for instance, the "pernicious" nature of online sexism, "regardless of the tone."[35] This effect was recognised similarly by Lewis, Rowe and Wiper, who reiterate that:

> [the] tactics of reluctant 'normalisation' of abuse reflect the wider tendency for both online and offline VAWG to be 'normalised' in ways which support heteronormativity and gender relations… and, arguably, increase the harm by communicating that it is not worthy of significant attention.[36]

As we said in 2019, these behaviours are "far from something that should become normalised"[37]—and yet it very much remains the case that it continues to be exactly that. In many respects, the acts that are manifested online and which comprise OVAW are nothing other than a continuation of old, established behaviours, albeit in 'new' spaces. The online environment has provided a new space for the centuries-old phenomenon of misogyny or, as Jane puts it, a "new form of old misogyny."[38] But we argue elsewhere that "misogyny as a phenomenon is not new—it has a persistent presence … [and] the online realm, too, is providing a home for online misogynistic behaviours."[39] While the root causes are the same, the legal tools to tackle OVAW are generally unsuitable, which is perhaps unsurprising given that no legal system (to date) specifically caters for instances of OVAW. As a result, legal provisions need to be adjusted to account for the specificity of OVAW, and the online context in particular. The legal tools should reflect that OVAW is not the same as

[34] Gianino (2017); Beckett and Whitty (2018).
[35] Fox et al. (2015, p. 436).
[36] Lewis et al. (2019, p. 130).
[37] Barker and Jurasz (2019a, p. 27).
[38] Jane (2017, p. 4).
[39] Barker and Jurasz (2019a, p. 24).

VAW, with specific and context-specific regulation required for the former. In contemporary society though—including Scotland—OVAW includes more than simply online misogynistic behaviours.[40] The range and breadth of behaviours which are categorisable as OVAW serves also as indicator that addressing VAW now includes addressing its digital and technologically facilitated versions too.

Terminology and widely agreed definitions of OVAW remain difficult to ascertain. Different international bodies refer to a similar collection of behaviours with alternative terms. The UN Special Rapporteur on violence against women refers to "behaviour online"[41] and lists things this includes, whereas varying studies (discussed above) interchangeably use terms such as harassment online, hate speech, online abuse or online harm—which is legally unhelpful. Moreover, such interchangeability captures behaviours which may fall within the purview of legal regulation, but also behaviours which, while harmful, may not be illegal.[42] To put it simply, not every online behaviour will amount to a legally actionable harm—but the use of terms to discuss all of these behaviours as one and the same is unhelpful in distinguishing between the severity of the acts. This poses additional problems for the legal regulation of OVAW.[43] Similarly, the disparity and inconsistency in the use of agreed-upon terms adds to the challenge of capturing—legally—the behaviours and associated concepts[44] complained of. For instance, some of these behaviours can include online misogyny, defined as "the manifestation of hostility communicated through online platforms, particularly social media and other participatory environments."[45] Similar to VAW (see Chap. 1), not all forms of online abuse will be misogynistic though, and while some may include misogyny, some will not. The absence of misogyny does not mean that such behaviour would not be abusive, harassing or even amount to online hate speech—it may still be any of those things, and still attract the need for legal intervention. Similarly, not all instances of

---

40 Barker and Jurasz (2020a).

41 United Nations Human Rights Council (2018, p. 5).

42 Barker and Jurasz (2021b, p. 58).

43 Barker and Jurasz (2020c, p. 55).

44 Barker and Jurasz (2022, forthcoming).

45 Barker and Jurasz (2019a, p. xiv).

online abuse will amount to online violence—there are some aspects of what Rowbottom refers to as "low-level"[46] speech which, while unpleasant, is not sufficiently serious enough or directed to a large enough audience[47] as to warrant the intervention of legal regulation. Other forms of online behaviour which could amount to OVAW include (non-exhaustively) acts such as gender-based abuse online,[48] text-based (sexual) abuse,[49] image-based sexual abuse,[50] text-based abuse,[51] sexist hate speech,[52] online hate and cyber discrimination[53] and cyberviolence against women,[54] as well as legislatively recognised (albeit not per se online) stalking and harassment. The list is non-exhaustive but so too is the breadth of interchangeable terminology used to describe similar behaviours, with some preferring OVAW and other suggestions including (online) technologically facilitated sexual violence (TFSV) or the "digital dimension of violence against women"[55] as alternatives.

The challenge of OVAW—as a term, but also as a collection of behaviours—is significant, with the Council of Europe elucidating this point in particular:

> To date, there is no universal typology/definition of behaviours or action that is considered to group together all forms of violence against women perpetrated online or through technology. Instead, discourses and approaches to abusive behaviour online and harms perpetrated via technology are marked by terms that are used interchangeably or inaccurately, creating a fragmentation that is reinforced by the diversity of aims and perspectives of the different stakeholders that are currently shaping the nar-

---

[46] Rowbottom (2012, p. 371).

[47] *Alinak v. Turkey* App no. 40287/98 (ECtHR, 29 March 2005); *Klein v. Slovakia* (2010) 50 E.H.R.R. 15.

[48] Barker and Jurasz (2021a).

[49] Barker and Jurasz (2019a, p. xiv); Barker and Jurasz (2021e, p. 254).

[50] McGlynn and Rackley (2017).

[51] Barker and Jurasz (2019a, p. xiv).

[52] Council of Europe (2016).

[53] Council of Europe Parliamentary Assembly (2017).

[54] Council of Europe (n.d.: https://www.coe.int/en/web/cyberviolence/cyberviolence-against-women).

[55] Council of Europe (2021, p. 15).

> rative. Many terms currently in use do not cover the full range of behaviour, nor do they highlight the gender pattern in the abuse. While describing some very relevant forms of violence against women perpetrated in digital spaces, they do not nearly cover all of the activities carried out online or through technology that harm women and girls.[56]

That said, there is some long overdue traction growing at European levels to address this fragmentation[57] challenge presented by OVAW. For instance, the Istanbul Convention includes within its definition of sexual harassment behaviours which are verbal or non-verbal as well as the non-physical. This allows some room for considerations of online behaviours to be captured within the remit of Article 40. In 2021, the GREVIO General Recommendation[58] on the digital dimension of violence against women was published. It considers a range of behaviours to fall within the remit of Article 40, including threats, rape threats, sexualised doxing, as well as the non-consensual sharing of intimate images or videos. The General Recommendation also includes clarifications relating to online stalking, particularly where it has been perpetrated with ICT means. Article 34 of the Istanbul Convention, for instance, now includes threatening behaviours, engaging in unwanted communications and pursuing contact through any means, but especially "ICT devices."[59] Ultimately welcome, the GREVIO Recommendation is significant because it sends clear signals that these behaviours will not be tolerated in online environments, though it does little to specifically affect the (current) Scottish legal landscape.

Legally capturing OVAW and behaviours that amount to VAW in online contexts is not straightforward, and while developments—and recognition—are important, they alone cannot effect change. More tangible mechanisms, including functional national criminal justice systems which specifically allow for "cyberviolence"[60] to be captured (and prose-

---

[56] Ibid.

[57] Barker and Jurasz (2020c, pp. 54–55).

[58] Council of Europe (2021).

[59] Ibid., p. 19.

[60] Council of Europe (n.d.: https://www.coe.int/en/web/cyberviolence/cyberviolence-against-women).

cuted) alongside other forms of VAW, are required. This is particularly important given the harmful impacts of OVAW, but also the pervasiveness of this digital epidemic. In a society where smartphones and connected devices mean that we are almost always online, the "ubiquity, portability and diverse capabilities" of such devices for "abuse and control strategies"[61] present an even greater challenge for law, law enforcement, regulation and women's safety online. This is recognised as Harvard and Lefevre make clear in the domestic abuse context,[62] but has not (yet) extended to non-domestic contexts of OVAW.

It is particularly striking then, that despite conceptualisations of domestic abuse as overwhelmingly physical and sexual, greater attention has not been paid (yet) to the online aspects. In Harvard and Lefevre's Power and Control Wheel (see Fig. 6.1), the emphasis has been designed to fall on the power and control elements of the physical and sexual abuse encountered in relationships where coercive control is at play. What is striking in this adapted wheel, from the perspective of OVAW, is the number of instances in which the behaviours have an OVAW dimension to them—irrespective of the domestic context. This indicates—above all else—that there is potential for OVAW beyond domestic abuse situations, but where this context is lacking, the OVAW element will also likely be overlooked. There are striking parallels here to the ways in which some characteristics are captured within hate crime provisions in Scots Law, but others are not. The gaps in the hate crime framework in respect of gender are mirrored with the gaps in the legal framework to tackle OVAW. To take an example, the law captures instances of racially aggravated hatred directed against Asian women, but not gender-based hate. Similarly, where that hatred is communicated through social media, the racially aggravated hatred would be captured, as would, potentially, other offences (see below) relating to communications misuse. None of these would address the OVAW aspect of the hatred. In domestic contexts, similar gaps also arise given the provisions within the Domestic Abuse (Scotland) Act 2018 (asp 5) (DA(S)A 2018), where coercive and controlling behaviours manifest themselves through the use of technology. For

[61] Harvard and Lefevre (2020, pp. 224–225).

[62] Ibid.

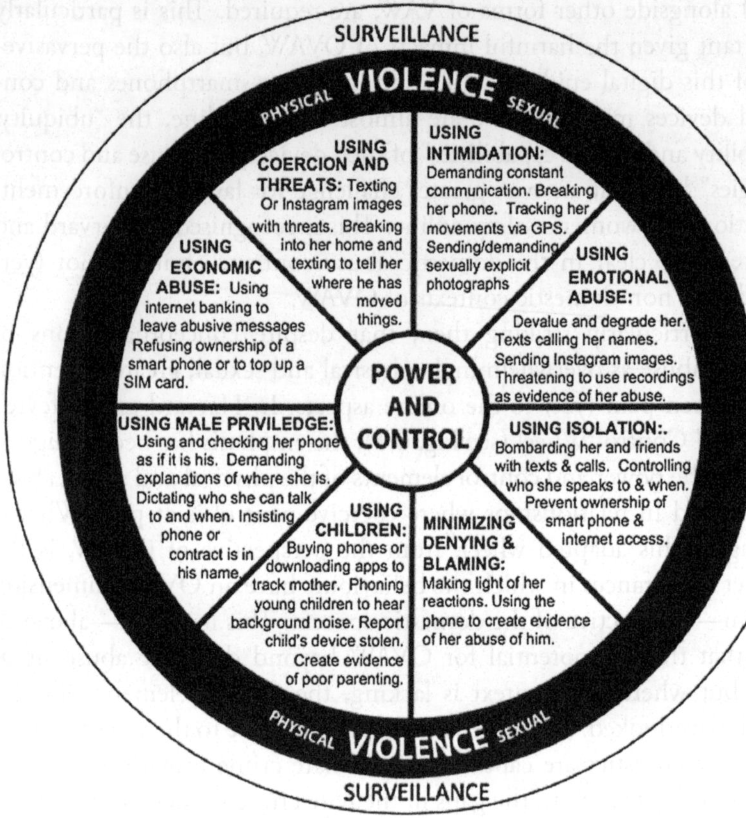

Fig. 6.1 Harvard and Lefevre's adapted Power and Control Wheel (Harvard and Lefevre (2020, pp. 233).)

instance, racially aggravated hatred can be communicated towards a partner through social media use and could be captured under either the hate crime provisions or the domestic abuse provisions. In neither situation is the OVAW element captured by the currently legislative provisions. Hatred (although not on the basis of gender) and coercive control (including through technological means) are captured, but the gendered and technological (online) aspects of violence directed at women are not. OVAW is therefore a significant gap in the patchwork of provisions in existence in Scots Law and not currently captured (see Sect. 6.3.2.).

The understandings of OVAW, its typologies and its terminology are growing. What is advancing perhaps more slowly is an understanding of why it is such a problem for women. This is not simply because of the increasingly digital societies in which we live—particularly in Scotland—but is due to the number of harmful effects being exposed to OVAW can have.

The impacts of OVAW are significant. Not only are women made to feel unsafe online, but there are broader harms that women suffer. For instance, by taking steps to protect themselves from exposure to online abuse, harassment, threats or other behaviours, their rights to free, public and equal participation are interfered with and, ultimately, curtailed. Self-censorship online or restricting who can access personal information via social media profiles may be one way of 'staying safe' and reducing the "real fear,"[63] but it is also the digital equivalent of safety work.[64] It can, at best, mitigate some of the potential harms suffered by those who are targeted through OVAW, but should not be necessary. Not only does self-censorship and silencing,[65] as the most likely response of women who are subjected to OVAW,[66] restrict participatory rights, but there are other harms at play beyond the physical and psychological violence that is understood for offline forms of VAW. For instance, for women in the public eye, such as Scottish politicians, Mhairi Black MP, Joanna Cherry QC and Nicola Sturgeon MSP, the OVAW they experience is incredibly sexualised but is also comprised of threats to physical safety. Black, for example, has openly reported the comments she receives, explicitly sharing the verbatim abuse, threats and harassment: "I struggle to see any joke in systematically being called a dyke, a rug muncher, a slut, a whore and a scruffy bint. I have been told, 'You can't put lipstick on a pig,' and: 'Let the dirty bitch eat shit and die'."[67]

---

[63] Women's Aid (2014).

[64] Barker and Jurasz (2021e, p. 256).

[65] Barker and Jurasz (2020b).

[66] Khoo (2021).

[67] HC Deb. 7 March 2018, vol. 637, col. 138WH (available at https://hansard.parliament.uk/commons/2018-03-07/debates/92236C51-2340-4D97-92A7-4955B24C2D74/MisogynyAsAHateCrime).

But Black's account goes on, with more explicit threats, harassment and abuse:

> I could soften some of this by talking about 'the C-word', but the reality is that there is no softening when I am targeted by these words: I am left reading them on my screen day in, day out. Someone said: 'She needs a kick in the cunt'.
>
> I have been called 'guttural cunt', 'ugly cunt' and 'wee animal cunt'. There is no softening just how sexualised and misogynistic the abuse is. Some guy called William Hannah—I have never heard of him in my life—commented: 'I've pumped some ugly burds in my time but I jist wouldn't'.
>
> I have been assured multiple times that I do not have to worry because I am so ugly that no one would want to rape me.
>
> All those insults were tailored to me because I am a woman. We can kid ourselves that those are comments by a few bad, anonymous people on Twitter, but they are not: this is everyday language.[68]

Black is not alone. Threats made via social media against Scottish MP Joanna Cherry QC have been serious enough to warrant her being given police protection.[69] Cherry is not an isolated example either. Prominent women in Scottish politics—both at Holyrood[70] and at Westminster[71]—have announced stepping down from politics because of the toll of the abuse and harassment, and the "impact"[72] it has on them, their careers and their families. This abuse and harassment extends to other prominent women, including television presenter Sonja McLaughlan who received a barrage of abuse that left her in tears for—in her own words—"doing her job."[73]

---

[68] HC Deb. 7 March 2018, vol. 637, col. 139WH (available at https://hansard.parliament.uk/commons/2018-03-07/debates/92236C51-2340-4D97-92A7-4955B24C2D74/MisogynyAsAHateCrime).

[69] Ward (2019).

[70] McLaughlin (2020).

[71] Taylor (2019).

[72] Barker and Jurasz (2020b).

[73] Barker and Jurasz (2021b, p. 54).

The barrage[74] of online harassment and abuse is not isolated to women in Scotland, nor to women in politics in Scotland—it is a widespread part of daily digital life for women generally. The impact of such constant and extremely sexualised threats of violence causes a significant impact on those who receive it. In our typology of harms caused by online abuse and harassment, we identify 12 categories of harm[75] that is inflicted on women as a result. This results in "enduring harm"[76] and reiterates the long-lasting effects of OVAW, but also a broader message to women everywhere that they and their voices are not welcome online. Amongst the 12 harms in our typology, OVAW imposes what we call reputational harm,[77] but also democratic, residential and economical harms[78]—due to the costs and inconvenience of having to disrupt personal lives in seeking alternative accommodation elsewhere (Fig. 6.2).

While these three harms are not the only harms, they are those which have been given the most attention—both in the press and in accounts sharing the experiences of women, but also in the limited number of cases dealing with instances of OVAW.[79] The cumulative impact is significant, with Jess Phillips MP highlighting the toll of being contactable around the clock via social media—especially when rape and death threats arrive in significant numbers—such as the 600 rape and death threats Phillips received in one night.[80] The impact of OVAW in its various forms has been described as amounting to a serious weather event: "each snarky comment, each spiteful tweet, is (as Zoe Quinn once put it)[81] just one snowflake in an avalanche."[82] Even in light of this, the over-

---

[74] Phillips (2017, p. 217).

[75] Barker and Jurasz (2021e, p. 256).

[76] Ibid.

[77] Ibid., p. 257.

[78] Ibid., p. 256.

[79] *R v. Nimmo and Sorley* (2014) (Westminster Magistrates' Court, 24 January 2014). (Sentencing Comments:https://www.judiciary.uk/wp-content/uploads/JCO/Documents/Judgments/r-v-nimmo-and-sorley.pdf). It should be noted that this is a case from England and Wales, rather than from Scotland, but the remarks of Judge Riddle relating to harm and impact are relevant to the discussion here.

[80] Allegretti (2016).

[81] Quinn (2015, at 19:05).

[82] Gardiner et al. (2016).

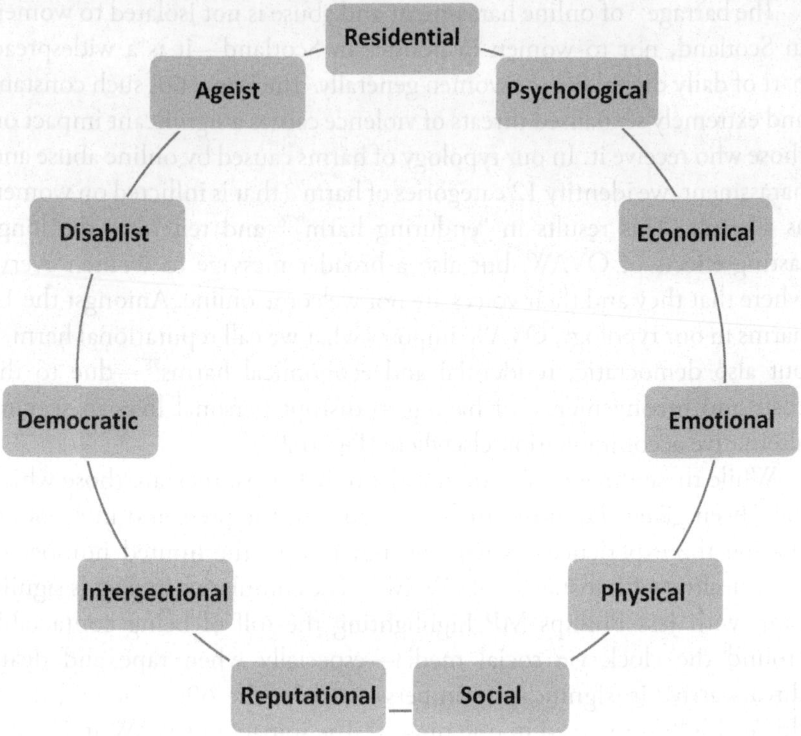

Fig. 6.2 Barker and Jurasz's 'Circle of Harms' (Barker and Jurasz (2022) (forthcoming).)

whelming response to OVAW remains one of indifference—it is seen very much as an everyday occurrence, and it is only the most extreme or shocking instances of OVAW that have any kind of wide-ranging effect on the public.[83]

With the increases in online misogyny, online gender-based hate and OVAW more generally, it remains perplexing that these behaviours have not been included within legislation. Where women receive online abuse, and online hate because they are women, that is the manifestation of misogyny, playing out through digital and online mechanisms. In online contexts, textual abuse takes on misogynistic forms, and the extreme

[83] Barker and Jurasz (2022, forthcoming).

versions of online misogyny amount to hatred of women (see Chap. 4) because they are women, reflecting the dissemination of hostility through—predominantly—social media platforms.[84] Given these inter-related behaviours—which are all based on the same, shared prejudice—that towards women—it is particularly important that OVAW is recognised by both hate crime and harassment branches of the law in Scotland (but also beyond).

6.3 From Images to Text: An Unfolding Scottish Legal Panoply?

The general approach adopted in Scots Law has been one that rests on tackling inequalities and addressing social cohesion. These ambitions have been aimed at reducing hostility. In some respects, the unfolding legislative competence and the accompanying creativity in legislation have seen some introductions to tackle aspects of OVAW. That said, not all aspects of OVAW are captured within Scots Law, despite a range of policy initiatives and some high-profile law reform proposals. In light of the emphasis that has been placed on addressing VAW in Scotland, the discussion here turns to exploring the unfolding panoply of policy and law which addressees, with shortcomings, some limited elements of OVAW.

6.3.1 Equally (Digitally) Safe?

Developments at European levels in offering greater recognition to digital elements of VAW have not seen—yet—reciprocal attention at national and domestic levels, especially in Scotland, despite ambitions to keeping up with EU legislation[85] (see Chap. 1). Patchy consideration is given to OVAW in leading policies addressing VAW across Scotland. In the otherwise leading policy initiative on VAW, *Equally Safe*, there are only two

---

[84] Barker and Jurasz (2019a, p. xiv).

[85] UK Withdrawal from the European Union (Continuity) (Scotland) Act 2021 (asp 4).

mentions of the 'online' dimension in the 2018 report.[86] The first mention refers to "online abuse"[87] in the definition of VAW offered by *Equally Safe*, while the second refers to "online technologies."[88] The *Equally Safe* 2020 report[89] makes more mentions of 'online' (totalling 9), but the majority of these relate to progress in delivering online resources to deliver the overall *Equally Safe* strategy—the emphasis falling less on addressing instances of OVAW. This, if viewed in isolation, while not encouraging, is not disastrous. However, when considered in conjunction with the increasing prevalence of OVAW as reported through various studies (on ever increasing scales), it seems remiss that such a flagship policy as *Equally Safe* has not delivered on online elements of VAW. That is an area where Scotland had the potential to act to address a contemporary societal challenge in the form of OVAW beyond image-based sexual abuse (IBSA). A unique opportunity presented itself to allow Scotland—historically an inherently misogynistic society[90]—to be progressive and forward-thinking by bringing together OVAW and (offline) VAW into the same policy and strategic delivery plan and, in doing so, tackle some of the underlying causes of (O)VAW.

Similarly, while the DA(S)A 2018 has been applauded for its "momentous"[91] and "gold standard"[92] changes to the law, and for capturing behaviours traditionally overlooked in domestic abuse legislation, it also does not address OVAW. While it has scope for capturing forms of violence that are perpetrated using technology, there still needs to be a domestic context for any legal action to be taken. This does not specifically address OVAW unless it falls within a domestic relationship, in which case, by virtue of the DA(S)A 2018, it will be irrelevant that it was OVAW *because of* the domestic aspect, which brings the behaviours

[86] Scottish Government and COSLA (2018).
[87] Ibid., p. 12.
[88] Ibid., p. 16.
[89] Scottish Government and COSLA (2020).
[90] Hills (2001, p. 30).
[91] Green (2018).
[92] Engender (2019, p. 32).

within the purview of the DA(S)A 2018 to begin with. It also, ultimately, reduces OVAW to a position of legal invisibility due to the dominant and prevailing domestic narrative.

6.3.2 An Unfolding Panoply of Scottish Provisions

Whereas action has been taken in Scots Law to implement a revised legal framework to tackle domestic abuse and, most recently, hate crime, the same cannot be said to have emerged—yet—for OVAW. Legislative developments have unfolded in a piecemeal, reactive fashion to address specific behaviours and acts which are considered to fall within the categorisation of OVAW, but there has been little coordination given to such developments. In ways similar to the unfolding of hate crime in the years immediately prior to and after devolution, the unfolding of reactionary stop-gap legislative measures has led to a number of disparate provisions that address in isolation limited aspects of behaviours that fall within OVAW.

(Online) Hate and Gender

While elements of the online aspects of hate crime and harassment have been mentioned in Scotland, these have almost always been passing considerations, rather than discussions of any substance. In the 2018 Independent Review of Hate Crime Legislation (Bracadale Review),[93] for instance, some—limited—consideration was given to the online dimension of hate crimes. Despite the breadth of his remit, and the scope to consider much more fully, the implications of hate crimes committed through digital and/or online means, Lord Bracadale concluded that he did "not consider any further legislative change necessary"[94] to address online hate crimes in Scotland. In reaching this conclusion, the focus was so clearly on the VAW aspects of hate, that there was all but complete ignorance of OVAW. Such a narrow focus on selected forms of VAW to

[93] Scottish Government (2018a).

[94] Ibid., p. 82.

the detriment of others and women is reflective of the seeming unwillingness or inability of law and policy-makers—both in Scotland and at European levels—to take a broader, more holistic approach[95] to tackling VAW.

What Lord Bracadale suggested, instead, was that there should be further attention paid to forthcoming considerations of reforming communications offences[96]—on the implied 'off-chance' that there was any need to reform anything specifically of benefit to Scots Law.[97] Lord Bracadale was of the opinion that the (then) range of statutory provisions in Scotland was adequate to address instances of hate crime, without needing any amendment to cater for the online aspect,[98] despite growing evidence of this emerging as an epidemic. Similarly, in the ensuing Scottish Government consultation on amending hate crime legislation, also in 2018, online hate reappeared as an area of concern.[99] The Scottish Government position in November 2018 was strikingly similar to the position adopted by the House of Lords[100] in 2014–15 when considering whether or not there was a pressing need to reform the communications offences. The Scottish Government position remained that:

> the starting point in considering what changes may be necessary as regards online hate crime is that what is criminal off-line is criminal on-line, and that an existing offence committed online can be aggravated in the same way as any other offence can be aggravated.[101]

Nevertheless, the Scottish Government posed the question to stakeholders as to whether specific legislative change was required or not. While some of the concerns of the Bracadale Review have been if not addressed then alleviated by the consolidating Hate Crime and Public Order (Scotland) Act 2021 (asp 14) (HCPOA 2021) (by bringing

95 Barker and Jurasz (2020c, p. 55).
96 Law Commission (2018, p. 1).
97 Scottish Government (2018a, para. 6.53).
98 Ibid., p. 82 at paras. 6.51–6.52.
99 Scottish Government (2018b, pp. 43 and 46).
100 Communications Select Committee (2014, para. 32).
101 Scottish Government (2018b, p. 43).

together hate crime provisions), little has changed in respect of the non-hate crime provisions in Scots Law to tackle online forms of hatred.

Similarly, there is nothing in the HCPOA 2021 that addresses specifically OVAW, nor gender, nor the online dimension of not gender-based hate crimes. While legislatively this may make for self-contained statutory provisions—an improvement on the disparate hate crime provisions pre-2021 (see Fig. 7 in Chap. 3)—it does little to address the notion that OVAW (including online hate) is dismissed by the legislature and the criminal justice systems in equal measure as insignificant and/or unimportant. The prevailing attitude that the 'online' dimension can be captured within pre-existing legislation also ignores the symbolic effect that such recognition within a statutory framework could offer to women, but also to sufferers of OVAW in particular. In not including OVAW in the reformed hate crime framework—despite hate crime being a flagship policy across Scotland since 2016, and *Equally Safe* being a leading aspect of governmental work since 2014—the Scottish Government has reinforced the attitude that OVAW is less significant and less serious. In so doing, it sends clear signals that VAW is to be tackled and addressed while repeating the notion that OVAW is a lesser concern, if a concern at all.[102]

As such, instances of OVAW continue to fall outside of the hate crime framework in Scots Law. While there are a number of other potential criminal offences which *may* offer a route towards prosecution in Scotland, it must be said here first, though, that given the failures of the HCPOA 2021 to include provisions relating to gender (see Chap. 4), that none of the provisions that are left to deal with instances of OVAW can be used as an underlying offence for the purposes of a hate crime where there is a demonstration of malice or ill will on the basis of gender. At best, given this omission in the HCPOA 2021, the other non-hate offences to which this discussion now turns, can only address the non-'W' component of OVAW. In sum, these offences are gender-blind—they do not and cannot address the VAW aspect of the behaviour, and instead have to address the behaviour, irrespective of the gender dimension. While this offers some equality before the law, it does little to address the phenomenon of OVAW, nor the specific and significant harms it causes.

[102] Barker and Jurasz (2021d, p. 786).

Image-Based Sexual Abuse

Where there are legislative provisions which can capture behaviours which may amount to instances of OVAW, these have almost all been introduced prior to the technological advances that have led to the emergence on a global scale, of the OVAW phenomenon itself. Some specific pieces of legislation have been introduced to deal with aspects of OVAW. For instance, Scotland recognised the role of technological advances when introducing legislation to tackle the non-consensual sharing of intimate images in 2016. The (then) Cabinet Secretary for Justice, Michael Matheson MSP, said, when introducing the Abusive Behaviour and Sexual Harm (Scotland) Bill (ABSHB) 2015, "our laws must also recognise that aspects of abusive behaviour can evolve as technology advances and our understanding of the different elements of abusive behaviour improves."[103] This recognition and awareness came almost a year before the ABSHB 2015 was presented to the Scottish Parliament, with First Minister, Nicola Sturgeon MSP, pledging that her government would "take a lead"[104] on ending VAW. To an extent, the delivery of this pledge was initiated by introducing legislation to ensure that IBSA was captured in Scots Law, but also by imposing harsher penalties of up to 5 years in prison for an offence in Scotland[105] compared to the maximum 2-year sentence introduced in England and Wales.[106] While not expressly recognising IBSA as a form of OVAW, there was, at least, recognition of the impact on women in Scotland, but also an awareness of the greater impact on women than men of IBSA.[107] Some recognition of the latter was present at the time, given the accompanying public awareness campaign—Not Yours To Share[108]—which was designed to influence attitudes and inform the public as to the shift in the law.

Given the manner in which IBSA has been legislated for in Scotland, it is disappointing that similar approaches have not been taken to address

---

[103] Meeting of the Scottish Parliament, 28 January 2016, Official Report, col. 63.

[104] Marshall (2015).

[105] Abusive Behaviour and Sexual Harm (Scotland) Act 2016, s. 2(7)(b) (asp 22).

[106] Criminal Justice and Courts Act 2015, s. 33(9)(a).

[107] Ross (2015, p. 9).

[108] Safer Scotland (n.d.: https://notyourstoshare.scot/).

other forms of OVAW. For instance, IBSA has been widely recognised as harmful, whereas the same cannot be said for text-based sexual abuse (TBSA).[109] While these forms of OVAW may be captured by offences dealing with the sending of threats, or harassment, or more commonly captured (if at all) as communications network misuse offences, to not have reciprocal provisions that capture the sexualised nature of the textual abuse creates a hierarchy within OVAW, but also within the perceptions of these types of abuse. The imbalance between the introduction of new provisions to deal with visual sexualised abuse compared to the stagnated law that does not offer specific provisions for sexualised forms of textual abuse reinforces the notion that some forms of OVAW are to be tolerated and accepted, whereas others are not.

Threatening Behaviour and Text-Based (Sexual) Abuse

While it is true that some forms of textual abuse may be captured by existing legislative provisions, this is not the case for all forms of text-based (sexual) abuse (TB(S)A). Threatening and abusive behaviour is captured in Scots Law by both common law breach of the peace and by the (now) statutory offence contained within Section 38 of the Criminal Justice and Licensing (Scotland) Act 2010 (asp 13) (CJL(S)A 2010). The Section 38 offence essentially operates as the statutory form of breach of the peace in Scotland and, as a result, covers a broad range of potential acts, from shouting, swearing, uttering threats or the brandishing of a knife.[110] The breadth of the potential behaviours that can be captured by this statutory offence suggest that it could apply to capture acts that may amount to forms of OVAW which are textual, especially given that the uttering of threats is captured here. That said, the offence is not concerned with any aspect of violence directed specifically at women but rather only with an objective assessment of the conduct of the accused. As confirmed in *Paterson v. Harvie*,[111] the actual impact of those experiencing the behaviour is irrelevant. As such, even if there were threats of, for

[109] Barker and Jurasz (2021e, p. 250).

[110] *Rooney v. Brown* [2013] HCJAC 57.

[111] [2014] HCJAC 87.

example, rape made, the substance of the threat is not the focus of the offence—it is instead, the making of the threat. In that, while there is potential for Section 38 to offer some mechanism of criminal redress in the event of online threats being made to women, whether it is the threat of rape or some other form of violence is irrelevant. Section 38 is of limited use in such instances, specifically because the impact of the threat of the rape is arguably the more significant aspect from the perspective of OVAW.

This raises concerns over the scope of the proposed misogynistic harassment offence, and its applicability to cases of OVAW. Were a stand-alone offence of—for example—misogynistic harassment to be in existence, it would still not address the situation in the rape threat example. The misogynistic harassment offence would require that harassment be exacerbated, or at the very least aggravated by misogynistic beliefs or prejudice—but in the example concerning rape threats, it would require that the threat of sexual violence (rape) is motivated or exacerbated by misogyny—somewhat self-defeating. Moreover, that hurdle aside, for an offence of misogynistic harassment to be workable, there would still need to be a grounding for a statutory harassment offence—which currently is not in existence (at the time of writing) in Scots Law. It is therefore difficult to know whether one instance of the making of rape threats would be sufficient for a potential prosecution under the offence of misogynistic harassment, but it is probable that more than one instance would be required. Moreover, were the rape threats made via social media, a similar result is likely to occur. The misogynistic motivation and/or prejudice is still going to be required, as is the underlying harassment offence. More problematically, the misogynistic harassment offence is not going to make any distinction between the online and the offline context. While this may be particularly encouraging from the perspective of making such an offence workable, it fails to capture fully the added harm from the so-called stranger danger and anonymity of online threats. In receiving online threats of physical and/or sexual violence (in the form of OVAW), misogynistic harassment, like the Section 38, offence would ignore the online context and focus purely on the threat itself. This suggests that the approach (at the time of writing) favoured by the Scottish Government, in introducing a stand-alone offence relating to misogynistic harassment, is one that seems set to continue the 'gender-blindness' of OVAW. Ultimately, a misogynistic harassment offence would not necessarily plug the current gap in Scots Law that fails to capture OVAW—in that, it seems incredibly short-sighted.

Similarly, just because there is an offensive comment made, that is not necessarily sufficient for a Section 38 contravention that could amount to a charge.[112] As such, once there has been offensive (or threatening) remarks, that is not the end of the matter—the Crown still has to establish that there has been behaviour in contravention of Section 38, that the behaviour would cause—objectively—a person to suffer fear or alarm and that the behaviour was intended or reckless as to the causing of fear or alarm.[113] Nevertheless, Section 38 has proved of use in situations addressing sexual violence (albeit before the introduction of the ABSHB 2015) where a prosecution followed for the sharing of intimate images without consent via Facebook.[114] All told, selected case law makes clear that there is potential for Section 38 to be used to address instances of OVAW, albeit with not so much emphasis on online or VAW aspects. This has been made clear in *Moneagle v. Procurator Fiscal, Elgin*,[115] where the use of technology was recognised in that the accused sent text messages that were inappropriate and sexual, and sufficient to amount to threatening and abusive behaviour under Section 38. The recognition of the use of technology here is significant, as is the sexual aspect, indicating that there is scope for these aspects to be captured by Scots Law even if there was no consideration of the VAW element in this case. The technological means by which the threatening and abusive behaviour was perpetrated here is important, but still does not suggest that online elements of VAW would fall within the Section 38 offence. In that, while the case law has not per se provided an opportunity for comment by a senior court on the remit of Section 38 in respect of OVAW, it seems unlikely that even were an instance of OVAW to appear, it would be considered. Where an instance of OVAW is to be prosecuted under Section

[112] *R v. Murphy* [2015] HJAC 47.
[113] Ibid. [16].
[114] *McHugh v. Harvie* [2015] HCJAC 86.
[115] [2017] SAC (Crim) 17.

38, it seems likely that consideration would fall on the threatening and/or abusive behaviour that was involved, but the court would not be able to consider the specific OVAW acts or implications. The Section 38 offence can operate broadly, but there are no indicators that it can be extended to considerations of OVAW.

Misusing Communications Networks

Given the limitations of the provisions in Scotland that address IBSA (but not TB(S)A) and threatening and abusive behaviours (but not OVAW), other provisions—well beyond hate crime and harassment—also have a role to play. The Communications Act (CA) 2003 in particular offers some potential to address instances of OVAW, such as online misogynistic abuse and online harassment. The Section 127 offence addresses instances where there is an improper use of a public electronic communications network. While it therefore offers some scope to tackle aspects of OVAW, it does not actually concern itself so much with the substance of the communication but rather focuses on the misuse of the network used in the making of the communication. While the Section 127 offence applies in Scotland and therefore can address online behaviours, it will—much like the Section 38 offence in the CJL(S)A 2010—not focus on addressing the OVAW element. For instance, "sick jokes" posted on social media,[116] including those with a strong sexual element, have been considered to be sufficient to satisfy the "grossly offensive" threshold under Section 127(1)(a). While this principle, discussed in *Rodgerson*,[117] touches on sexual elements and on social media sites as the medium on which the communication appeared, the focus rests—as it must under the CA 2003—on the network misuse. A similar conclusion was reached in *Brown*[118] where, again, a social media platform was involved. In this instance, the messages sent via Facebook were threatening, rather than grossly offensive, but still serious enough to warrant a conviction. While the conviction in *Brown* demonstrates that threatening

[116] *Rodgerson v. Dunn* [2016] HJAC 12.

[117] Ibid.

[118] *Brown v. Procurator Fiscal, Ayr* [2016] SAC (Crim) 32 (a.k.a. *Brown v. MacPherson*).

communications will be captured, again this arose in respect of a situation that did not involve OVAW. The ultimate outcome of the communication itself must be one which has messages of "menacing content"[119] under Section 127, as the offence is that of sending—there is no requirement that communications are received by the intended recipient or anyone else, and the reaction of the complainer is "not the determining factor."[120] Even if messages are sent via social media that threaten the rape or death of a woman because she is stupid, for example, the Section 127 offence is not concerned purely with any substantive content which amounts to OVAW. Similarly, in *Sutherland v. HM Advocate*,[121] while there was a conviction under Section 127(1)(a), and some of the behaviour related to the posting on Facebook of a picture of the complainer's vagina (without consent), the conviction was not for this act. This case is a further indicator that the Section 127 offence does not focus on this aspect of behaviour—even if such acts could amount to OVAW as IBSA. It does not capture TB(S)A behaviours, nor online misogyny.[122]

In sum, the CA 2003, like other Scots-law-specific legislation, does not address comprehensively, nor effectively, OVAW in its myriad forms. Given that the Communications Act 2003, together with the Abusive Behaviour and Sexual Harm (Scotland) Act 2016 (asp 22) and Criminal Justice and Licensing (Scotland) Act 2010 (asp 13), does not capture OVAW, the gap in Scots Law remains. While it is technically possible for an offence under one of these pieces of legislation to operate as an underlying criminal act for a hate crime (see Fig. 8 in Chap. 3), given that gender does not feature in the HCPOA 2021, there can be no gender-based hatred factored in to the non-OVAW provisions either. Consequently, there is no consideration in the current legal provisions to capture (or address) online misogyny, online gender-based hate or OVAW more broadly. While harassment exists as a breach of the peace offence at common law in Scotland (rather than in statute) (see Chap. 5), it too

[119] *DPP v. Collins* (2006) 4 All ER 602.

[120] *Brown* (n. 121) [9]; *Collins* (n. 122) [8] (Lord Bingham).

[121] [2017] HJAC 22.

[122] Barker and Jurasz (2019a); Barker and Jurasz (2021c, pp. 86–87).

overlooks OVAW. In many respects, legal provisions "designed to tackle threats, abusive behaviour, [and] harassment … have shown that much of the existing legislation is not suited to dealing with social media abuse."[123]

Draft Codes and Verbal Injury

Other potential routes exist in Scots Law for addressing OVAW. For instance, as far back as 2003, proposals were outlined to include a codified gender aggravation. The Draft Criminal Code for Scotland included the suggestion that there was scope for a codified aggravation that could be applied to offences on the basis of "hatred or contempt for, or malice, or ill-will towards a group of persons defined by reference to … gender."[124] Had the Draft Criminal Code been actioned, an aggravation on the basis of gender would have filled a gap that (still) remains in Scots Law (at the time of writing). It would have allowed for more severe sentencing following the commission of a criminal offence where there was an aggravation because of gender. In that respect, it would have allowed for gender-based prejudice to have been legislatively captured in Scotland very quickly after devolution. Had the Draft Criminal Code been implemented, the discussions surrounding hate crime reform could—potentially—also have been resolved much earlier. Such an inclusion would have provided some degree of future proofing—it would for instance have allowed instances of VAW and OVAW to be captured through underlying criminal offences, such as the misuse of communications networks. For example, a Section 127 offence could—had the Draft Criminal Code been implemented—have resulted in a more severe penalty where there was, for instance, hatred of gender involved.

OVAW may be addressed beyond the criminal law. For instance, the now—largely—overlooked civil remedy of verbal injury could offer some potential for victims of OVAW. Verbal injury provides a cause of action for a pursuer who can prove that a false statement has been made which was intended to injure the pursuer, and the injury was in fact sustained.

[123] Barker and Jurasz (2019a, p. 74).

[124] Clive et al. (2003, p. 25: see s. 7(2)(b)).

While this is not a criminal method of redress and has its roots in delict, there is potential for this to apply to instances of OVAW. In order for it to be of use in the context of OVAW, the verbal injury would have to be "to feelings by exposure to public hatred, contempt or ridicule. Verbal injury has been the matter of some debate and remains notoriously uncertain as to what can fall within it."[125] Vagueness aside, the utility of verbal injury remains a moot point—even if OVAW could fall within it, a civil action does not really address, nor contribute to, tackling OVAW, and offers, at most, one-off redress, rather than systemic change.

Ultimately, Scots Law contains an almost continuously unfolding panoply of provisions which might offer some scope to capture and tackle OVAW. The reality is that Scots Law actually contains an array of piecemeal provisions showing little joined up thinking, or cohesiveness—largely resulting from a system of legislative provisions that have been implemented in response mode. The range of provisions is not so much impressive, as it is ineffective in addressing OVAW.

Back to (d)Evolution: The 'Online' Provisions

As outlined above, there has been little strategic thought given to the ways in which provisions are enacted or enforced where they cut across legal jurisdictions. There are still some powers which are reserved by the UK Government at Westminster which could make addressing OVAW—at least legislatively—a much more convoluted process in Scots Law. For instance, while the Scottish Government has the legislative competence to tackle VAW, it has less legislative power as a result of the reservations to Westminster to address aspects of the criminal justice, such as communications offences, that intersect with OVAW. As such, while criticism for not addressing, holistically, all forms of VAW can be levied at the Scottish Government, the same cannot follow for OVAW given the restricted ability to address all facets—at least legislatively.

That said, in addressing the online aspects of VAW, and moving beyond the specific legislative panoply (see Sect. 6.3.2.), the context of UK-wise

[125] Scottish Government (2019, p. 39).

legislative developments must be borne in mind. Reform discussions have been an almost constant feature at a UK level surrounding communications, social media, online harms and Internet regulation over the last 5 years. There has, however, been a noticeable shift in stance from circa 2015 when the position was that the current legislative framework was regarded as adequate to tackle the Internet[126] (although it should be noted here that neither the Bracadale Review nor *Equally Safe* captures this). The momentum shifted significantly from 2019 onwards with the advent of the (then) "landmark"[127] policy proposal that encompassed the online harms proposals, designed to "make Britain the safest place in the world to be online."[128] The earliest discussions of these proposals indicated that they would take a broad approach to online behaviours. Had the initial consultation on the Internet Safety Strategy (2017) included OVAW, it would have addressed—at least in part—some of the gaps in Scots Law. Unfortunately, "only scant attention was paid to issues of online misogyny"[129] and OVAW. This disappointment continued with the full Online Harms White Paper (OHWP) in April 2019[130] which, despite including 23 online harms, made no mention of any of the behaviours which could amount to OVAW.[131] While the OHWP has led to a renamed Online Safety Bill (OSB),[132] it is still a disappointing piece of legislation—not just in terms of filling in the gaps in Scots Law to address online forms of VAW, but as a piece of draft legislation, it fails to capture OVAW generally and, as we say elsewhere, "does not go far enough to ensure the safety of women and girls online" (Fig. 6.3).[133]

Amendments to the OSB will follow and include provisions (affecting all jurisdictions of the UK, including Scotland) to address "illegal content"[134] which, it has been announced, will encompass "new harmful

[126] Communications Select Committee (2014, para. 32).

[127] Barker and Jurasz (2021a, p. 532).

[128] Martin (2017).

[129] Barker and Jurasz (2021a, p. 532).

[130] HM Government (2019).

[131] Barker and Jurasz (2021a, p. 534).

[132] Department for Digital, Culture, Media and Sport (2021).

[133] Barker and Jurasz (2021f, para. 1.1).

[134] Department for Digital, Culture, Media and Sport and Home Office (2022).

Fig. 6.3 Girlguiding sign for #saferinternetday 2022

online communications offences."[135] While there is some room for optimism given the February 2022 announcement of adding offences to the Draft OSB, the OSB itself is not a one-stop solution for online harms, and especially not for OVAW. The provisions within the OSB *may* address the current, dominant and, in our opinion, "incredibly fragmented and selective approach"[136] previously adopted towards online harms, but given that the proposed legislation itself is—at least purportedly—focused on the imposition of statutory duties[137] rather than online content, it would seem that OVAW remains unlikely to be captured here either. Even if OVAW were captured within the OSB, its provisions would essentially outsource decisions about whether or not OVAW is harmful because "commercial platforms are being trusted with decisions on what is—or is not—permitted speech,"[138] allowing the law to

[135] Ibid.

[136] Law Commission (2021, p. 144); Barker and Jurasz (2021a, p. 536).

[137] Joint Committee on the Draft Online Safety Bill (2021, para. 52).

[138] British and Irish Law, Education and Technology Association (2021); Joint Committee on the Draft Online Safety Bill (2021, para. 165).

continue to overlook the "disproportionate impact of online abuse and online violence on women."[139] While there is some evidence of joined-up thinking by bringing together hate crime offences (albeit those in operation in England and Wales) together with online regulation, the OSB itself is not a piece of legislation targeting OVAW, online misogyny or online hate and, as such, does not, in its current form, offer much in the way of improvement for the legislative capture of OVAW.

In the Scottish context, there is little that can be done to address aspects of legal competence covered by the Draft OSB. Similarly, the proposed reforms to the Communications Act 2003 offences—which are now set to feature in the Draft OSB—are also developments beyond the competence of the Scottish Parliament, and as such, it is a waiting game for Scotland in terms of the regulation of online behaviours and OVAW. With a new offence proposed to address "genuinely threatening" communications, and

> to better capture online threats to rape, kill and inflict physical violence or cause people serious financial harm … [the proposed offence] addresses limitations with the existing laws which capture 'menacing' aspects of the threatening communication but not genuine and serious threatening behaviour.[140]

The other proposed offences to address shortcomings with the current Communications Act 2003 offences include: "A harm-based communications offence to capture communications sent to cause harm without a reasonable excuse" and "[a]n offence for when a person sends a communication they know to be false with the intention to cause non-trivial emotional, psychological or physical harm."[141] Whether these offences address instances of OVAW remains to be seen. There are—at least—glimmers of hope that the capture of online threats to rape and/or cause physical violence may allow for the inclusion of OVAW. In reality, these offences are still concerned with the threat-making, and the use of communications networks, so, at least initially, appear to do little differently in terms of substance than the existing provisions.

[139] Barker and Jurasz (2021f, para. 1.1); Joint Committee on the Draft Online Safety Bill (2021, para. 25).

[140] Department for Digital, Culture, Media and Sport, and Home Office (2022).

[141] Ibid.

The Department for Culture, Media & Sport, and the Home Office seem confident that the new

> harm-based communications offence ... will consider the context in which the communication was sent. This will better address forms of violence against women and girls, such as communications which may not seem obviously harmful but when looked at in light of a pattern of abuse could cause serious distress.[142]

While the sentiment is welcome, this feels like tokenism, rather than any meaningful attempt to seriously address OVAW. In that respect, the UK Government proposals do little to radically alter the legislative landscape for addressing OVAW. It therefore seems that irrespective of reserved powers or otherwise, both the UK and Scottish Governments have sidestepped—repeatedly—opportunities to address OVAW.

6.4 The 2020s in Scots Law: (Re)Reclaiming?

While law reform discussions relating to matters of 'online' traditionally have been ringfenced or dealt with as though detached from areas of policy, there are emerging glimmers that online aspects of OVAW, including hatred, harassment and gender-based prejudice (at least in Scots law), do now feature in policy discussions. That they remain only indicators is a further sign of the limited consideration that the digital and online aspects of hate crime or of harassment have received to date.

Scotland *could* have legislated to include aspects of gender within hate crime, which would have allowed for some of the behaviours of OVAW to be treated accordingly. Not pursuing this opportunity means that OVAW, including gender-based abuse, hatred and harassment, can continue all but unabated online, with no specific legislative provision in Scots Law (at the time of writing) to address it.

As we stated in 2019, in response to the Scottish Government consultation on hate crime, and in particular the capture of the online

[142] Ibid.

dimensions of hate crime in Scots Law: "We are of the view that legislative change is essential in respect of online conduct, particularly where it concerns instances of gender-based online abuse and/or gender-based hostility online."[143] Our view remains unchanged. The need for law reform to address OVAW is more pressing. It is time to redress the imbalance in Scots Law by ensuring that the focus of Section 38 of the CJL(S) A 2010 no longer rests on offline behaviours. While the Internet extends well beyond Scotland's physical borders, and beyond some of its legislative competence, that is no excuse for not acting, where it has competence to do so, to address OVAW, and its harms, within its borders, laws and policies.

References

Allegretti, Aubrey. 2016. Jess Phillips Responds to Trolls Who Sent Her Rape Threats on Twitter. *HuffPost*, May 31. https://www.huffingtonpost.co.uk/entry/jess-phillips-rape-threats-twitter_uk_574d95c6e4b03e9b9ed6262c. Accessed 10 February 2022.

Amnesty International. 2017. Social Media Can Be a Dangerous Place for UK Women. Amnesty International UK. https://www.amnesty.org.uk/files/Resources/OVAW%20poll%20report.pdf. Accessed 10 February 2022.

———. 2018. Toxic Twitter – The Silencing Effect. https://www.amnesty.org/en/latest/news/2018/03/online-violence-against-women-chapter-5/. Accessed 10 February 2022.

Barker, Kim, and Olga Jurasz. 2019a. *Online Misogyny as a Hate Crime: A Challenge for Legal Regulation?* London: Routledge.

———. 2019b. Submission of Evidence to One Scotland Consultation on Amending Scottish Hate Crime legislation. https://consult.gov.scot/hate-crime/consultation-on-scottish-hate-crime-legislation/consultation/view_respondent?show_all_questions=0&sort=submitted&order=ascending&_q__text=jurasz&uuId=167846602. Accessed 10 February 2022.

———. 2020a. Concept Paper to Inform the First General Recommendation on the Implementation of the Istanbul Convention in Relation to Online and Technologically-Facilitated Violence Against Women. On File with Authors.

[143] Barker and Jurasz (2019b, p. 16).

———. 2020b. Gendered Misinformation & Online Violence Against Women in Politics: Capturing Legal Responsibility? University of Stirling Public Policy Blog. https://policyblog.stir.ac.uk/2020/03/23/gendered-misinformation-online-violence-against-women-in-politics-capturing-legal-responsibility/. Accessed 10 February 2022.

———. 2020c. Online Violence Against Women as an Obstacle to Gender Equality: A Critical View from Europe. *European Equality Law Review* 1: 47–60.

———. 2021a. Gender-Based Abuse Online: An Assessment of Law, Policy and Reform in England and Wales. In *The Palgrave Handbook of Gendered Violence and Technology*, ed. Anastasia Powell, Asher Flynn, and Lisa Sugiura, 529–544. London: Palgrave Macmillan.

———. 2021b. *Online Misogyny as a Hate Crime: An Obstacle to Equality? GenIUS: Rivista di studi giuridici sull'orientamento sessuale e l'identità di genere* 1: 51–66.

———. 2021c. Online Misogyny as a Hate Crime: #TimesUp. In *Misogyny as Hate Crime*, ed. Irene Zempi and Jo Smith, 79–98. London: Routledge.

———. 2021d. Sexual Violence in the Digital Age: A Criminal Law Conundrum? *German Law Journal* 22 (5): 784–799.

———. 2021e. Text-Based (Sexual) Abuse and Online Violence Against Women: Toward Law Reform? In *The Emerald Handbook of Technology-Facilitated Violence and Abuse*, ed. Jane Bailey, Asher Flynn, and Nicola Henry, 247–264. Bingley: Emerald Publishing.

———. 2021f. Written Evidence to the Draft Online Safety Bill Committee. https://committees.parliament.uk/writtenevidence/39198/html/. Accessed 10 February 2022.

———. 2022, forthcoming. Online Text-Based (Sexual) Abuse. In *Comprehensive Guide to Gender-Based Violence*, eds. Parveen Ali and Michaela M. Rogers. Springer.

Beckett, Jennifer, and Monica Whitty. 2018. #MeToo Must Also Tackle Online Abuse. *The Conversation*, March 21. https://theconversation.com/metoo-must-also-tackle-online-abuse-93000. Accessed 10 February 2022)

Booth, Robert. 2022. Fifth of Young Women and Girls 'cyberflashed' in Past Year, UK Study Reveals. *The Guardian*, February 9. https://www.theguardian.com/society/2022/feb/09/online-sexual-abuse-cyber-flashed-young-women. Accessed 10 February 2022.

British and Irish Law, Education and Technology Association. 2021. Written Evidence to the Draft Online Safety Bill Committee. https://committees.parliament.uk/writtenevidence/39201/html/. Accessed 10 February 2022

Clive, Eric, Pamela Ferguson, Christopher Gane, and Alexander McCall Smith. 2003. A Draft Criminal Code for Scotland with Commentary. Scottish Law Commission. https://www.scotlawcom.gov.uk/files/5712/8024/7006/cp_criminal_code.pdf. Accessed 10 February 2022.

Communications Select Committee. 2014. Social Media and Criminal Offences. HL 2014–15, 37. https://publications.parliament.uk/pa/ld201415/ldselect/ldcomuni/37/37.pdf. Accessed 10 February 2022.

Council of Europe. 2016. Combating Sexist Hate Speech. Council of Europe Gender Equality Strategy. https://rm.coe.int/CoERMPublicCommonSearchServices/DisplayDCTMContent?documentId=0900001680651592. Accessed 10 February 2022.

———. 2021. GREVIO General Recommendation No. 1 on the Digital Dimension of Violence Against Women. https://rm.coe.int/grevio-rec-no-on-digital-violence-against-women/1680a49147. Accessed 10 February 2022.

———. n.d. Cyberviolence Against Women. https://www.coe.int/en/web/cyberviolence/cyberviolence-against-women. Accessed 10 February 2022.

Council of Europe Parliamentary Assembly. 2017. Ending Cyberdiscrimination and Online Hate. Resolution 2144. Council of Europe. http://assembly.coe.int/nw/xml/XRef/Xref-XML2HTML-en.asp?fileid=23456. Accessed 10 February 2022.

Cybersmile Foundation, The. 2017. Stop Cyberbullying Day Survey 2017: A Major International Survey into Bystander Experiences of Bullying, Abuse and Harassment on the Internet. https://www.cybersmile.org/wp-content/uploads/Stop-Cyberbullying-Day-Survey-2017.pdf. Accessed 10 February 2022.

Department for Digital, Culture, Media and Sport. 2021. Draft Online Safety Bill. Cm 405, 2021. https://assets.publishing.service.gov.uk/government/uploads/system/uploads/attachment_data/file/985033/Draft_Online_Safety_Bill_Bookmarked.pdf. Accessed 10 February 2022.

Department for Digital, Culture, Media and Sport and Home Office. 2022. Online Safety Law to Be Strengthened to Stamp Out Illegal Content. https://www.gov.uk/government/news/online-safety-law-to-be-strengthened-to-stamp-out-illegal-content. Accessed 10 February 2022.

Economist Intelligence Unit, The. 2021. Measuring the Prevalence of Online Violence Against Women. *The Economist*, March 1. https://onlineviolencewomen.eiu.com/. Accessed 10 February 2022.

Engender. 2019. Making Women Safer in Scotland: The Case for a Standalone Misogyny Offence. https://www.engender.org.uk/content/publications/

Making-Women-Safer-in-Scotland%2D%2D-the-case-for-astandalone-misogyny-offence.pdf. Accessed 10 February 2022.

Fawcett Society. 2020. Reclaim the Internet. https://www.fawcettsociety.org.uk/reclaim-the-internet. Accessed 10 February 2022.

Fox, Jesse, Carlos Cruz, and Ji Young Lee. 2015. Perpetuating Online Sexism Offline: Anonymity, Interactivity and the Effects of Sexist Hashtags on Social Media. *Computers in Human Behavior* 52: 436–442.

Gardiner, Becky, Mahana Mansfield, Ian Anderson, Josh Holder, Louter Daan, and Monica Ulmanu. 2016. The Dark Side of Guardian Comments. *The Guardian*, April 12. https://www.theguardian.com/technology/2016/apr/12/the-dark-side-of-guardian-comments. Accessed 10 February 2022.

Gianino, Laura. 2017. I Went Public with My Sexual Assault. And Then the Trolls Came for Me. *The Washington Post*, October 18. https://www.washingtonpost.com/news/posteverything/wp/2017/10/18/i-went-public-with-my-sexual-assault-and-then-the-trolls-came-for-me/. Accessed 10 February 2022.

Girlguiding. 2021. Girls' Attitudes Survey 2021: A Snapshot of Girls' and Young Women's Lives. https://www.girlguiding.org.uk/globalassets/docs-and-resources/research-and-campaigns/girls-attitudes-survey-2021-report.pdf. Accessed 10 February 2022.

Girlguiding Scotland. 2018. Girls in Scotland 2018. https://www.girlguiding-scotland.org.uk/wp-content/uploads/2020/08/Girls-in-Scotland-survey-2018.pdf. Accessed 10 February 2022.

Girlguiding UK. 2022. Young People Polling – Report 2022. https://drive.google.com/file/d/1HnCQpxnoYv1dTTESyjfI2jNh-WNvGvwD/view. Accessed 10 February 2022.

Green, Chris. 2018. Scottish Parliament Passes 'world leading' Domestic Abuse Law. *iNews*, February 1. https://inews.co.uk/news/uk/scottish-parliament-passes-world-leading-domestic-abuse-law-122769. Accessed 10 February 2022.

Harvard, Tirion, and Michelle Lefevre. 2020. Beyond the Power and Control Wheel: How Abusive Men Manipulate Mobile Phone Technologies to Facilitate Coercive Control. *Journal of Gender-Based Violence* 4 (2): 223–239.

Hills, Leslie. 2001. Why Engender? In *Women and Contemporary Scottish Politics: An Anthology*, ed. Esther Breitenbach and Fiona Mackay, 29–33. Edinburgh: Polygon.

HM Government. 2019. Online Harms White Paper. White Paper, Cm 57, 2019. https://assets.publishing.service.gov.uk/government/uploads/system/

uploads/attachment_data/file/973939/Online_Harms_White_Paper_V2.pdf. Accessed 10 February 2022.
Jane, Emma A. 2017. *Misogyny Online: A Short (and Brutish) History*. London: SAGE Publications.
Joint Committee on the Draft Online Safety Bill. 2021. Draft Online Safety Bill. 2021–22, HL 129, HC 609. https://committees.parliament.uk/publications/8206/documents/84092/default/. Accessed 10 February 2022.
Khoo, Cynthia. 2021. Deplatforming Misogyny: Report on Platform Liability for Technology-Facilitated Gender-Based Violence. LEAF. https://www.leaf.ca/publication/deplatforming-misogyny/. Accessed 10 February 2022.
Laville, Sandra. 2016. Research Reveals Huge Scale of Social Media Misogyny. *The Guardian*, May 26. https://www.theguardian.com/technology/2016/may/25/yvette-cooper-leads-cross-party-campaign-against-online-abuse. Accessed 10 February 2022.
Law Commission. 2018. Abusive and Offensive Online Communications: A Scoping Report. Law Com. No. 381. https://s3-eu-west-2.amazonaws.com/lawcom-prod-storage-11jsxou24uy7q/uploads/2018/10/6_5039_LC_Online_Comms_Report_FINAL_291018_WEB.pdf. Accessed 10 February 2022.
———. 2021. Modernising Communications Offences: A final report. Law Com. No. 399. https://s3-eu-west-2.amazonaws.com/lawcom-prod-storage-11jsxou24uy7q/uploads/2021/07/Modernising-Communications-Offences-2021-Law-Com-No-399.pdf. Accessed 10 February 2022.
Lewis, Ruth, Elizabeth Sharp, Jenni Remnant, and Rhiannon Redpath. 2015. 'Safe Spaces': Experiences of Feminist Women-Only Space. *Sociological Research Online* 20 (4): 105–118. https://doi.org/10.5153/sro.3781.
Lewis, Ruth, Mike Rowe, and Clare Wiper. 2019. In *Online Othering – Exploring Digital Violence and Discrimination on the Web*, ed. Karen Lumsden and Emily Harmer, 121–142. London: Palgrave Macmillan.
Marshall, Chris. 2015. Moves to Tackle Domestic Abuse and 'revenge porn'. *The Scotsman*, March 26. https://www.scotsman.com/news/moves-tackle-domestic-abuse-and-revenge-porn-1509145. Accessed 10 February 2022.
Martin, Alexander J. 2017. Conservatives Pledge 'Digital Charter' Crackdown on Social Media Companies. *Sky News*, May 18. https://news.sky.com/story/conservatives-pledge-digital-charter-crackdown-n-social-media-companies-10883078. Accessed 10 February 2022.
McGlynn, Clare, and Erika Rackley. 2017. Image-Based Sexual Abuse. *Oxford Journal of Legal Studies* 37 (3): 534–561.

McLaughlin, Mark. 2020. Quitting MSPs Blame Online Trolls and Long Hours. *The Times*, March 9. https://www.thetimes.co.uk/article/quitting-msps-blame-online-trolls-and-long-hours-fzw9zcm37?utm_medium=Social&utm_source=Twitter#Echobox=1583739212. Accessed 10 February 2022.

Phillips, Jess. 2017. *Everywoman: One Woman's Truth About Speaking the Truth*. Hutchinson.

Plan International. 2020. Free to Be Online? Girls' and Young Women's Experiences of Online Harassment. https://plan-international.org/publications/freetobeonline. Accessed 10 February 2022.

Quinn, Zoe. 2015. Crash Override – XOXO Festival. https://www.youtube.com/watch?v=vAcdKTXtx1k. Accessed 10 February 2022.

Ross, Graham. 2015. Abusive Behaviour and Sexual Harm (Scotland) Bill. SPICe Briefing 15/74. https://archive2021.parliament.scot/ResearchBriefingsAndFactsheets/S4/SB_15-74_Abusive_Behaviour_and_Sexual_Harm_Scotland_Bill.pdf. Accessed 10 February 2022.

Rowbottom, Jacob. 2012. To Rant, Vent and Converse: Protecting Low Level Digital Speech. *The Cambridge Law Journal* 71 (2): 355–383.

Safer Scotland. n.d. Not Yours to Share. Scottish Government. https://notyourstoshare.scot/. Accessed 10 February 2022.

Scottish Government. 2018a. Independent Review of Hate Crime Legislation in Scotland: Final Report. https://www.gov.scot/binaries/content/documents/govscot/publications/progress-report/2018/05/independent-review-hate-crime-legislation-scotland-final-report/documents/00535892-pdf/00535892-pdf/govscot%3Adocument/00535892.pdf. Accessed 10 February 2022.

———. 2018b. One Scotland: Hate Has No Home Here: Consultation on Amending Scottish Hate Crime Legislation. https://www.gov.scot/publications/one-scotland-hate-home-here-consultation-hate-crime-amending-current-scottish-hate-crime-legislation/pages/1/. Accessed 10 February 2022.

———. 2019. Defamation in Scots Law: A Consultation. https://www.gov.scot/publications/defamation-scots-law-consultation/documents/. Accessed 10 February 2022.

———. 2021. A Study into the Characteristics of Police Recorded Hate Crime in Scotland. https://www.gov.scot/binaries/content/documents/govscot/publications/research-and-analysis/2021/02/study-characteristics-police-recorded-hate-crime-scotland/documents/study-characteristics-police-recorded-hate-crime-scotland/study-characteristics-police-r. Accessed 10 February 2022.

Scottish Government and COSLA. 2018. Equally Safe: Year One Update Report. https://www.gov.scot/publications/equally-safe-year-one-update-report/. Accessed 10 February 2022.

———. 2020. Equally Safe: Year Three Update Report. https://www.gov.scot/publications/equally-safe-final-report/pages/9/. Accessed 10 February 2022.

Southern, Rosalynd, and Emily Harmer. 2019. Othering Political Women: Online Misogyny Towards Women in Public Life. In *Online Othering – Exploring Digital Violence and Discrimination on the Web*, ed. Karen Lumsden and Emily Harmer, 187–210. London: Palgrave Macmillan.

Taylor, Rohese Deverux. 2019. 'Abused and dehumanised' Female MPs Stand Down. *The Herald*, November 15. https://www.heraldscotland.com/news/18037983.abused-dehumanised-female-mps-stand/. Accessed 10 February 2022.

UN Women and APPG for UN Women. 2021. Prevalence and Reporting of Sexual Harassment in UK Public Spaces. https://www.unwomenuk.org/site/wp-content/uploads/2021/03/APPG-UN-Women-Sexual-Harassment-Report_Updated.pdf. Accessed 10 February 2022.

United Nations Human Rights Council. 2018. Report of the Special Rapporteur on Violence Against Women, Its Causes and Consequences on Online Violence Against Women and Girls from a Human Rights Perspective. UN Doc. A/HRC/38/47. https://digitallibrary.un.org/record/1641160. Accessed 10 February 2022.

Verdegem, Pieter. 2021. Tim Berners-Lee's Plan to Save the Internet: Give Us Back Control of Our Data. *The Conversation*, February 5. https://theconversation.com/tim-berners-lees-plan-to-save-the-internet-give-us-back-control-of-our-data-154130. Accessed 10 February 2022.

Ward, Sarah. 2019. SNP MP Joanna Cherry Given Police Protection After Online 'death threat'. *Daily Record*, May 6. https://www.dailyrecord.co.uk/news/scottish-news/snp-mp-joanna-cherry-given-15004326. Accessed 10 February 2022.

Women's Aid. 2014. Virtual World, Real Fear: Women's Aid Report into Online Abuse, Harassment and Stalking. https://1q7dqy2unor827bqjls0c4rn-wpengine.netdna-ssl.com/wp-content/uploads/2015/11/Women_s_Aid_Virtual_World_Real_Fear_Feb_2014-3.pdf. Accessed 10 February 2022.

7

Tackling VAW Through Scots Law: Alternative Proposals

7.1 Introduction

> Comprehensive legislation provides the foundation for a holistic and effective response. Such legislation must be consistently enforced and monitored, and adequate resources must be allocated to address the problem. Personnel and officials working in the field must have the skills, capacity and sensitivity to apply the spirit and letter of the law. Laws must inform a concerted effort that includes education, awareness raising and community mobilization. They must also contribute to tackling discriminatory stereotypes and attitudes, and they must man- date the research and knowledge-building that are necessary to support policy development.[1] (Asha-Rose Migro, Deputy Secretary-General, United Nations)

In assessing violence against women (VAW), its online forms (OVAW) and the underlying causes, we have examined the development of the legal (and policy) responses in Scots Law. These responses have led to a situation (at the time of writing) whereby the focus of law reform rests on—ultimately—proposals relating to a stand-alone offence of misogynistic harassment. As we have outlined in Chap. 5, there are number of

[1] United Nations (2010, p. iii).

K. Barker, O. Jurasz, *Violence Against Women, Hate and Law*, Palgrave Hate Studies,
https://doi.org/10.1007/978-3-030-99375-7_7

concerns over this. The immediate concern is one of focus—not all forms of VAW are misogynistic. Similarly, an offence of misogynistic harassment cannot, and will not, capture all forms of VAW. In choosing to focus efforts on such a legislative invention, not only has the Scottish Government set itself up for a prolonged battle relating to definitions—of misogyny and of harassment—but it has also positioned itself to have to address, again and in not so remote future, hate crime reform. The latter is likely to arise as a topic of law reform repeatedly, as it has done to date, given the continued failure to incorporate gender as a protected characteristic. This omission, effectively excluding women from hate crime legislation, means that the question of hate crime reform in Scotland has not yet been comprehensively settled.

Given that the current Scottish approach focuses on, first, misogynistic harassment and, second, hate crime, that leaves—as we have outlined in this book—significant gaps in the legislative system to capture behaviours amounting to VAW, both online and offline. Consequently, we propose an alternative vision, one more in keeping with the *Equally Safe* mission, and the initiatives which have flowed from it, including the notion of holding the Scottish Government to account on gender-competent policy-making.[2]

To that end, we propose amendments that take on a dual approach to addressing, legislatively, VAW. First, we propose amendments to the Hate Crime and Public Order (Scotland) Act 2021 (asp 14) (HCPOA 2021) to incorporate gender as a protected characteristic. Second, we propose a more radical and forward-looking statutory offence of harassment (rather than misogynistic harassment).

The position taken in this book is that the most appropriate avenue of addressing harassment of women (because they are women) is through a two-stage process:

(1) the creation of a statutory, stand-alone offence of harassment (not misogynistic harassment) and
(2) the addition of gender as a protected characteristic to hate crime legislation through amendment of HCPOA 2021.

[2] Scottish Government (2019, p. 29).

This proposed new statutory offence of harassment (discussed at Sect. 3) would then be able to be used in situations where there are harassing behaviours generally—to capture incidents of harassment, stalking, threatening and abusive behaviours (both on and offline), as well as being subject to an aggravation on the basis of gender. In this respect, our proposals remedy the gap in the HCPOA 2021 *and* address the broader gap in Scots Law by proposing a harassment offence which works for instances of harassment well beyond those motivated by misogynistic prejudice. These proposals could work in conjunction to offer provisions that would allow a much broader range of behaviours—on- and offline—to be captured (and prosecuted where the relevant threshold is satisfied) than under the current limited provisions of Scots Law.

This chapter presents our proposals for an amended HCPOA 2021, together with our draft harassment offence. In offering this alternative vision for addressing hate, harassment and VAW in Scots law, this chapter demonstrates that the current approach adopted by the Scottish Government is likely to leave gaps in the law. These gaps will continue to be to the detriment of not only women but also, by failing to address the omission of gender in the HCPOA 2021 and offer a wider, general statutory offence of harassment, to other groups in society too. In offering an amended set of legislative proposals, this chapter offers commentary on the approach adopted, together with an illustration of the workability of the proposals in combination to address VAW and OVAW.

7.2 Amending the HCPOA 2021: Gender as a Protected Characteristic

To give effect to gender appearing as a protected characteristic in Scots Law, and to allow it to operate as an aggravation where there is an underlying criminal offence of—for example—harassment, it is necessary to amend the HCPOA 2021. Accordingly, we propose to amend Section 1(2) so that it reads:

(2) The characteristics are—
(a) age,
(b) disability,
(c) race, colour, nationality (including citizenship), or ethnic or national origins,
(d) religion or, in the case of a social or cultural group, perceived religious affiliation,
(e) sexual orientation,
(f) transgender identity,
~~(g) variations in sex characteristics.~~
(g) gender.

This amendment removes the current (as at the time of writing) category of 'variations in sex characteristics.' This is replaced by a new Section 1(2)(g) category of 'gender.' In light of the amendment to include gender, we do not propose to amend Section 2, so that the consequences apply equally to all of the categories in our amended Section 1(2). This amendment would allow gender to be captured through the penalty enhancement model already in operation in Scots Law, contained within Section 2(d)(i).

We would also propose to amend Section 11(8) as it addresses directly the meaning of a person who is a member of the group defined by reference to variations in sex characteristics. By amending Section (1)(2) to remove this group, we would also amend Section 11(8) accordingly:

(8) A reference to gender includes reference to persons of all genders.

We would also remove Section 12 given that the category of variation in sex characteristics has been amended in our revised HCPOA 2021 proposal.

Our proposals move beyond an almost singular focus on hate and misogyny and look beyond those two aspects. It also allows us to look beyond misogyny as the sole underlying motivation for hate directed at women and VAW (including OVAW). Our approach, embodied within the proposed amendments to the HCPOA 2021, and the new proposed harassment offence employ a different focus. Our intent in offering the proposed statutory sections is to draft a law that works for women, but not just for women. The proposals we offer here also work for others, particularly the proposed harassment offence. In amending HCPOA 2021, we do not seek to undergo (another) protracted consultation, debate and proposals, but rather fill the gaps left by continued Scottish Government inaction. Similarly, we have adopted the language of 'gender' (see Chaps. 1 and 4), following the lead of the Scottish Government expressed in key policy documents on VAW.

Our approach also offers future scope to avoid significant legislative redrafting, especially of, albeit not limited to, hate crime. It offers the potential to be future-proofed, but also to pave the way for other VAW legislation to be implemented in Scotland. For instance, if there is in the future, for example, an Economic Abuse (Scotland) Act, with the addition of gender as a protected characteristic, an offence of economic abuse could be subjected to an aggravation at the sentencing stage where there is hatred on the basis of gender involved in the abuse offence.

7.3 ~~Misogynistic~~ Harassment and the Law: A Proposal

It is important that a modern and clear offence of harassment is introduced in Scots Law on a statutory basis to enable the capture of lived experiences of harassment, especially those recounted by women. Introducing an offence of harassment in Scotland on a statutory basis also provides additional opportunities to modernise this area of the law without restricting it to 'misogynistic' harassment only. Our rationale for this approach is that not all harassment experienced by women is misogynistic per se, as argued in Chap. 5. In our view, legislating specifically for misogynistic harassment would forego the opportunity to timeproof the offence and would unnecessarily restrict this avenue of redress only to women whose harassment was proven to be misogynistic in nature. In so doing, an offence of misogynistic harassment would be unnecessarily restrictive and, rather than address the harassment of women, could inadvertently trigger more harassment, as observed in relation to the backlash of #MeToo.

Accordingly, in our proposal, harassment can then be prosecuted alone or, in cases where there is a clear gender-based hate aspect, a gender aggravation can be applied to signal this, as well as to be reflected in sentencing. The latter aspect can only be possible if an aggravation based on gender/gender hostility (to follow the terminology used by Lord Bracadale)[3] is introduced into Scots Law. We elaborated upon the reasons for favouring the characteristic of gender over that of sex in Chap. 4 and outlined the various and significant shortcomings of the proposed standalone offence of misogynistic harassment in Chap. 5. Building on this critique, the alternative, two-stage approach proposed here presents a solution to overcoming these problems whilst also enabling better and more accurate capturing of the nature of harassment experienced by women in contemporary Scotland as well as the range of impacts and harms that it carries.

With that in mind, our proposed formulation of the harassment offence captures the required course of conduct as well as the harm and impact arising from the offence (Sect. 7.3.1), reflecting the cause and effect of harassment. The proposed offence was designed to capture the effects that harassment—especially experiences in the public sphere—has on women, as reflected in reported lived experiences of the victims and relevant literature on the subject.

To that end, the proposed offence gives recognition to the economic consequences of harassment—including the economic costs of measures undertaken by women to improve their safety and economic loss resulting from harassment (e.g., loss of earnings or loss of employment resulting from reporting workplace sexual harassment).[4] It also recognises and captures (Section 1(3)(a) below) women's 'safety work' that is undertaken to 'stay safe' and/or to prevent harm to themselves, which is so aptly articulated in the work of Liz Kelly and Fiona Vera Grey.[5] Finally, the proposed offence reflects that harassment can occur online as well as offline (section 1(1) below). Therefore, it builds on our earlier critique of

[3] Scottish Government (2018, p. vii: Recommendation 9).

[4] See, for example, Hegewisch et al. (2021).

[5] Kelly (2012); Vera-Grey (2018); Vera-Gray and Kelly (2020).

the 'online blindness' of the contemporary laws and policies targeting VAW in Scotland (Chap. 6) and makes the new offence fit for the future.

However, one element which is not captured is the conduct required in our proposed offence is the threshold for the frequency of harassing behaviour, that is, whether, as a minimum, it needs to occur at least once (as per the 'gold standard' Domestic Abuse (Scotland) Act 2018 (asp 5)) or on at least two occasions (as per the Protection from Harassment Act 1997).

There are advantages and disadvantages to both approaches but also a number of aspects of women's lived experiences of harassment that need careful consideration. For instance, is the requirement of repetition of harassing conduct (i.e., on at least two occasions) adequate for online harassment where, whilst it is likely to be repeatable, it might not be by the same perpetrator? To put it into context, a perpetrator online can be anonymous or, even if initially blocked on social media, can easily start a new profile and continue the harassment. Equally, in an offline setting, would not a single incident of street harassment—however terrifying and life-changing to the victim—be sufficient to establish harassment? Our proposal does not seek to answer these questions here, but should the Scottish Government decide to pursue much needed law reform in this area, in reaching any future decision on this matter, a consultation with stakeholders, including women who were subjected to harassment, would be advisable.

7.3.1 Proposed Draft Statutory Offence of Harassment

1. *(1) An individual must not harass any other person by any means online or offline ('offence of harassment').*

(2) Harassment for the purposes of this section is taken to include one or more of the following—

(a) causing alarm and/or distress,

(b) using threatening, abusive or insulting words,

(c) using threatening, abusive or insulting behaviour(s),

(d) making threatening, abusive or insulting communications.

(3) *An individual commits the offence of harassment where the harassment results in at least one of the following—*

(a) *a change of behaviour of the victim,*
(b) *the taking of measures by the victim to improve their safety, including additional expense,*
(c) *economic loss to the victim,*
(d) *changes or disruption to everyday activity of the victim.*

2. (1) *For the purposes of section 1(3), changes of behaviour and/or the taking of measures to improve the safety of the victim include one or more of the following—*

(a) *increased home security,*
(b) *increased personal security,*
(c) *increased work-related security,*
(d) *reduction in visibility,*
(e) *reduction in public profile,*
(f) *reduction in social interaction(s) of the victim and/or of associated persons as defined in subsection (2).*

(2) *Associated persons include, but are not limited to, dependants, family members, friends, professional contacts and / or co-workers.*

7.4 Conclusion

The aim of this chapter was to demonstrate that an alternative approach to tackling (O)VAW, including harassment and gender-based hate, is possible in Scots Law. Our approach strives to be pragmatic in creating simple but modern and fit-for-the-future legislation that works for women, and is reflective not only of women's reported experiences but also the wealth of (feminist) research on the subjects of VAW, OVAW and (online) gender-based hate. In doing so, we hope to show that Scots Law is capable of meaningful change in these areas, building on some of the demonstrated and aspirational areas of legislative progressivism.

Although not all acts of VAW amount to harassment, the pervasiveness of harassment of women—especially in public spaces, both online and offline—reaffirms the need for Scots Law to respond to this challenge. As such, the proposal above would enable several outcomes:

(1) prosecution of online and offline harassment of women on the basis of a statutory offence which is both modern and captures the multi-dimensional nature of harassment;
(2) prosecution of harassment as a gender-aggravated offence, where applicable and proven;
(3) prosecution of acts of VAW as a gender-aggravated offence, where such conduct is criminalised under Scots Law;
(4) prosecution of any future offences in Scots criminal law as gender-aggravated.

Nonetheless, as emphasised throughout this book, law is only one of the tools in the toolbox for dismantling the structures that enable VAW to thrive and that perpetuate it. As such, law alone cannot fix this problem, although it has a significant role to play in signalling the societal progress in perceiving the harmfulness of (O)VAW and capturing a range of motivations and harms applicable to (O)VAW.

References

Hegewisch, Ariane, Jessica Forden, and Eve Mefferd. 2021. Paying Today and Tomorrow: Charting the Financial Costs of Workplace Sexual Harassment. Institute for Women's Policy Research and Time's Up Foundation. https://timesupfoundation.org/wp-content/uploads/2021/07/Paying-Today-and-Tomorrow_Charting-the-Financial-Costs-of-Workplace-Sexual-Harassment_FINAL.pdf. Accessed 10 February 2022.

Kelly, Liz. 2012. Standing the test of time? Reflections on the concept of the continuum of sexual violence. In *Handbook on Sexual Violence*, ed. Jennifer Brown and Sandra Walklate, xvii–xxvi. London: Routledge.

Scottish Government. 2018. Independent Review of Hate Crime Legislation in Scotland: Final Report. https://www.gov.scot/binaries/content/documents/govscot/publications/progress-report/2018/05/independent-review-hate-crime-legislation-scotland-final-report/documents/00535892-pdf/00535892-pdf/govscot%3Adocument/00535892.pdf. Accessed 10 February 2022.

———. 2019. Scottish Government's Response to the First Minister's National Advisory Council on Women and Girls. https://www.gov.scot/publications/

scottish-governments-response-national-advisory-council-women-girls/documents/. Accessed 10 February 2022.

United Nations. 2010. Handbook for Legislation on Violence against Women. https://www.un.org/womenwatch/daw/vaw/handbook/Handbook%20for%20legislation%20on%20violence%20against%20women.pdf. Accessed 10 February 2022.

Vera-Grey, Fiona. 2018. *The Right Amount of Panic: How Women Trade Freedom for Safety*. Bristol: Policy Press.

Vera-Gray, Fiona, and Liz Kelly. 2020. Contested Gendered Space: Public Sexual Harassment and Women's Safety Work. *International Journal of Comparative and Applied Criminal Justice* 44 (4): 265–275.

8

Conclusion: Towards Ending Violence Against Women

While Europe's eye is fix'd on mighty things,
The fate of Empires and the fall of Kings;
While quacks of State must each produce his plan,
And even children lisp the Rights of Man;
Amid this mighty fuss just let me mention,
The Rights of Woman merit some attention. Robert Burns[1]

Through examining the law from the perspective(s) of women in Scotland, thorough scrutiny suggests that there remains significant room for improvement in tackling violence against women (VAW) and its online forms (OVAW). The question remains: just how far has Scotland come and how much further has it to go?

This book began by outlining the unfolding of VAW alongside the rise of the women's movement in modern Scotland. It set out to identify why women, but especially VAW, have been overlooked by Scots Law. To

[1] Burns (1792). It must be noted though that while Burns had a point in 1792, some of his behaviour, especially that displaying misogynistic tendencies, is not without criticism: see, for example, Ferguson (2022).

K. Barker, O. Jurasz, *Violence Against Women, Hate and Law*, Palgrave Hate Studies,
https://doi.org/10.1007/978-3-030-99375-7_8

answer that question, the discussion here has investigated the rise of recognition of VAW as a phenomenon both within and outside Scotland. It also, uniquely, explores the impact of Devolution on Scotland, Scots law- and policy-making and Scottish politics in respect of women's rights. These aspects were discussed against the backdrop of societal changes in Scotland post-Devolution. As we have identified, the ways in which Scots Law addresses issues of VAW, harassment and hatred require a wider consideration than purely exploring the relevant statutory provisions. The context in Scotland—legally and societally—is unique, and so too are discussions relating to how Scotland has tried—and continues to try—to address VAW. In exploring the historical exclusion of gender to date, both within hate crimes and harassment, Scots Law has shown itself to be unwilling to address contemporary phenomena such as online misogyny, gender-based hate and OVAW.

Despite having implemented "gold-standard"[2] legislation for addressing domestic abuse, and having introduced a leading programme of work to address aspects of gender inequality in *Equally Safe*,[3] Scotland has not shown the same commitment to capturing gender-based aspects of VAW directed at women specifically within its growing panoply of law. This omission continues to be perplexing, not least because of the forward-thinking approaches adopted in respect of other areas of policy addressing VAW, but also when considered alongside other progressive policies—including the smacking ban,[4] ending period poverty[5] and the smoking ban.[6] It is equally baffling as to why women—and gender—do not feature more prominently in statutory provisions in Scotland, though this book has shed some light on the myriad of reasons for this absence. Legislative creativity and boldness in the form of Scottish proposals for a misogynistic harassment[7] offence that stands alone from the hate crime

---

[2] Engender (2019, p. 32).

[3] Scottish Government and COSLA (2020).

[4] Children (Equal Protection from Assault) (Scotland) Act 2019 (asp 16). Although it should be noted that there is no creation of a new offence in the 2019 Act, rather it removes the defence previously available to those charged with assault.

[5] Period Products (Free Provision) (Scotland) Act 2021 (asp 1).

[6] Smoking, Health and Social Care (Scotland) Act 2005 (asp 13).

[7] Scottish Government (2018b, p. 17).

framework (where gender remains missing as a protected characteristic)—while potentially valuable—cannot address in the same way as hate crimes, the gender-based prejudice directed at women because they are women.

In assessing the progress made in Scotland in addressing VAW, our attention has fallen on the development of hate crimes, as well as other criminal provisions which have potential applicability to behaviours that are encapsulated within VAW. While hate crimes and their justification are far from easy to navigate, Scotland has shown openness and willingness to engage in discussions of hate crime law reform on an almost constant basis since 2002, all while resisting the inclusion of gender within its provisions. Alongside these persistent discussions, the Scottish Government (and its predecessor, the Scottish Executive) has shown that it is not averse to engaging with the public to address issues relating to tolerance, equality and public awareness relating to societal challenges such as hate crime, intolerance and prejudice.

Triggered by the incredibly successful (and initially localised) Zero Tolerance Campaign (see Chap. 2) of the early 1990s, another almost constant theme in post-Devolution Scotland is the use of public awareness campaigns generally. Partly, these latter campaigns have been tailored to target aspects of intolerance within Scottish society, but they have also been used in targeted campaigns. For example, in respect of hate crime, the 'Dear Haters'[8] campaign was a prominent feature. This is not an isolated example, with the 'Not Yours to Share'[9] campaign unveiled to increase public awareness of new offences criminalising image-based sexual abuse (IBSA), introduced through the Abusive Behaviour and Sexual Harm (Scotland) Act 2016 (asp 22). Both of these campaigns, while not specifically focused on the overarching theme of VAW (and yet contributing to it), were based on the incredibly impactful forerunner, the Zero Tolerance Campaign launched in the early 1990s by Edinburgh District Council to raise awareness of VAW in the form of domestic violence. While not specifically designed to address VAW, the use of public awareness tools as mechanisms outside of legislation indicates again that

[8] One Scotland (n.d.: https://onescotland.org/campaigns/hate-crime-campaign/resources/).

[9] Safer Scotland (n.d.: https://notyourstoshare.scot/).

Scotland is prepared to do things differently in order to effect policy ambitions. They are also a further sign that Scotland is willing to discuss and enact reform to capture emerging behaviours—such as IBSA—which are incredibly harmful and damaging, especially when manifested as forms of VAW. It is therefore incredibly disappointing that Scotland has not built on this momentum to address gaps in its legal approach to VAW, either offline or online.

The repeated returns to hate crime reform across the relatively short history of the re-established Scottish Parliament are an indicator of the apparent paralysis which seems to emerge at a national level when issues of gender-based hate appear, but also signify a one-dimensional focus on isolated aspects of VAW, even though not all forms of VAW are motivated by hate. Throughout discussions in 2002,[10] 2004,[11] 2009,[12] 2016,[13] 2018,[14] right through to 2021,[15] hate crime working groups, reports and consultations have all seemed to skirt around the issue of gender within the Scottish hate crime framework. Worse, in contemporary society, they have also ignored the nuance of OVAW and have seen fit either to ignore the online dimension in its entirety, reinforce the false perception (intentionally or otherwise) or assume—unadvisedly—that there is no difference between offline and online VAW.

From leading the way with a progressive and modern hate crime approach in the early 2000s, the Scottish Government has descended into a quagmire whereby its favoured approach seems to be to 'duck' the issue of gender. Most recently, despite engaging with the language of 'gender,' the Scottish Government has retreated to the language of the Equality Act 2010 and chosen to hide behind 'sex'[16] while attempting to redirect public discourse to questions over the potential to legislate

---

[10] Scottish Executive (2002).

[11] Working Group on Hate Crime (2004).

[12] The Sentencing of Offences Aggravated by Prejudice (Scotland) Bill was lodged on 2 October 2007, becoming the Offences (Aggravation by Prejudice) (Scotland) Act 2009 (asp 8).

[13] Scottish Government (2016).

[14] Scottish Government (2018a); Scottish Government (2018b).

[15] Hate Crime and Public Order (Scotland) Act 2021 (asp 14).

[16] Scottish Government (2020). The Equality Act 2010, s. 11 mentions 'sex' as a protected characteristic. In contrast, 'gender' appears under protected characteristics only in relation to 'gender reassignment' (ibid., s. 7).

specifically on offences of misogynistic harassment.[17] This again avoids addressing head-on the non-inclusion of gender as a protected characteristic in Scots Law. In avoiding engaging with the debate surrounding sex/gender, the Scottish Government has repeated a pattern, initially triggered in the early 2000s, of falling back on the notion that further research into VAW is required.[18] This is not the only repeated behaviour that is displayed by the Scottish Government. In fact, in attempting to 'future-proof' the Hate Crime and Public Order (Scotland) Act 2021 (asp 14) by including powers to add variations in protected characteristics,[19] all the Scottish Government has done is act on a recommendation from 2016 to do exactly that.[20] Again, the ineffectiveness of Scottish Government action is difficult to reconcile given the speed with which flagship legislation addressing domestic abuse[21] or IBSA[22] (also forms of VAW) was enacted.

We have outlined in this book the unfolding story of VAW, hate, harassment and women's equality in Scotland. This story serves to highlight that there is not yet an end in sight, that VAW and OVAW have not been eradicated and that there is potential to develop more innovative and progressive legislation to address VAW, including gender-based hate and harassment, both on and offline. This potential would also reflect more broadly than current legislative proposals in Scotland, the ambition that the Scottish Government has voiced to maintain progress with the European Union,[23] but also to cement its ambitions to implement international standards and human rights treaties including CEDAW[24] into domestic law. For these aspirations to be more than tokenistic, the Scottish Government needs to adopt—we suggest—a different approach to tackling VAW in Scots Law.

[17] Scottish Government (2018b, p. 17).

[18] Barker and Jurasz (2021, p. 7).

[19] Hate Crime and Public Order (Scotland) Act 2021, s. 12 (asp 14).

[20] Working Group on Hate Crime (2004, p. 4: Recommendation 1).

[21] Domestic Abuse (Scotland) Act 2018 (asp 5).

[22] Abusive Behaviour and Sexual Harm (Scotland) Act 2016 (asp 22).

[23] UK Withdrawal from the European Union (Continuity) (Scotland) Act 2021 (asp 4).

[24] Scottish Government (2021, p. 27).

Our proposal to make two significant alterations to Scots Law to address both gender-based hate *and* harassment (generally, as well as gender-based) shows that there is potential for Scotland to adopt a different approach, and to step outside of the constant report-consult-legislate cycle of hate crime reform. For Scotland to develop a set of legislative provisions that are complementary to the ambition shown through the *Equally Safe* programme of work requires a different approach. It will also require a broader societal engagement extending well beyond the criminal justice system, but also filtering into educational and policing sectors. As innovative as a set of legislative provisions may be, they are only as effective as the system in which they are asked to operate and the police force asked to enforce them.

Perhaps, therefore, the associated issues surrounding policing, police attitudes and behaviours are also a significant challenge for Scotland in seeking to end VAW and OVAW. While addressing and eradicating VAW will require much more than a set of legislative provisions—though they do offer a start—it will also require buy-in, understanding and support from the police. That is likely to be a much greater hurdle to tackling VAW than enacting legislation to introduce gender as a protected characteristic for hate crime in Scots Law. Recent issues exposing misogynistic, harassing, sexually deviant and abusive attitudes and behaviours in the police (both in Scotland and in England) do little to suggest that Scotland's ambition to end VAW (and OVAW) is realistic.[25] If those charged with enforcing the law relating to VAW and OVAW—including the police—are also those demonstrating abusive, insulting, threatening and sexual behaviours towards women, it is unlikely that women who have already been subjected to VAW will be willing to trust in law-enforcement bodies. As such, the true impact of VAW is unlikely to be accurately captured. Similarly, if those charged with law enforcement are unwilling to understand it, or the causes that have led to its implementation, again, it is unlikely that accurate records can or will be kept or victims/complainants taken seriously.

[25] Court Reporter (2021); HM Inspectorate of Constabulary in Scotland (2021, p. 55); Vesty (2022).

This all suggests—pessimistically—that the ambition to end VAW and OVAW is just that. In some respects, the damage done to the confidence women have in the police is symptomatic of the confidence women have in the Scottish Government to substantively act to end all forms of VAW and gender-based hate. Equally, the damaging reports of police attitudes and culture have at the very least given attention to the significant and substantial challenge in implementing change. Burying these behaviours and these reports is unhelpful, but, as Rose suggests, recognising the problem is a necessary step even if it does not in itself lead to change:

> If sexual violence arises from a form of tunnel vision, and from burying those aspects of the inner life that are most difficult to acknowledge or see, it is also the case that raising violence to the surface of public consciousness is not always transformative in the ways we would want it to be.[26]

Irrespective of the difficulty of the policy ambition[27] of eradicating all forms of VAW, together with the long-standing societal misogynistic attitudes,[28] institutional misogyny evident in the police and law enforcement bodies[29] and the paralysis evident when legislators are faced with addressing the 'gender question,' VAW remains a pressing societal challenge. While some progress has been made in Scotland, especially since Devolution, much more can—and *must*—be done.

In a society which has seen the rise of women and women's voices, those voices are yet to be reflected in legislative provisions Robert Burns elucidated in 1792, that the 'Rights of Woman'[30] merit attention—such consideration is well beyond long overdue. And yet, in 2022, the same remains very much true. For as long as this remains the case, Scotland cannot hope to achieve its ambition of eradicating VAW and making it a matter of 'historical curiosity.'

---

[26] Rose (2021).

[27] Breitenbach (2006, p. 17).

[28] Hills (2001, p. 30).

[29] HM Inspectorate of Constabulary in Scotland (2021, p. 55).

[30] Burns (1792).

References

Barker, Kim, and Olga Jurasz. 2021. Misogynistic Harassment: A Stumbling Block for Scots Hate Crime Reform? *Juridical Review* 1: 1–17.

Breitenbach, Esther. 2006. Developments in Gender Equality Policies in Scotland Since Devolution. *Scottish Affairs* 56 (1): 10–21.

Burns, Robert. 1792. The Rights of Woman. https://www.bbc.co.uk/arts/robertburns/works/the_rights_of_woman/. Accessed 10 February 2022.

Court Reporter. 2021. East Kilbride police officer jailed for explicit messages. *Glasgow Evening Times*, December 14. https://www.glasgowtimes.co.uk/news/19784026.east-kilbride-police-officer-jailed-explicit-messages/. Accessed 10 February 2022.

Engender. 2019. Making women safer in Scotland: The case for a standalone misogyny offence. https://www.engender.org.uk/content/publications/Making-Women-Safer-in-Scotland%2D%2D-the-case-for-astandalone-misogyny-offence.pdf. Accessed 10 February 2022.

Ferguson, Brian. 2022. 'Misogyny' of Robert Burns tackled by female Scottish poets in new work exploring bard's treatment of women. *Edinburgh Evening News*, January 25. https://www.edinburghnews.scotsman.com/whats-on/arts-and-entertainment/misogyny-of-robert-burns-tackled-by-female-scottish-poets-in-new-work-exploring-bards-treatment-of-women-3539535. Accessed 10 February 2022.

Hills, Leslie. 2001. Why Engender? In *Women and Contemporary Scottish Politics: An Anthology*, ed. Esther Breitenbach and Fiona Mackay, 29–33. Edinburgh: Polygon.

HM Inspectorate of Constabulary in Scotland. 2021. Thematic Inspection of Hate Crime. https://www.hmics.scot/sites/default/files/publications/HMICS%20Thematic%20Inspection%20of%20Hate%20Crime%202021.pdf. Accessed 10 February 2022.

One Scotland. n.d. *Dear* Haters, You're Going to Hate This, But We've Had Enough. *Yours, Scotland*. Scottish Government. https://onescotland.org/campaigns/hate-crime-campaign/resources/. Accessed 10 February 2022.

Rose, Jacqueline. 2021. Damage: The Silence Forms of Violence Against Women. *The Guardian*, March 30. https://www.theguardian.com/news/2021/mar/30/damage-the-silent-forms-of-violence-against-women. Accessed 10 February 2022.

Safer Scotland. n.d. Not Yours to Share. Scottish Government. https://notyourstoshare.scot/. Accessed 10 February 2022.

Scottish Executive. 2002. Report of the Cross-Party Working Group on Religious Hatred. http://image.guardian.co.uk/sys-files/Politics/documents/2002/12/05/crosspartyreport.pdf. Accessed 10 February 2022.

Scottish Government. 2016. Report of the Independent Advisory Group on Hate Crime, Prejudice and Community Cohesion. https://www.gov.scot/publications/report-independent-advisory-group-hate-crime-prejudice-community-cohesion/documents/. Accessed 10 February 2022.

———. 2018a. Independent Review of Hate Crime Legislation in Scotland: Final Report. https://www.gov.scot/binaries/content/documents/govscot/publications/progress-report/2018/05/independent-review-hate-crime-legislation-scotland-final-report/documents/00535892-pdf/00535892-pdf/govscot%3Adocument/00535892.pdf. Accessed 10 February 2022.

———. 2018b. One Scotland: Hate Has No Home Here: Consultation on Amending Scottish Hate Crime Legislation. https://www.gov.scot/publications/one-scotland-hate-home-here-consultation-hate-crime-amending-current-scottish-hate-crime-legislation/pages/1/. Accessed 10 February 2022.

———. 2020. Hate Crime and Public Order (Scotland) Bill: Information Note: Sex/Gender. https://www.gov.scot/binaries/content/documents/govscot/publications/factsheet/2020/04/hate-crime-bill-what-it-will-do/documents/hate-crime-bill-sex-and-gender/hate-crime-bill-sex-and-gender/govscot%3Adocument/Hate%2BCrime%2BBill%2B-%2BInformation%2BNote%2BPdf%2B-%2BSex-Gender%2B-%2BRevised%2BAugust%2B2020.pdf. Accessed 10 February 2022.

———. 2021. National Taskforce for Human Rights Leadership Report. https://www.gov.scot/binaries/content/documents/govscot/publications/independent-report/2021/03/national-taskforce-human-rights-leadership-report/documents/national-taskforce-human-rights-leadership-report/national-taskforce-human-rights-leadership-report. Accessed 10 February 2022.

Scottish Government, and COSLA. 2020. Equally Safe: Year Three Update Report. https://www.gov.scot/binaries/content/documents/govscot/publications/progress-report/2020/11/equally-safe-final-report/documents/equally-safe-year-three-update-report-november-2020/equally-safe-year-three-update-report-november-2020/govscot%3Adocument/equ. Accessed 10 February 2022.

Vesty, Sarah. 2022. Police Scotland inspector appears in court charged with 'stalking' fellow officer. *Daily Record*, February 12. https://www.dailyrecord.co.uk/news/scottish-news/police-scotland-inspector-appears-court-26205228. Accessed 12 February 2022.

Working Group on Hate Crime. 2004. Working Group on Hate Crime Report. Scottish Executive. https://www.hatecrimescotland.org/wp/wp-content/uploads/2014/08/Scottish-Working-Group-on-Hate-Crime-Report-2004.pdf. Accessed 10 February 2022.

Index[1]

[1] Note: Page numbers followed by 'n' refer to notes.

K. Barker, O. Jurasz, *Violence Against Women, Hate and Law*, Palgrave Hate Studies,
https://doi.org/10.1007/978-3-030-99375-7

K

L

M

N

The manufacturer's authorised representative in the EU is Springer Nature Customer Service Centre GmbH, Europaplatz 3, 69115 Heidelberg, Germany. If you have any concerns regarding our products, please contact ProductSafety@springernature.com

Printed and bound by CPI Group (UK) Ltd, Croydon, CR0 4YY
30/09/2026
02225499-0014